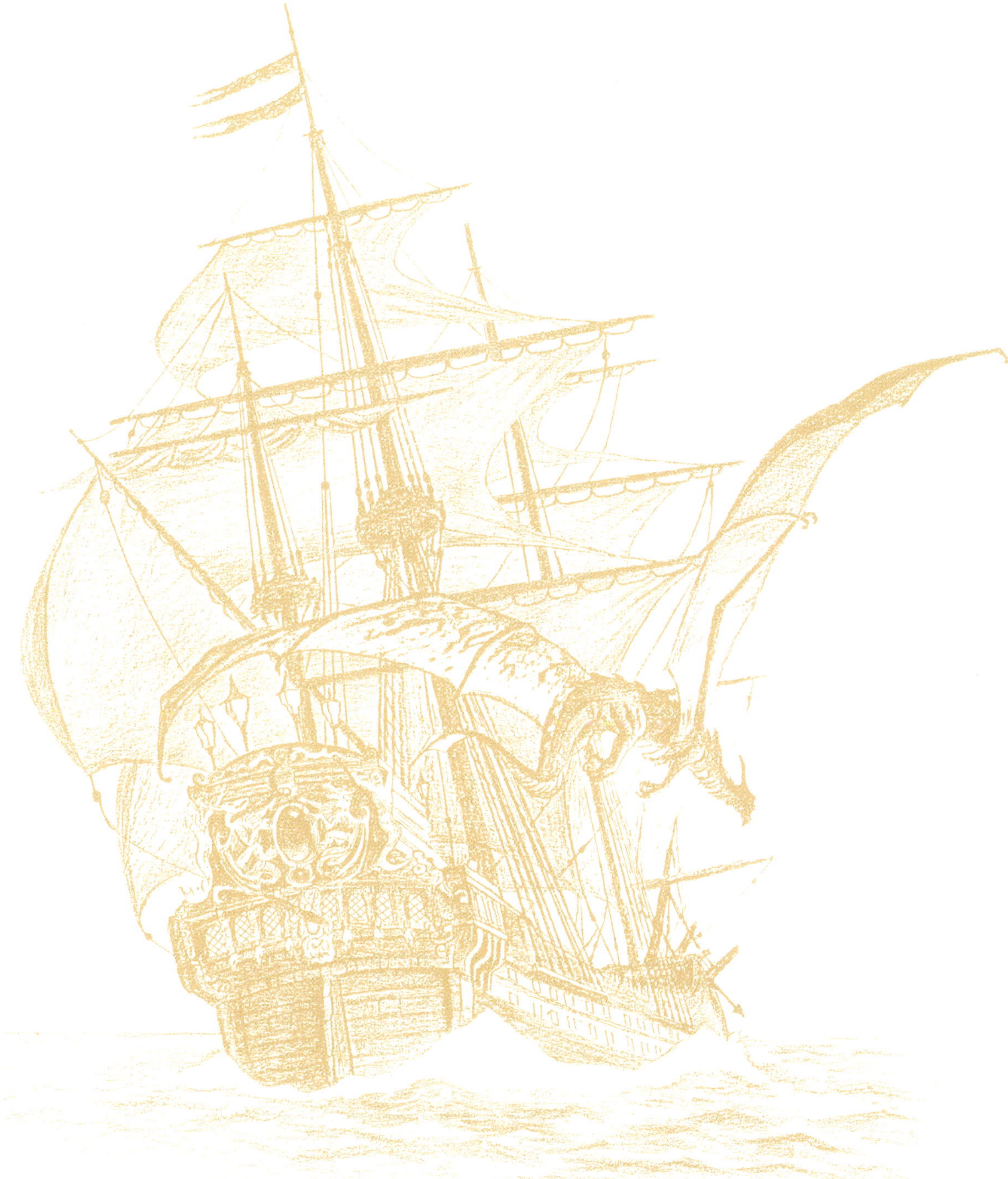

THE ART OF STEPHEN YOULL

PARADOX

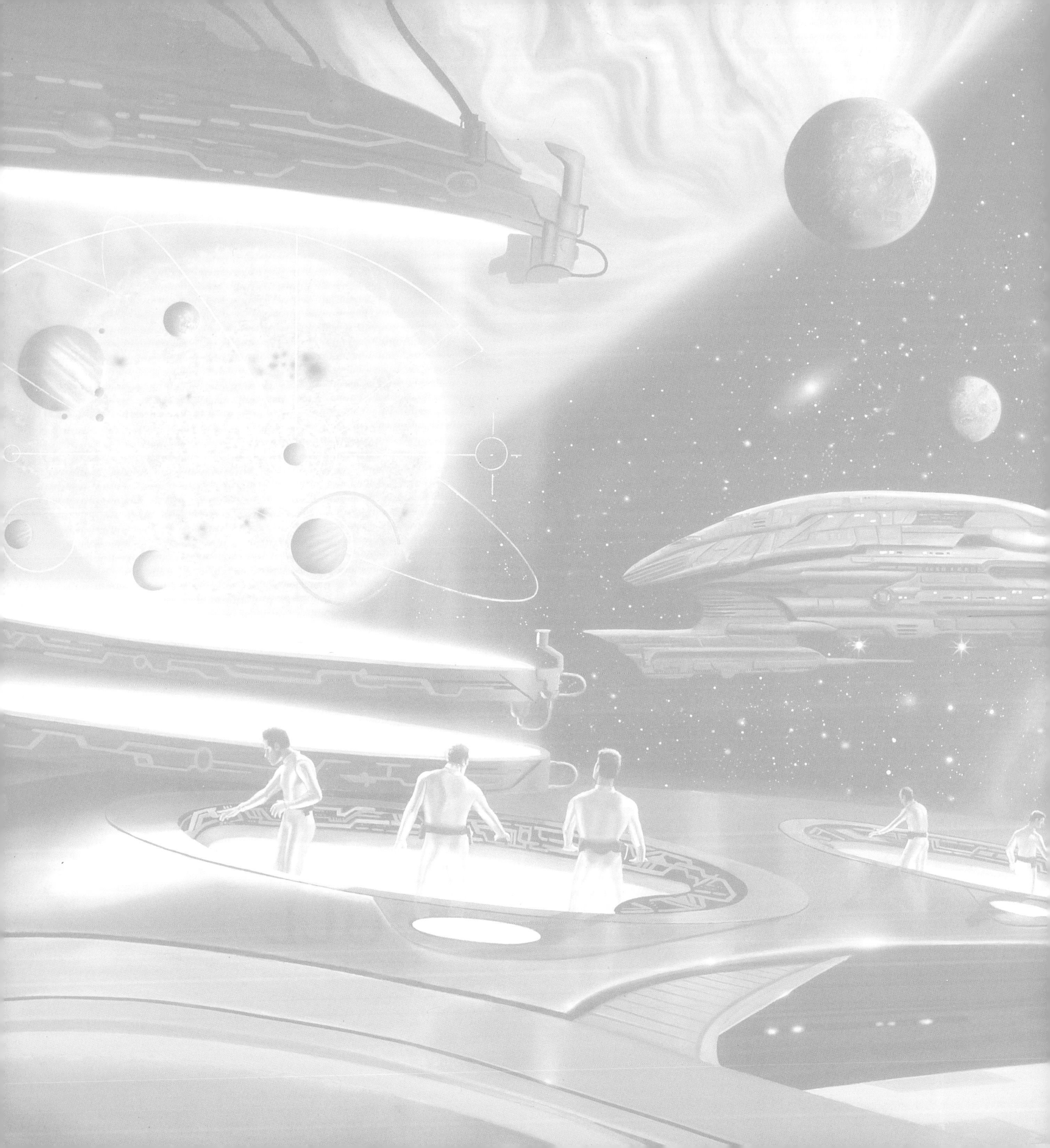

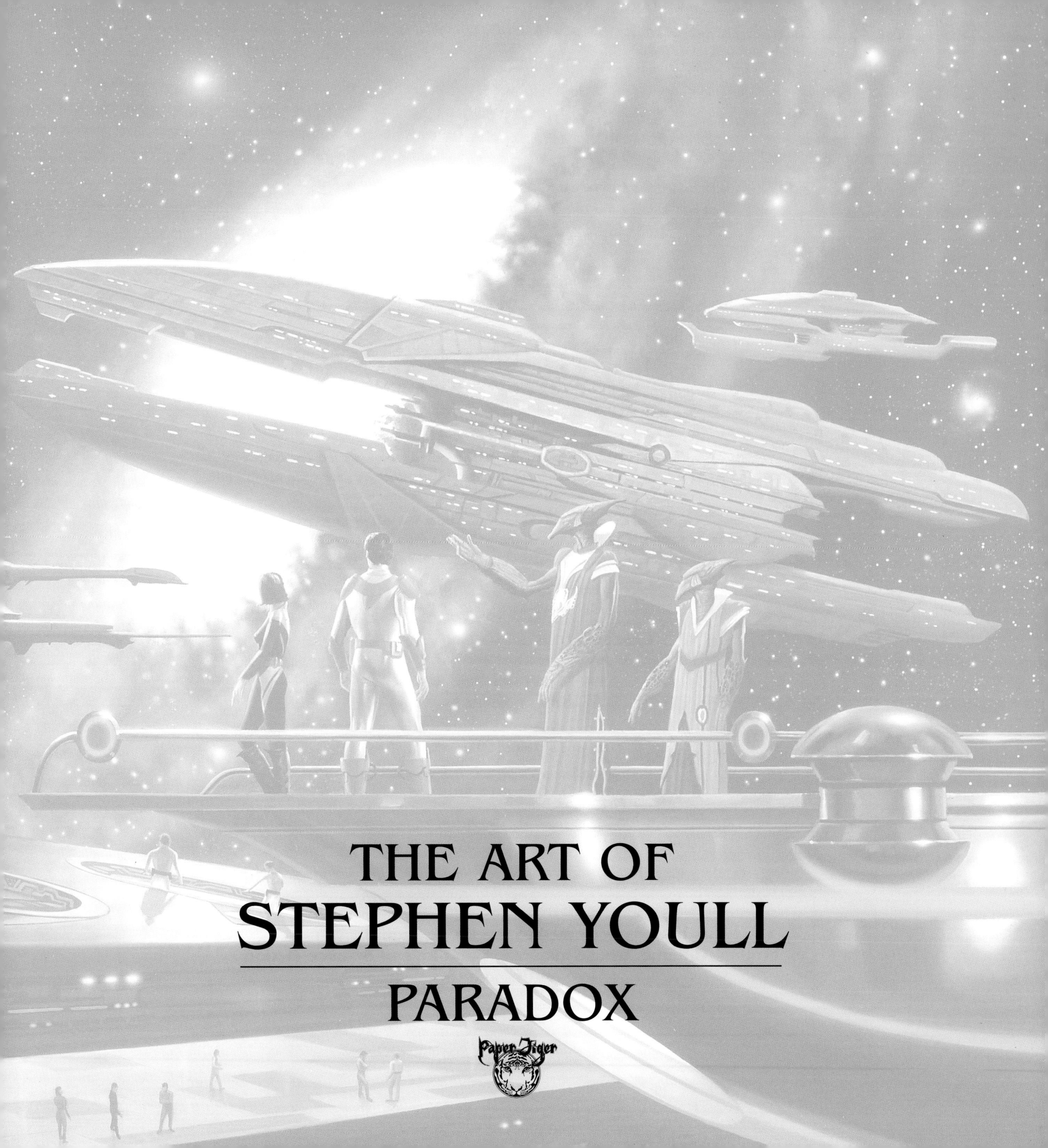

THE ART OF
STEPHEN YOULL

PARADOX

Paper Tiger

First published in Great Britain in 2001
by Collins & Brown Limited
London House
Great Eastern Wharf
Parkgate Road
London SW11 4NQ

Distributed in the United States and Canada by Sterling Publishing Co.,
387 Park Avenue South, New York, NY 10016, USA

1 3 5 7 9 8 6 4 2

British Library Cataloguing-in-Publication Data:
A catalogue record for this book
is available from the British Library.

ISBN 1 85585 916 5

Designed by Jamie S. Warren Youll

Reproduction by Classicscan in Singapore
Printed by Craftprint in Singapore

This book is dedicated to the loving memory of my brother, Graeme, whose inspiration and love of Science Fiction live on through me.
1957–1986

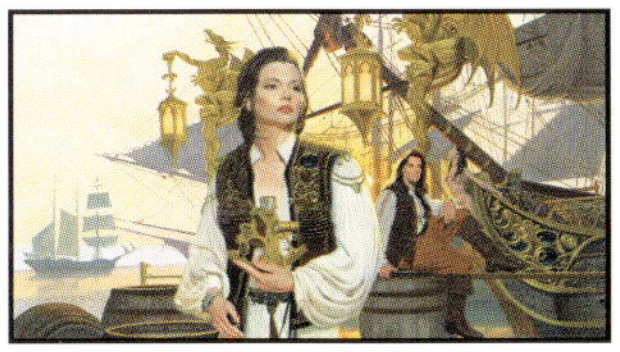
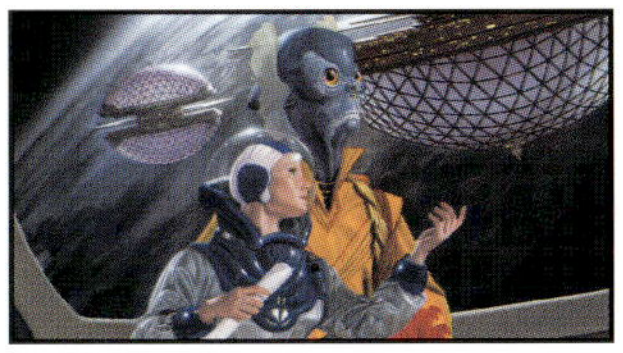
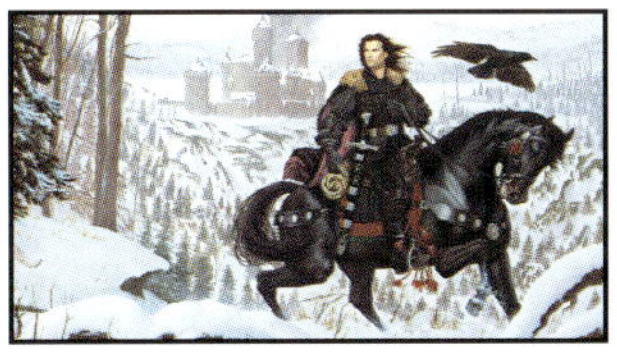
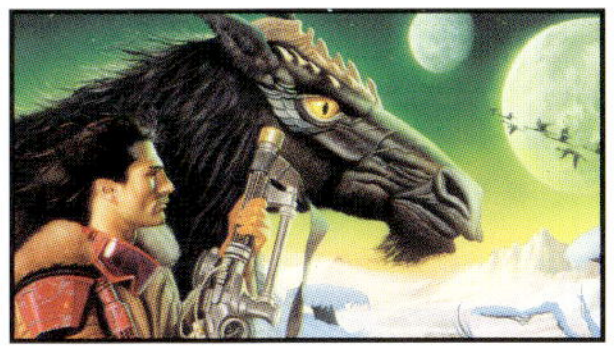
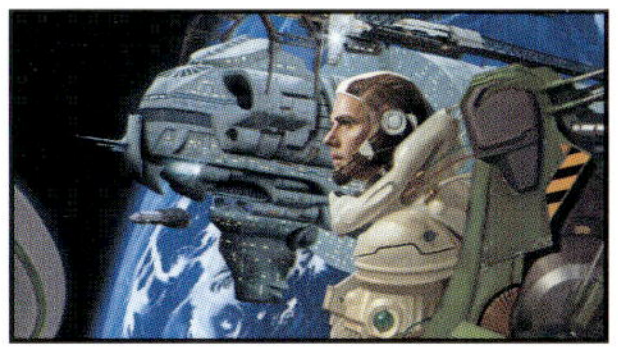

CONTENTS

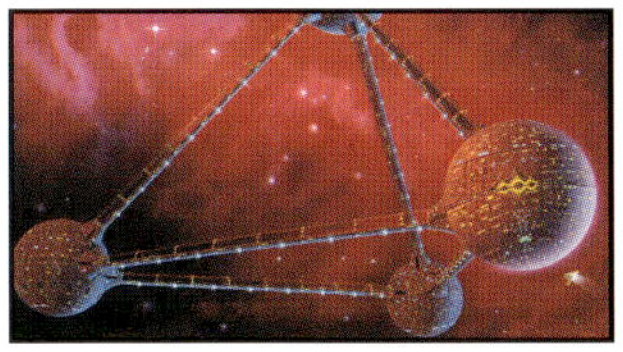
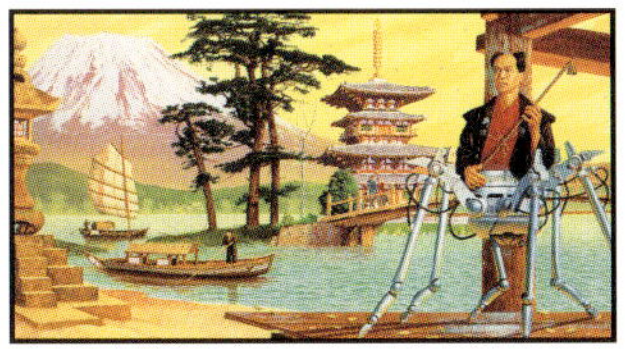
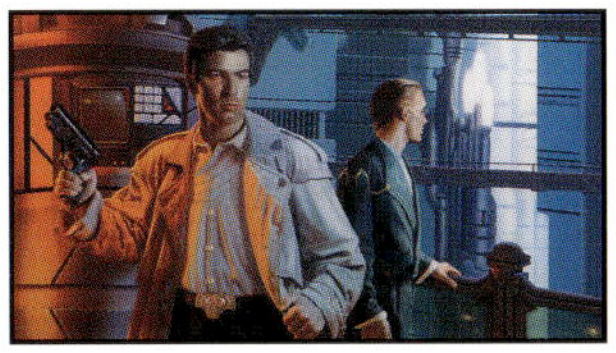
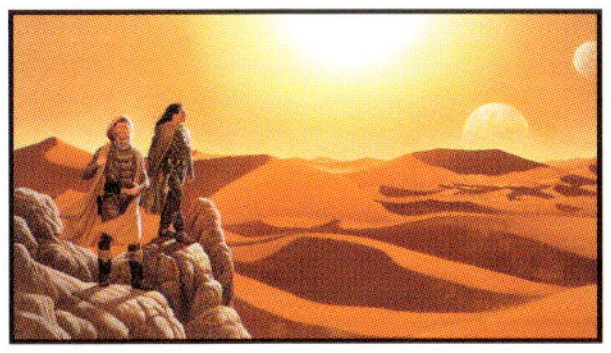
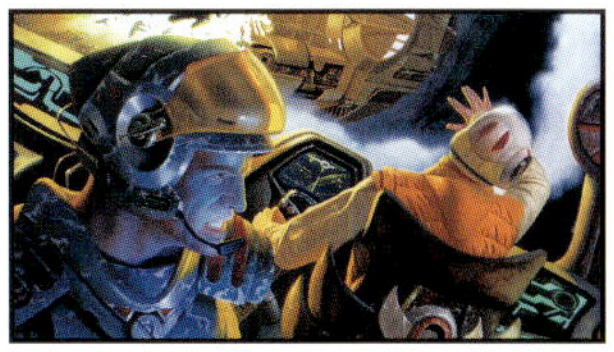

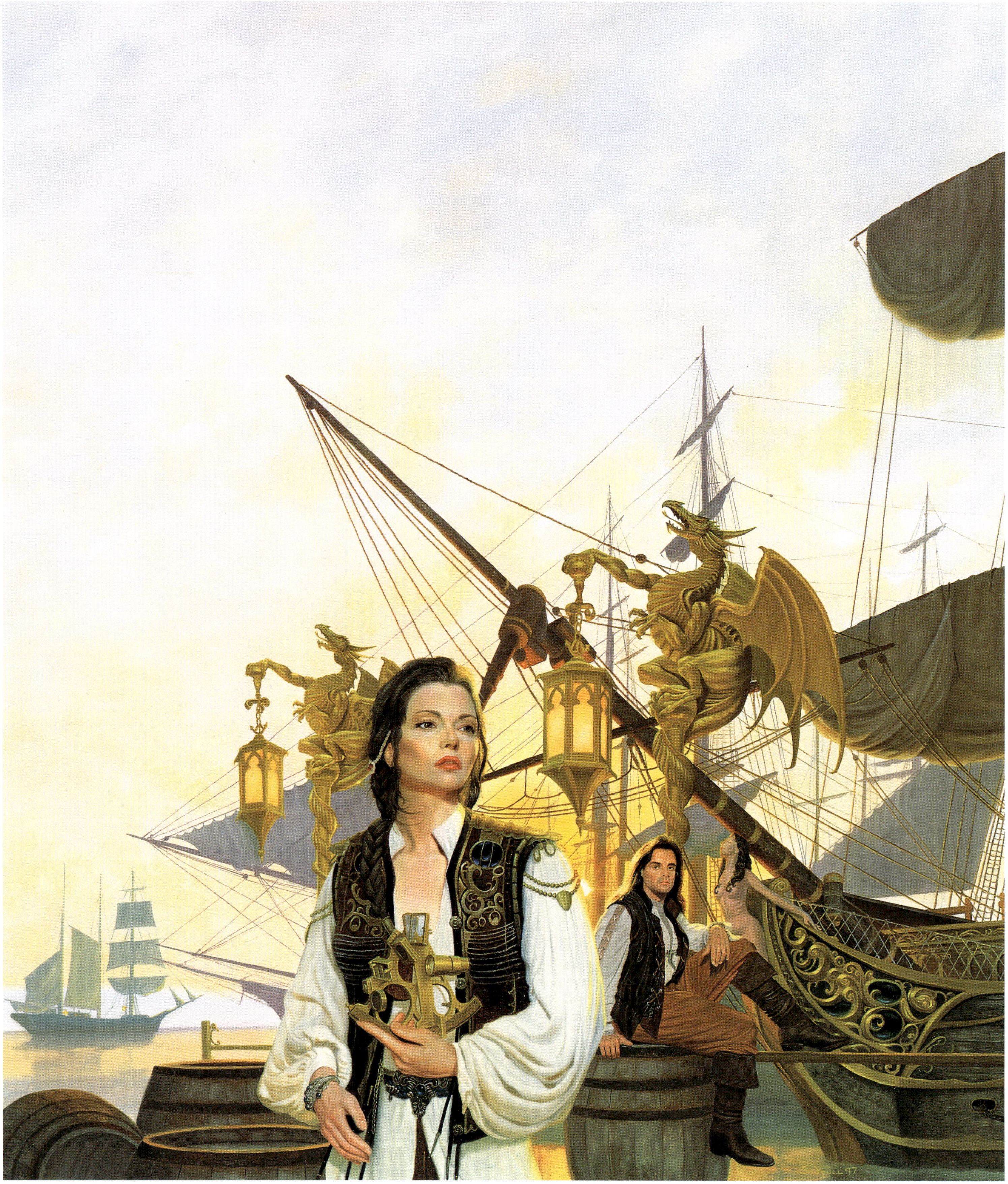

SHIP OF MAGIC

ROBIN HOBB, BANTAM, 1997

OIL ON ILLUSTRATION BOARD, 30 x 25in (76 x 64cm)

FOREWORD BY KEVIN J. ANDERSON

A PICTURE IS WORTH MORE THAN A THOUSAND WORDS

Stephen Youll lives in his imagination, and in the imaginations of countless authors. This is your chance to take a journey to the strange places he sees in his mind's eye.

Coming at it from an author's perspective, when I finally get to see the cover of a new novel there's always that long 'cringe' moment when I open the envelope and hope I won't find too many slavering monsters, garish robes, and brass brassieres – you know, the stuff that some art director once thought would sell copies. Not so when I know Steve is the artist. He understands what he's doing; he actually reads the manuscript he's supposed to illustrate, and he often consults with the writer.

Stephen Youll has painted the covers of seven of my novels: three Dune prequels, three *Star Wars* anthologies and an original science-fiction novel, *Blindfold*. The first cover he did for one of my works, *Tales from the Mos Eisley Cantina,* was published in August 1995, and the book immediately became the best-selling science-fiction anthology of all time. Steve's painting for my follow-up anthology, *Tales from Jabba's Palace,* won him a Gold Award from the Magazine and Booksellers Newsstand Cover Competition for most outstanding cover of the year.

Check out his painting for Ian McDonald's *Speaking in Tongues* (page 48). Look at it. Stare at it. This was the first piece of Steve's I ever noticed, hanging in a Worldcon art show in San Francisco in 1993. The alien is weird and detailed and wonderful – but the human is unbelievable! A painting, not a photo? That's hard to swallow. It's so incredibly realistic.

An editor at Bantam recently sent me some books she thought I'd like, the *Assassin* trilogy by Robin Hobb. When I received them, I told her I especially liked the covers, which I thought had been done by a particularly well-known artist in the genre. She said, 'One of them is by Stephen Youll.' Time for a double-take, go back to the shelf, study the paintings one more time. Sure enough, it's that Youll guy again. Steve certainly is versatile – from photorealistic science fiction to beautiful fantasy.

Born in Hartlepool, England, in 1965, Steve made up his mind to become a science-fiction and fantasy artist at an early age, and then he went on to enter and win art contests all through his college years. After graduating at the top of his class at the Durham New College of Art and Design, he worked as a historical reconstruction artist at Durham Cathedral, one of the oldest cathedrals in England. As part of his work, he painted numerous portraits of important people in the Church throughout British history. Many of his paintings and sketches are on display in churches and cathedrals around Great Britain. His ambitious aerial view of a cutaway of Durham Cathedral took him a full year to complete, relying on ancient texts and sketches.

Apparently tired of respectability, however, Steve decided to jump into the world of SF and fantasy artwork. He painted many samples and exhibited them for the first time at the World Science Fiction Convention in Brighton, England, in 1987. There he made such a splash that he landed several assignments from major US publishing companies. Shortly afterwards, he was receiving so many cover jobs that he quit his cathedral work.

For two years he often collaborated on paintings with his identical-twin artist brother, Paul. In 1989 Stephen got married and moved to the United States, where he has continued to build up an impressive portfolio of work for virtually every major SF publisher, illustrating books by Arthur C. Clarke, Isaac Asimov, C.J. Cherryh, George R.R. Martin, Margaret Weis and Tracy Hickman, Robert Silverberg, Ben Bova and many others.

Not only is his artwork superb, but from an author's perspective Steve is also a great artist to work with. More often than not, the cover artist and author have no contact with each other.

In far too many cases, the artist reads only a blurb or a summary of the novel at hand. Steve is an exception.

He takes a genuine interest in the books themselves, and he's a reader. He has often called me to ask about details for an illustration for one of my novels, to brainstorm what scenes might make the best cover

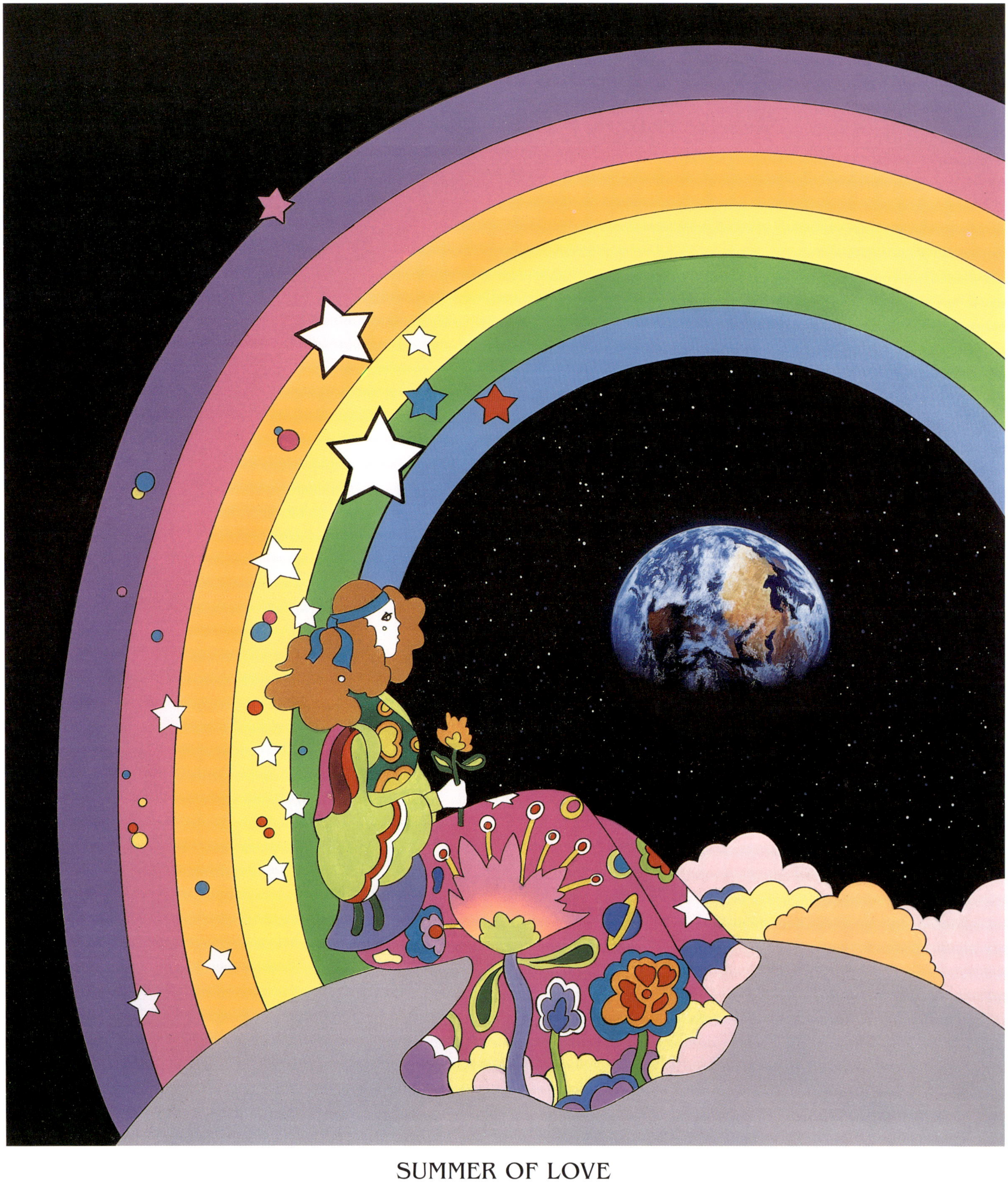

SUMMER OF LOVE
LISA MASON, BANTAM, 1993
ACRYLIC ON ILLUSTRATION BOARD, 12½ x 15in (32 x 38cm)

painting – sometimes this is even before the manuscript itself is completed. For *Dune: House Corrino* we talked about possible images that would convey the right look before I had delivered the novel to the publisher. I sent him draft chapters even without the rest of the manuscript, just to get him started, though I knew he would still read the entire novel.

The scenes and arrangements he chooses for his covers not only exemplify excellence in artwork but they also tell a story. Glancing at the paintings makes you want to pick up the book and see what it's about – something for which we authors are obviously greatly appreciative.

You need only look at the range of his work to see a consistent level of amazing detail and sheer pageantry. He uses sweeping colours and intricate reflections, all of which convey the sense that Steve Youll actually lives in these fabulous worlds. He has been nominated for just about every major award in the field, has received certificates of merit and has won numerous art show competitions. He has exhibited his work at numerous SF conventions in the United States and in Britain. His work has journeyed around the United States in several travelling SF art shows under the aegis of such bodies as the Society of Illustrators and the Frank Collection, and has also been seen in New York City at the Society of Illustrators and the Illustration House. When you look at the examples in this book, you'll certainly see why.

Well, if a picture is worth a thousand words… you've just finished my thousand-word introduction, which is worth exactly one picture. Now go look at the pictures themselves.

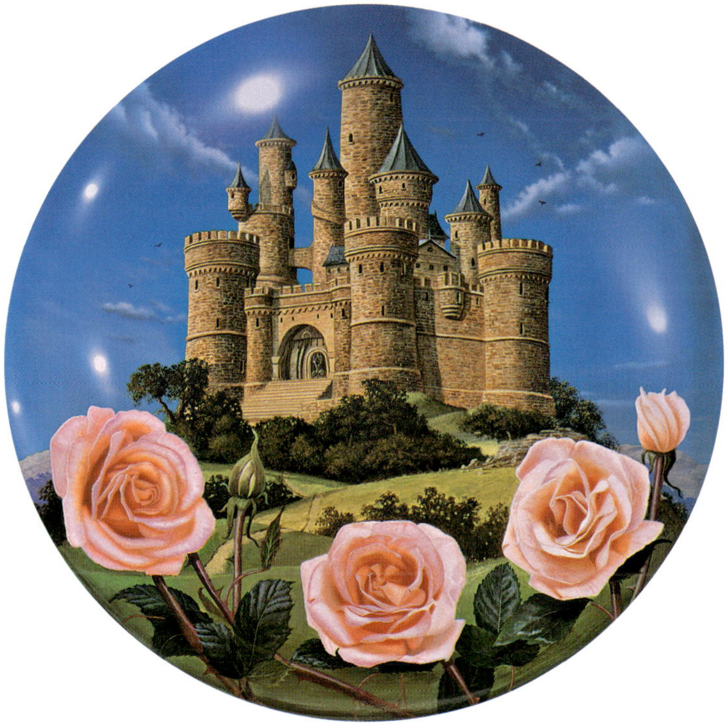

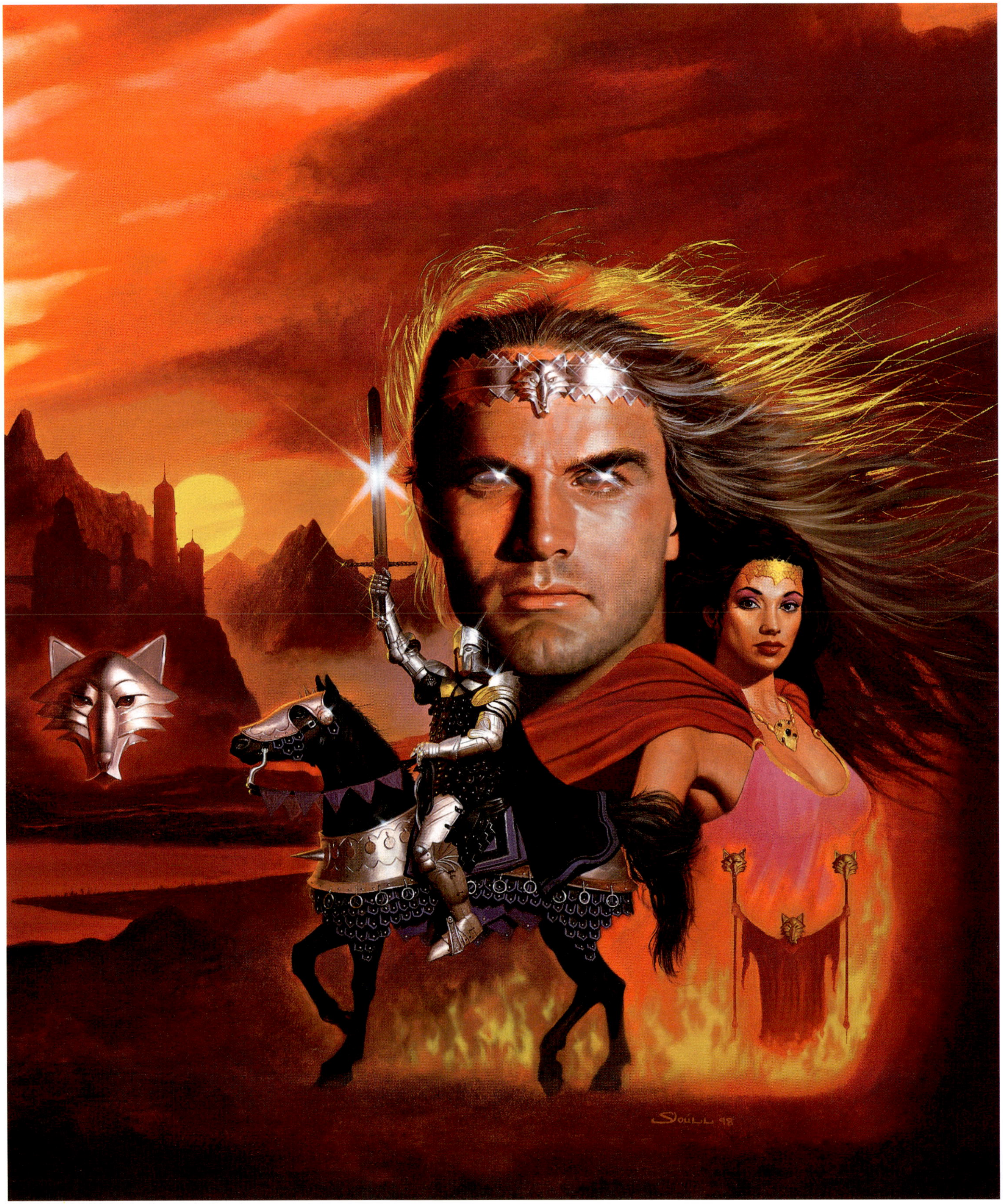

EYES OF SILVER

MICHAEL A. STACKPOLE, BANTAM, 1998

OIL ON MASONITE, 30 x 40in (76 x 102cm)

LIFE DREAMS

I was born the elder of a pair of identical twins in Hartlepool, England, in 1965. I grew up in the village of Wheatley Hill, cradled between woods, hills and farmland, about seven miles (eleven kilometres) from the city of Durham in the northern part of the country. There was nothing remarkable about the village except for one thing: there was an old Royalty cinema within walking distance of my home.

It was the Royalty that gave me my earliest recollections of being introduced to the world of the fantastic. My twin brother, Paul, and I frequented this old, mouldy, rundown establishment in search of action and adventure, which we duly found every Saturday in the form of those old black-and-white SF serials: classics like *Flash Gordon, Buck Rogers in the 25th Century* and *Rocket Man* created an imaginative addiction that would last the rest of our lives.

My mother had a total of three sets of twins, all boys, although she unfortunately lost one of those boys at birth. Having three older brothers and my twin, I naturally had to face a good deal of competition, which is why I became an overachiever.

Paul and I have always shared, as most twins do, the same interests. So it was with science fiction. As kids we loved to go walking over fields and meadows, across streams and through woods. However, in the middle of one of those hikes, it would take only a sudden realization that *Star Trek* was due on television for us to run home in a panic and throw ourselves in front of the screen to watch our favourite show. Our idea of complete bliss! Most of our childhood was filled with a steady diet of classic SF television shows. *Doctor Who, Thunderbirds, Captain Scarlet and the Mysterons, Space: 1999, Lost in Space* and *Battlestar Galactica* all kindled our imaginations and reinforced our love for the genre.

With the exception of comics – notably *2000 A.D., Vulcan* and *Valiant* – I can't remember reading any SF as a boy. In fact, most of my reading interests lay in science proper; I avidly read books on astronomy, archaeology and biology. However, my childhood hero, my older brother Graeme, loved SF and fantasy and was a great reader in these genres. I found myself fascinated by the covers of the books he read.

At secondary school I discovered a kindred spirit and mentor in my art teacher, Denis Fox. Foxy, as the students fondly called him, introduced me to a whole world of illustrators producing off-world visions. He brought in books of art by Bruce Pennington and Chris Foss, so fuelling an ever-evolving passion in me. His encouragement to study various artists' visions and create my own work in their tradition was the catalyst that started me on the road to an artistic career.

When it came time for me to consider what I should do on leaving school I was torn between a love of art and a love of science, but Foxy pleaded with my parents to send me to art college. My parents had very little money in those days, and the idea of finding the funds for further education seemed daunting. My three older brothers had all gone to work at age sixteen. Though my mum and dad knew I had a tenacious appetite to create, they worried that, if I went to art college, I would have no prospects for gainful employment afterwards. My family, you must remember, was strictly blue-collar: not a professional artist in sight on the family tree. In the end, nevertheless, my parents decided that Paul and I should have the chance to apply to art college.

In the summer of 1981, when we were sixteen, Paul and I won second and third place in an art contest. We were both working in pastels and tempera paints at the time, and the artist who had judged the competition showed us his portfolio of airbrush art. We marvelled at his finishes, and he advised us to get an airbrush.

I had a part-time job delivering newspapers, and I was able to earn enough money to pay for the airbrush itself. However, I couldn't afford the compressor. So for a compressor I used the inner tube of a bus-tyre, given to me on permanent loan by the owner of a bus company headquartered at the end of our street when I promised him I would airbrush him a 'sexy' woman to hang on his garage wall. To fit the air hose to the airbrush gun I had to use a car tyre adapter. Unfortunately, though, the air lasted for only about fifteen minutes, so over the next year Paul and I were constantly to be seen, at all hours of the day and night, wheeling that inner tube up and down the street as we went to get refills of air. Occasionally the owner of

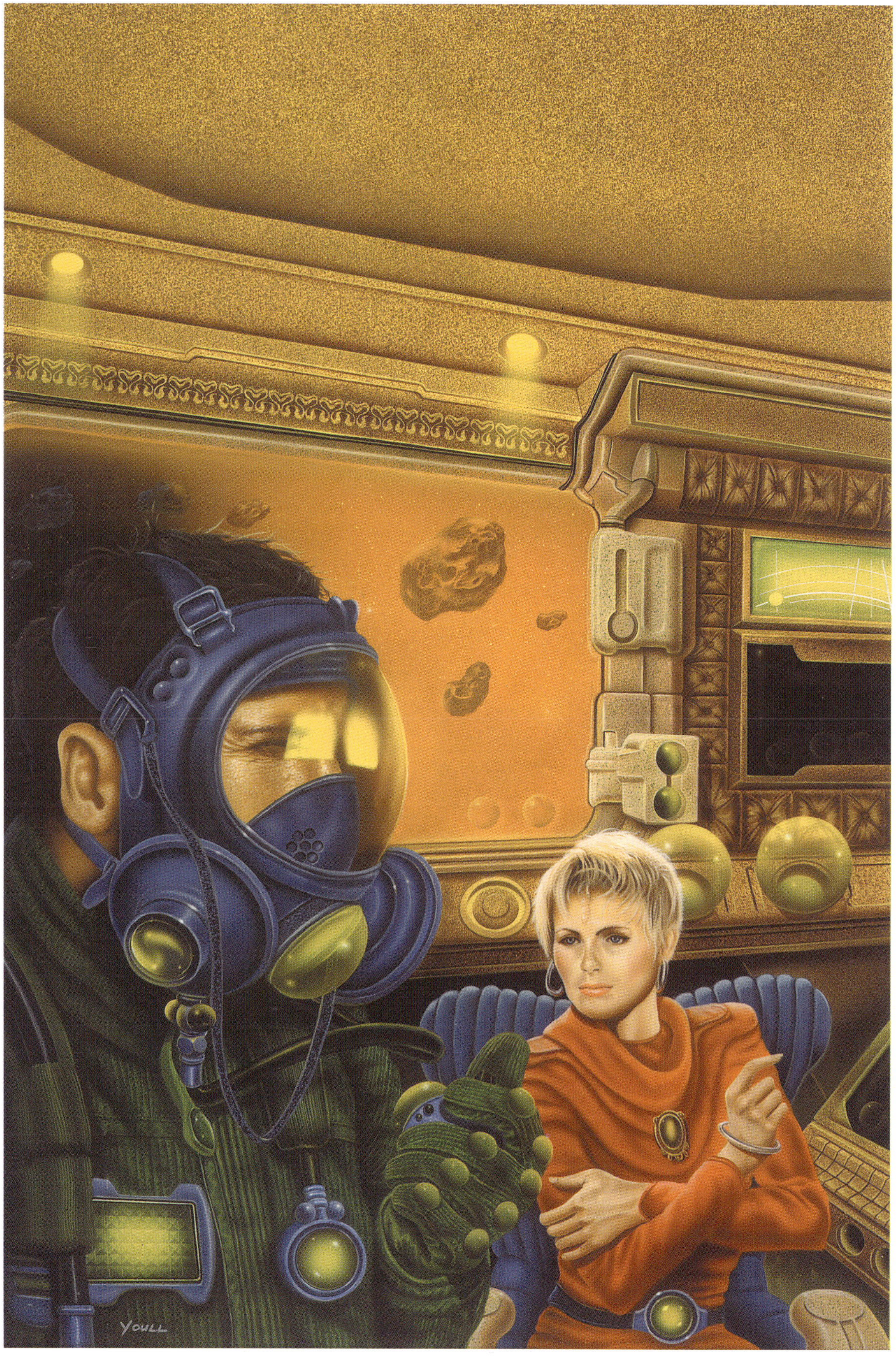

MAN IN THE BLUE MASK

PORTFOLIO SAMPLE, 1987

ACRYLIC ON ILLUSTRATION BOARD, 17½ x 11in (44 x 28cm)

the garage would hear noises at two o'clock in the morning and come running out of his house in a dressing gown yelling, 'Who's there?' We would yell back, 'It's only us... not a burglar.' I can still hear him shouting as he walked back to his house, 'Where's my naked lady?' Shameful to say, he never got her, though, deep down, I don't think he minded.

Later that same summer, armed with dozens of pastel drawings and tempera paintings and enough enthusiasm to put someone on the moon, we joined the art school of New College, Durham. The college, just a short bus ride away from our home, provided instruction in a broad range of disciplines, including life drawing and painting in a wide range of media.

Doing art at home proved to be difficult, as I had no formal place to paint or airbrush and had to use the bathroom floor or the kitchen table. Luckily my being an artist was never made to seem an inconvenience to my family – not even when I finally got a little compressor that used to vibrate the ceiling so much that my mother's chandelier would shake or the paint would go flying and stain the carpets. Each new painting was always met with praise and encouragement.

After I had gained my diploma from New College I wanted to improve my technical-drawing skills, and found that Sunderland University had one of the finest programmes for technical illustration in the country. I was accepted there, and in due course, in 1985, graduated with a degree in Visual Information Design.

During my time at university I freelanced, through one of my instructors, for a number of professional clients, and this gave me valuable experience: I acquired more practical knowledge from these few real assignments than from the entire range of lectures and classes at university. However, I had produced very little SF art during my years of formal art training, and certainly not enough to gain employment from the SF publishing industry, even though my plan was to pursue a career in SF book-cover art.

It took Paul and me six months of steady work at home after we'd left university to get a whole new group of paintings together. We then showed our work to several art agencies in London, and received much-needed criticism from these experienced art representatives. They encouraged us to do additional samples and show them at the forthcoming World Science Fiction Convention, to be held in Brighton in August 1987. While we were working on these new paintings, our brother and constant supporter Graeme was killed in a motorcycle accident. I felt that the only way to honour his memory and his dream of Paul and I becoming artists was to get our art to that convention.

Going to Worldcon would cost money, however, and neither of us had any, so we both took jobs that summer as reconstruction artists at Durham Cathedral. This entailed painting portraits of various religious dignitaries, making drawings of religious artefacts and doing hours of research both at the cathedral and at various locations all over England. So during the day I was working for the cathedral and at night I was doing my own SF paintings for the upcoming convention. It was an exhausting time, but it helped to be working as I would otherwise have dwelt on the grief of losing my brother.

That convention at Brighton still remains my favourite Worldcon; I met new friends, professional artists and potential clients. Two months after the convention Paul and I got a call from a New York publisher, Bantam, and received our first professional cover assignment, for *Emerald Eyes* by Daniel Keys Morgan (page 102). Several months later we were hired by another company in New York, Byron Preiss Visual Publications, and then several London publishing houses also called. Paul and I found we worked well together, painting side by side in a symbiotic manner. We could even match colours without premixed palettes and work from different sides of the canvas to meet seamlessly in the centre. It certainly made deadlines easier! Sometimes one of us would sleep while one stayed up painting, then we'd switch so the other could rest.

As our first Worldcon had been such a success, my brother and I decided to attend the next one, held in New Orleans in 1988. One of the New York art directors I worked with, Jamie Warren, was attending as well – I had been hired by her to do a cover for George Alec Effinger's *A Fire in the Sun*. We planned to meet her at the convention and show her the sketch. As a consequence of this meeting, Jamie and I fell in love;

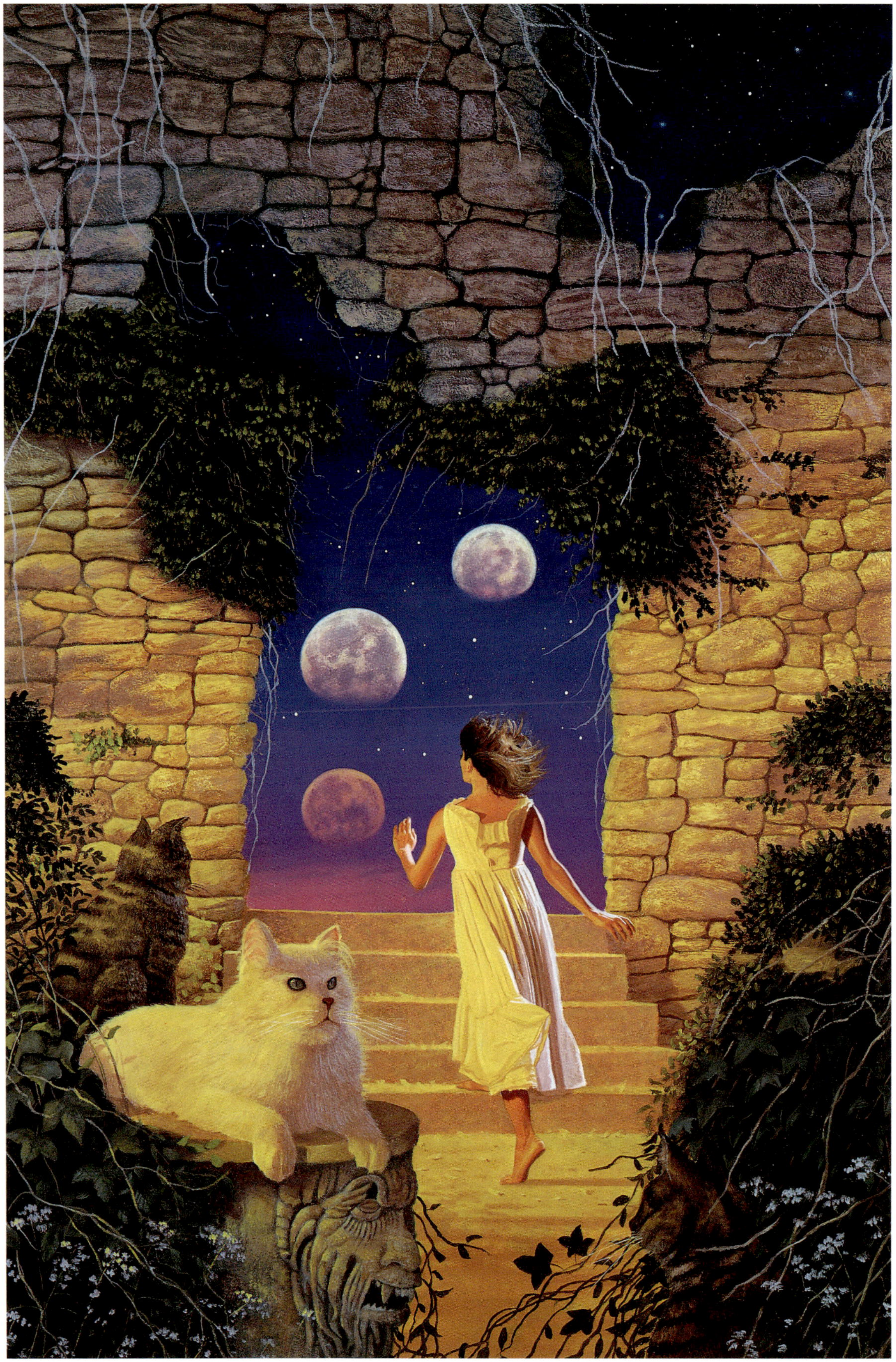

RELUCTANT VOYAGERS
ELISABETH VONARBURG, BANTAM, 1995
OIL ON ILLUSTRATION BOARD, 24 x 15in (61 x 38cm)

we were married a year and a half later. After the wedding I moved to the United States, in the winter of 1989, and became a 'legal alien' – it does seem an appropriate term for an SF artist, doesn't it?

It was the toughest thing I ever did, leaving behind my family, my country and my brother, Paul, who was also my painting partner. There was culture shock, too: I had moved from a tiny village to the metropolitan city of New York. I can still remember my reaction. It was as if I had been projected into the future. Here was a place where my mind was in a constant ferment of ever-evolving images. The city itself had a profound effect on the development of the style and content of my work. Our apartment was on the Upper East Side, and I shared a studio with a terrific illustrator, Jerry LoFaro, down in the SoHo district. He and I shared the same love for movie soundtracks, and would blast them out well into the small hours of the morning while working on some crazy deadlines.

An artist is always searching for a sense of place, both inside and as part of the art community. Affected by my new surroundings, I adopted a new approach to my art, an approach that I like to call 'movie-istic'. I found using various lighting effects I had so often seen in movies gave my art a more three-dimensional and modern look.

Jamie and I stayed in the city for two years, and then moved to New Jersey and into our own home. I have now been a professional artist for fifteen years – years of occassional frustration and frequent fulfilment – and plan to continue the adventure for many more. I used to feel that being an artist was like being stuck in purgatory, what with the deadlines, the late hours and the pressure to produce better and better paintings. I now know that the key to happiness comes via hard work and a devotion to doing your best. If other people enjoy looking at my paintings as much as I have enjoyed creating them, then all my efforts are worthwhile.

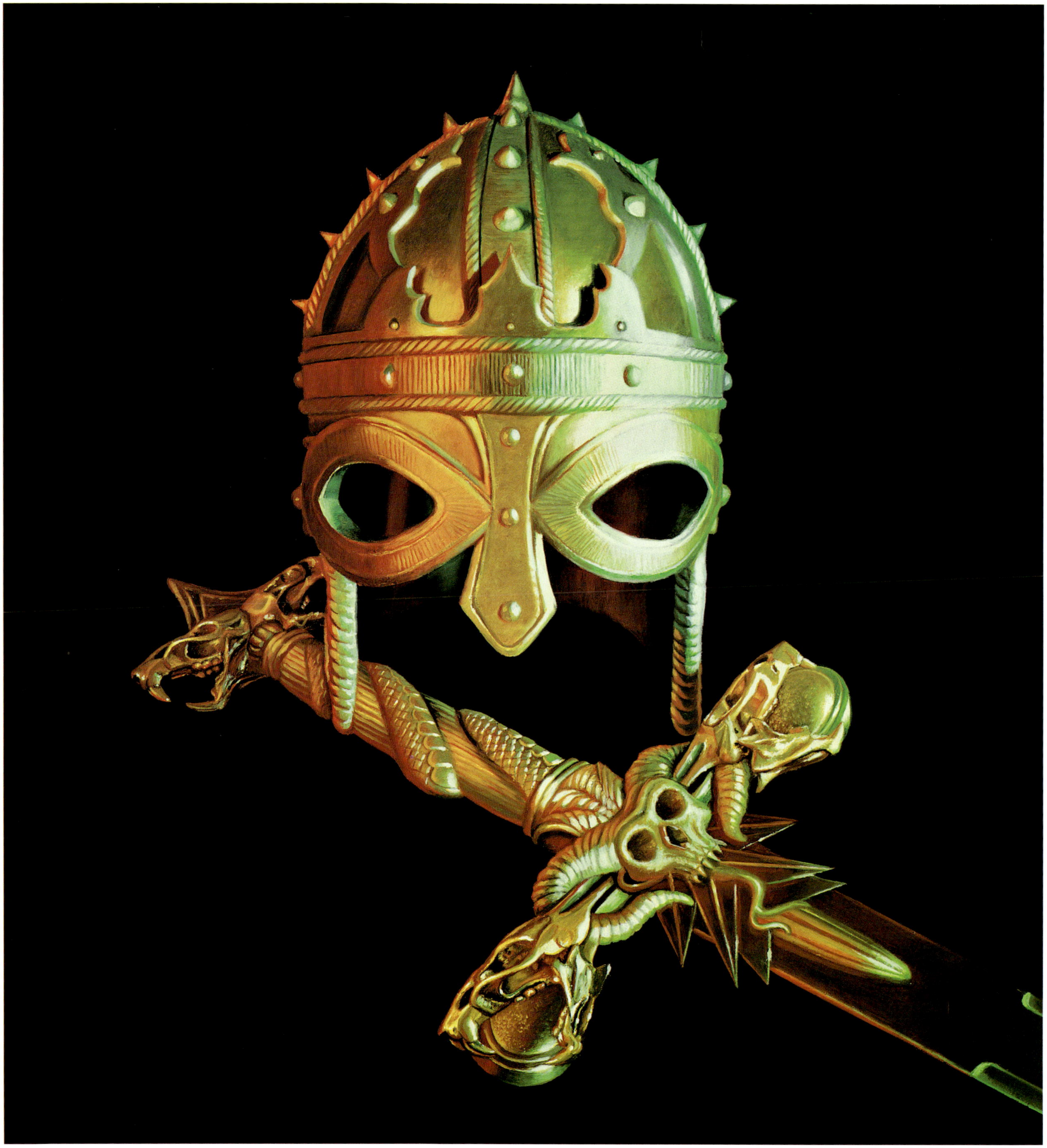

THE WARRIOR KING

CHRIS BUNCH, WARNER, 1998

OIL ON MASONITE, 26¼ x 17½in (67 x 44cm)

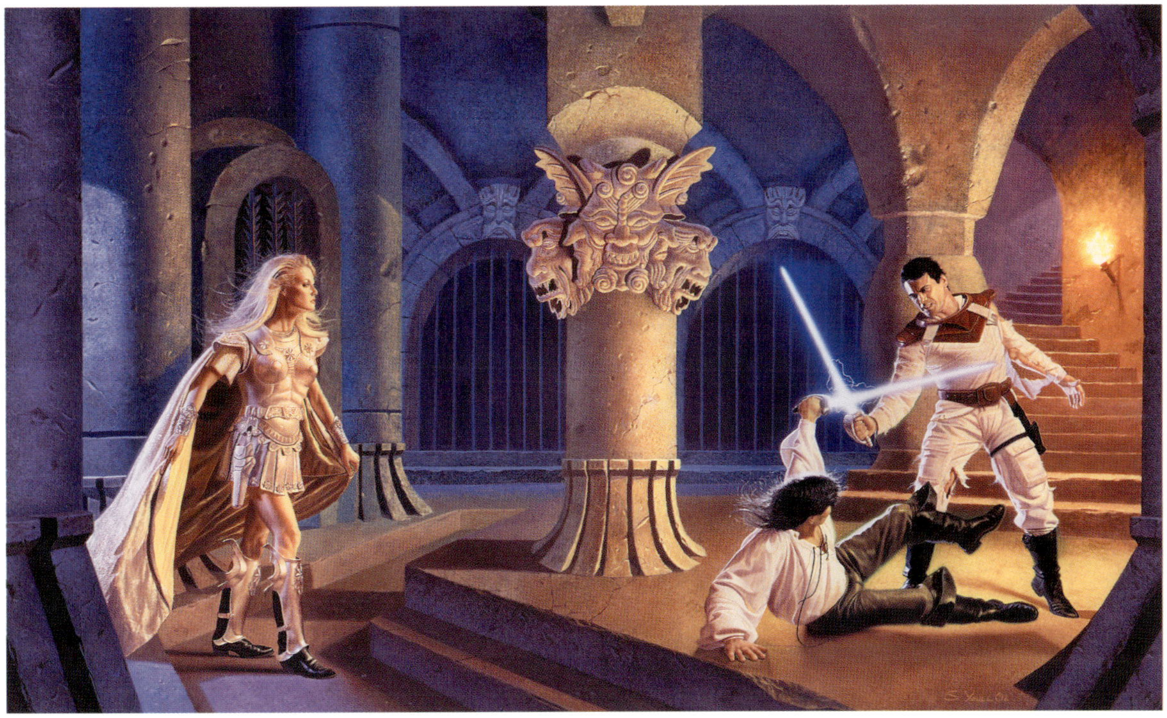

GHOST LEGION
MARGARET WEIS, BANTAM, 1992
ACRYLIC AND OIL ON ILLUSTRATION BOARD, 27 x 40in (69 x 102cm)

THE WARRIOR KINGS

Being a Gemini, I can seemingly go from one personality to another – it drives me crazy! However, I've learned to live with my astrologically determined quirks, and instead of fighting them I use them. When I'm working as an SF artist, most of the images I paint are flashy, polished and highly energetic. But when I'm painting fantasy I like to portray mood, a feeling of subdued passion and a sense of history.

After I left college my brother Graeme gave me his treasured copy of what I think is the greatest fantasy novel ever written: *The Lord of the Rings* by J.R.R. Tolkien. Every page of its pure genius has coloured my way of seeing fantasy art. I love to illustrate fantasy stories classically, especially when it's the kind of novel that lends itself to a more historical feel, like George R.R. Martin's saga *A Song of Ice and Fire*. The opening books in this continuing story are stylish and sombre, and have an upscale quality that I wanted to reflect in the cover illustrations. I deliberately chose more muted colour schemes, and used contrasts in value and tone to enhance the mood and flavour of the novels.

The works of the nineteenth-century masters J.W. Waterhouse and Jean-Léon Gérôme have been a great source of inspiration for me since my early days at art college. The figures in their paintings seem neither posed nor self-conscious, captured in their natural state of being. For some time I have adopted this approach when composing my figures, with the hope of giving my art a timeless quality. I use posed models for the characters in all my illustrations, but maintain a sense of caution when rendering them in the painting. Since I'm illustrating characters from a book, not aiming to depict the model I've hired to pose for me, I alter and subtly change the person to fit the image of the character I have formed in my imagination, based on what the author has written.

Several years ago, while visiting my family in England, I discovered an unusual attachment to my past, a renewed sense of appreciation for my rural beginnings. Being driven towards the technological side of science fiction, my imagination had always felt stifled by my surroundings in the village where I grew up. Moving to New York City, with its canyons of glass and steel, had cured that. But now I found many of the places I had frequented as a boy – the woods, the valleys, the misty lakes – were finding their way into my fantasy work. I had never given much thought to the true value of my rural past; now I have come to rely on it.

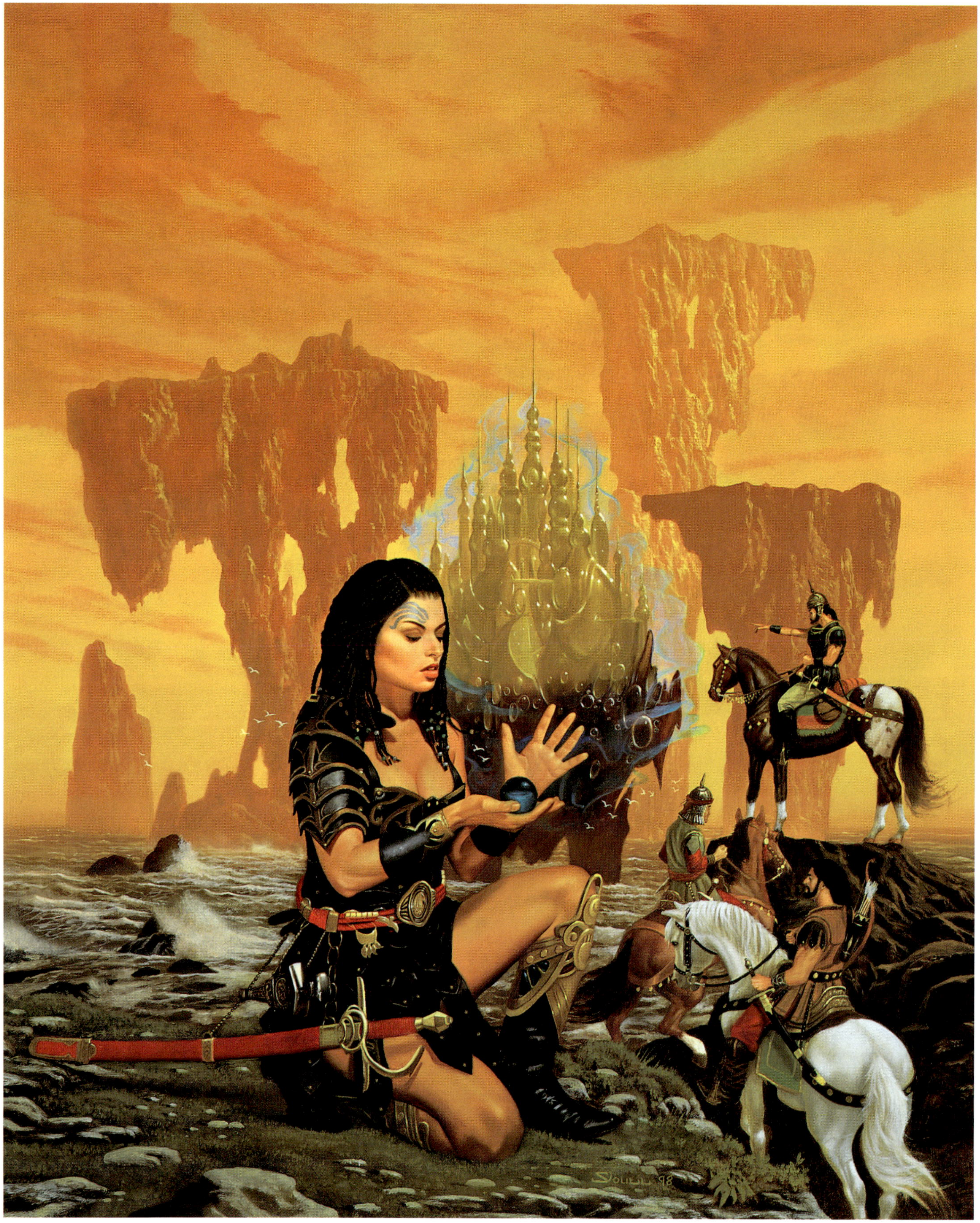

THE COMPANY OF GLASS
VALERY LEITH, BANTAM, 1998
OIL ON MASONITE, 21 x 17in (53 x 43cm)

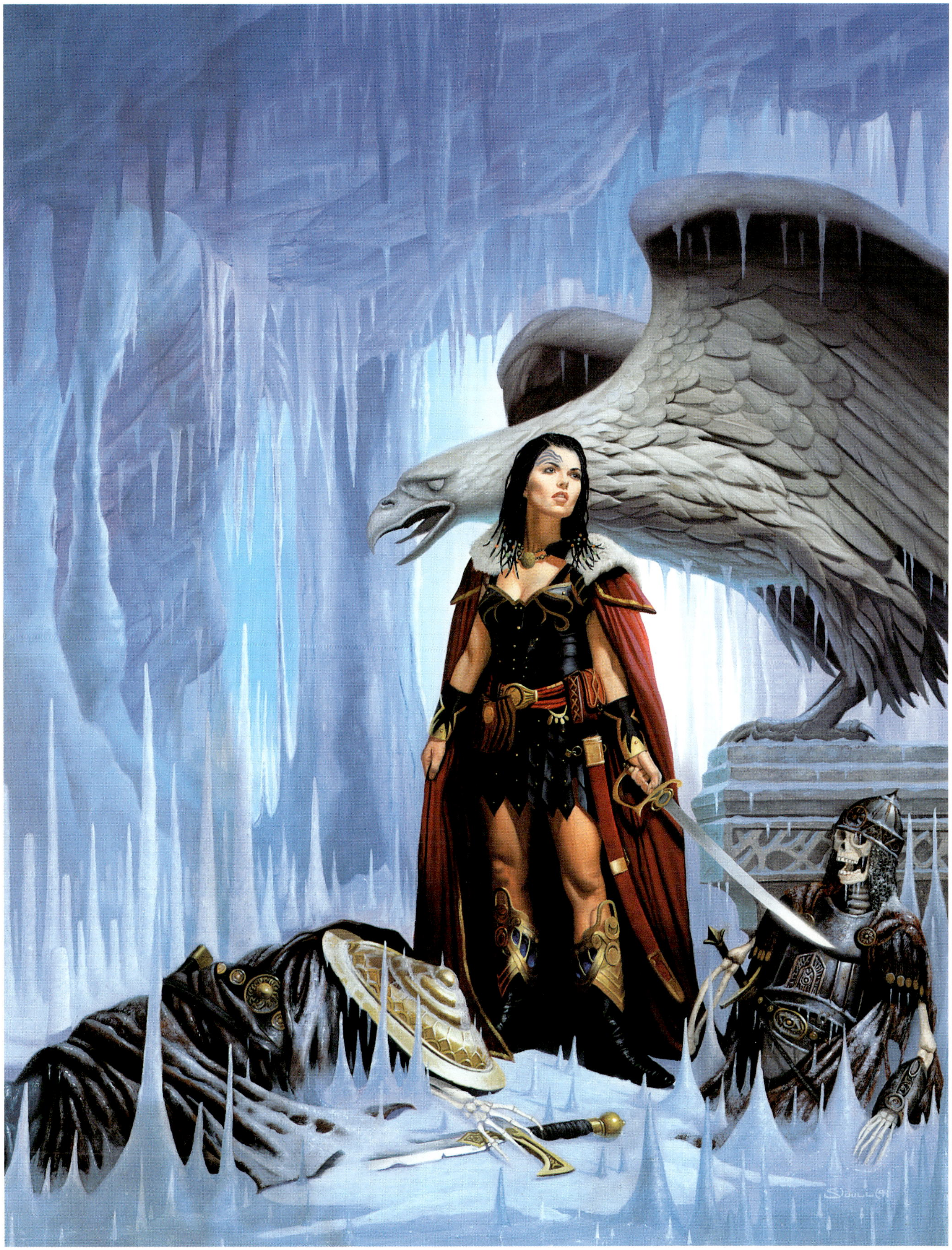

THE RIDDLED NIGHT

VALERY LEITH, BANTAM, 1999

OIL ON MASONITE, 26¼ x 17½in (67 x 44cm)

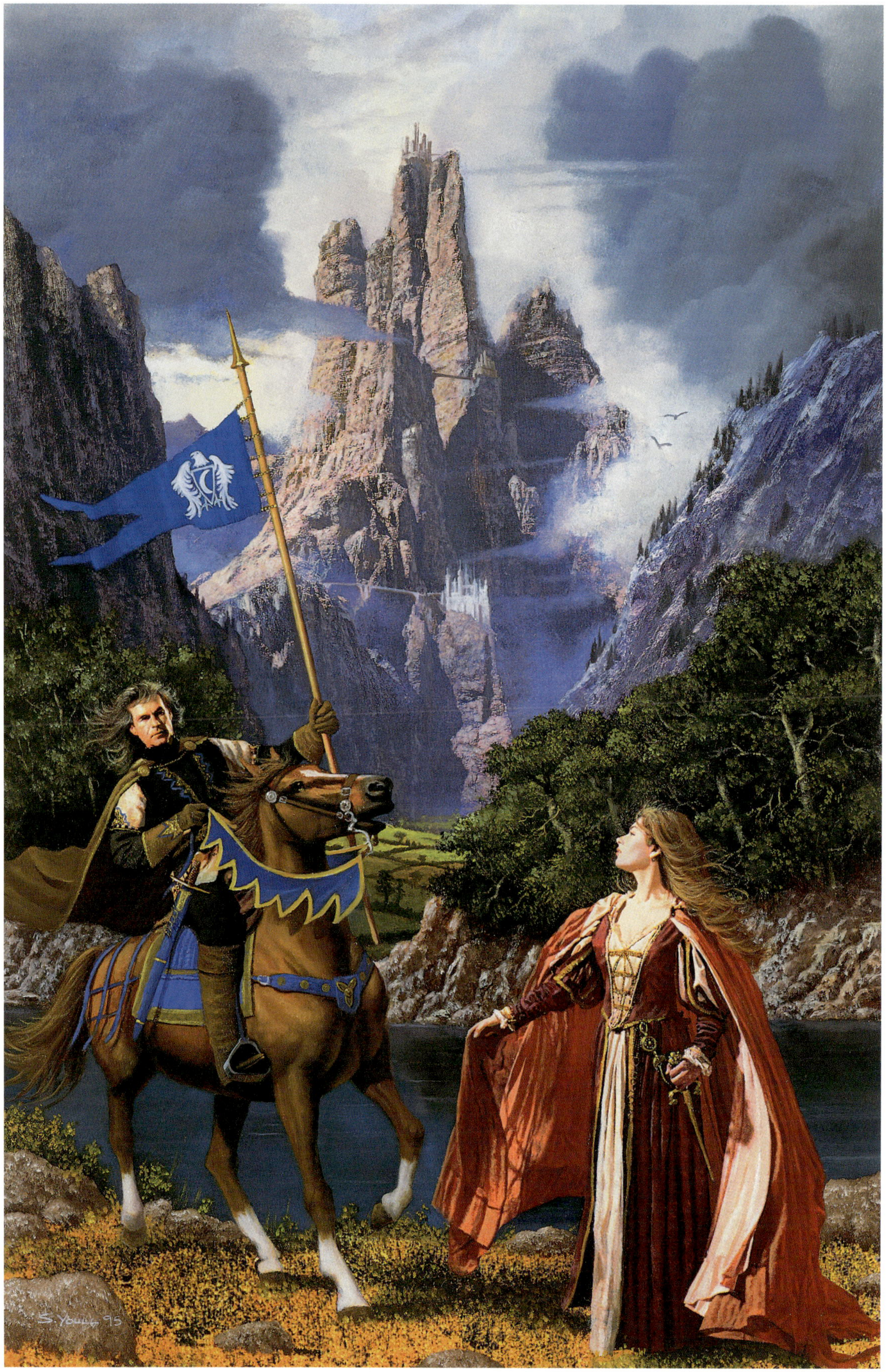

A GAME OF THRONES (1)

GEORGE R.R. MARTIN, BANTAM, 1995

INK AND OIL ON ILLUSTRATION BOARD, 17 x 11in (43 x 28cm)

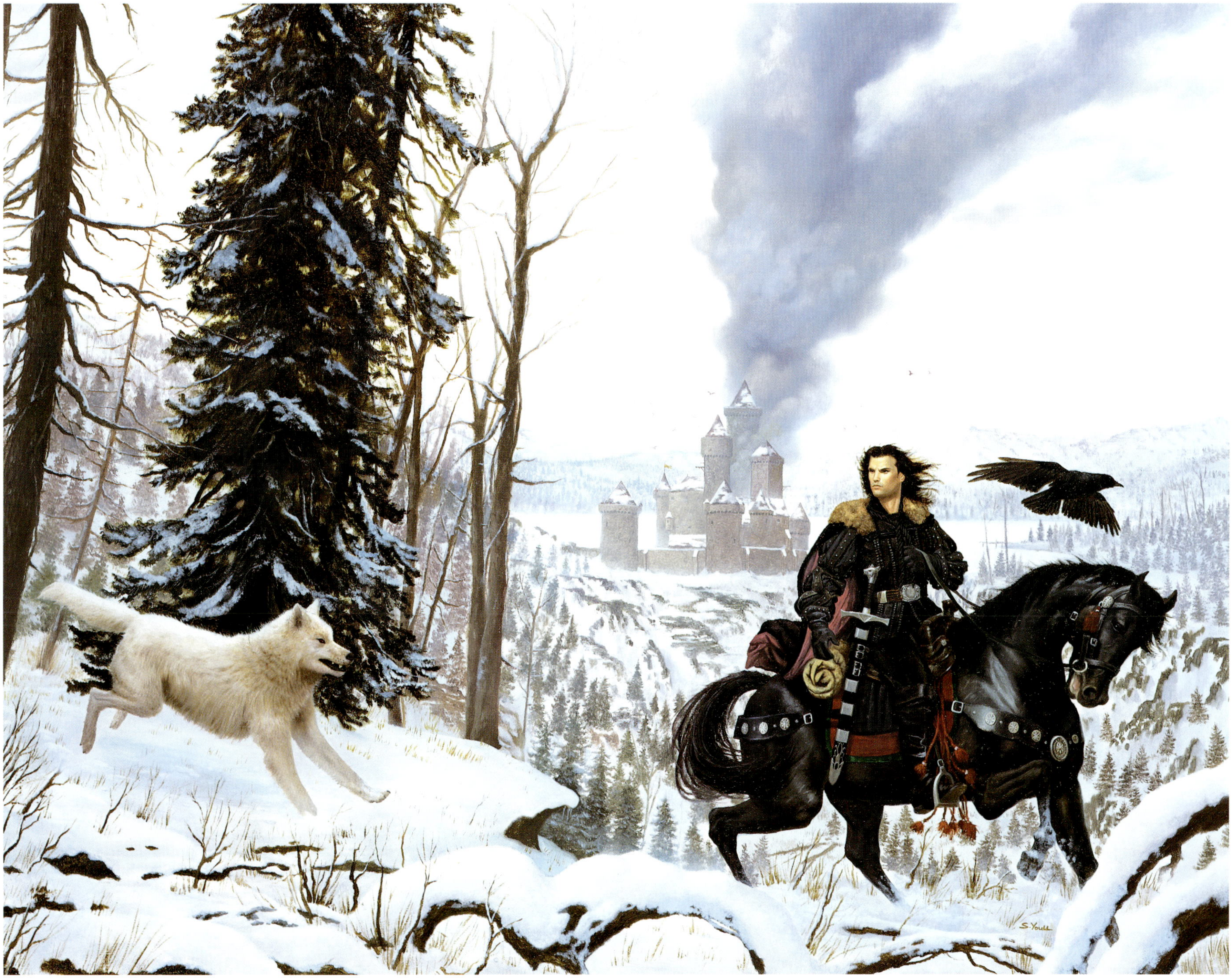

A GAME OF THRONES (2)
GEORGE R.R. MARTIN, BANTAM, 1996
OIL ON ILLUSTRATION BOARD, 24 x 33½in (61 x 85cm)

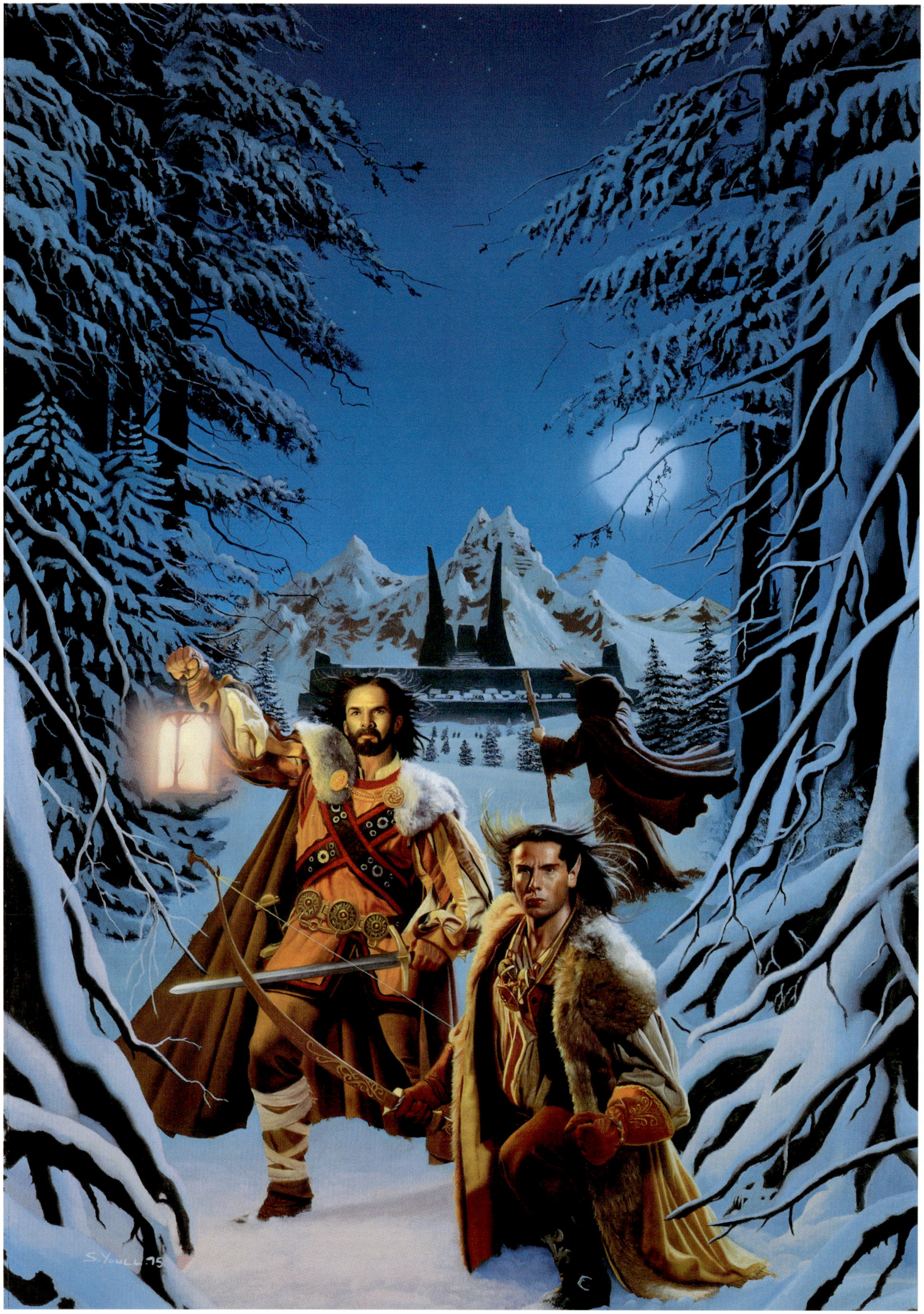

THE SHAMAN

CHRISTOPHER STASHEFF, BALLANTINE, 1995
OIL ON ILLUSTRATION BOARD, 32 x 21in (81 x 53cm)

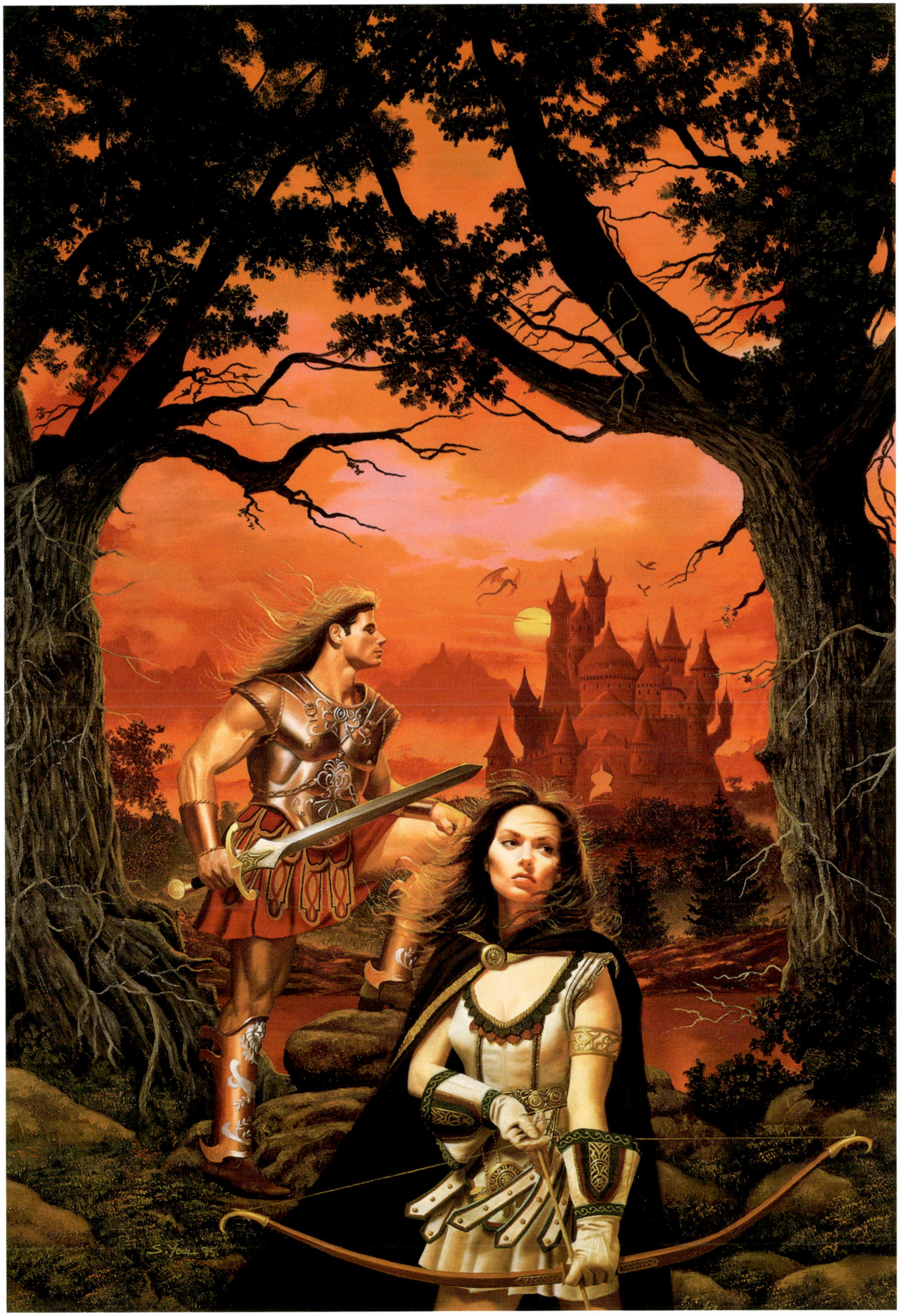

THE SAGE

CHRISTOPHER STASHEFF, BALLANTINE, 1995

OIL ON ILLUSTRATION BOARD, 25½ x 16½in (65 x 42cm)

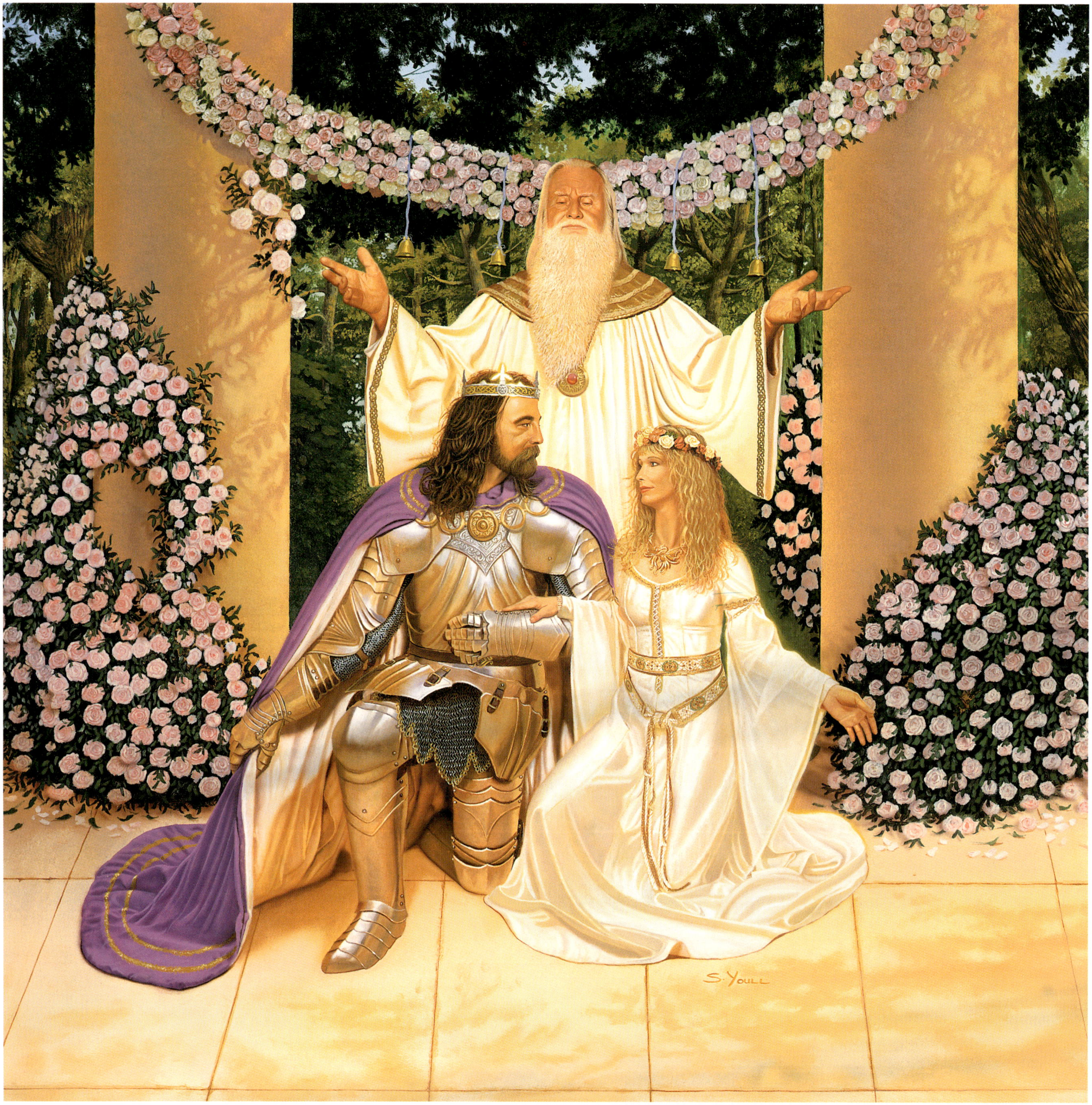

THE BLESSING

HAMILTON PLATES, 1993

OIL ON ILLUSTRATION BOARD, 24 x 23½in (61 x 60cm)

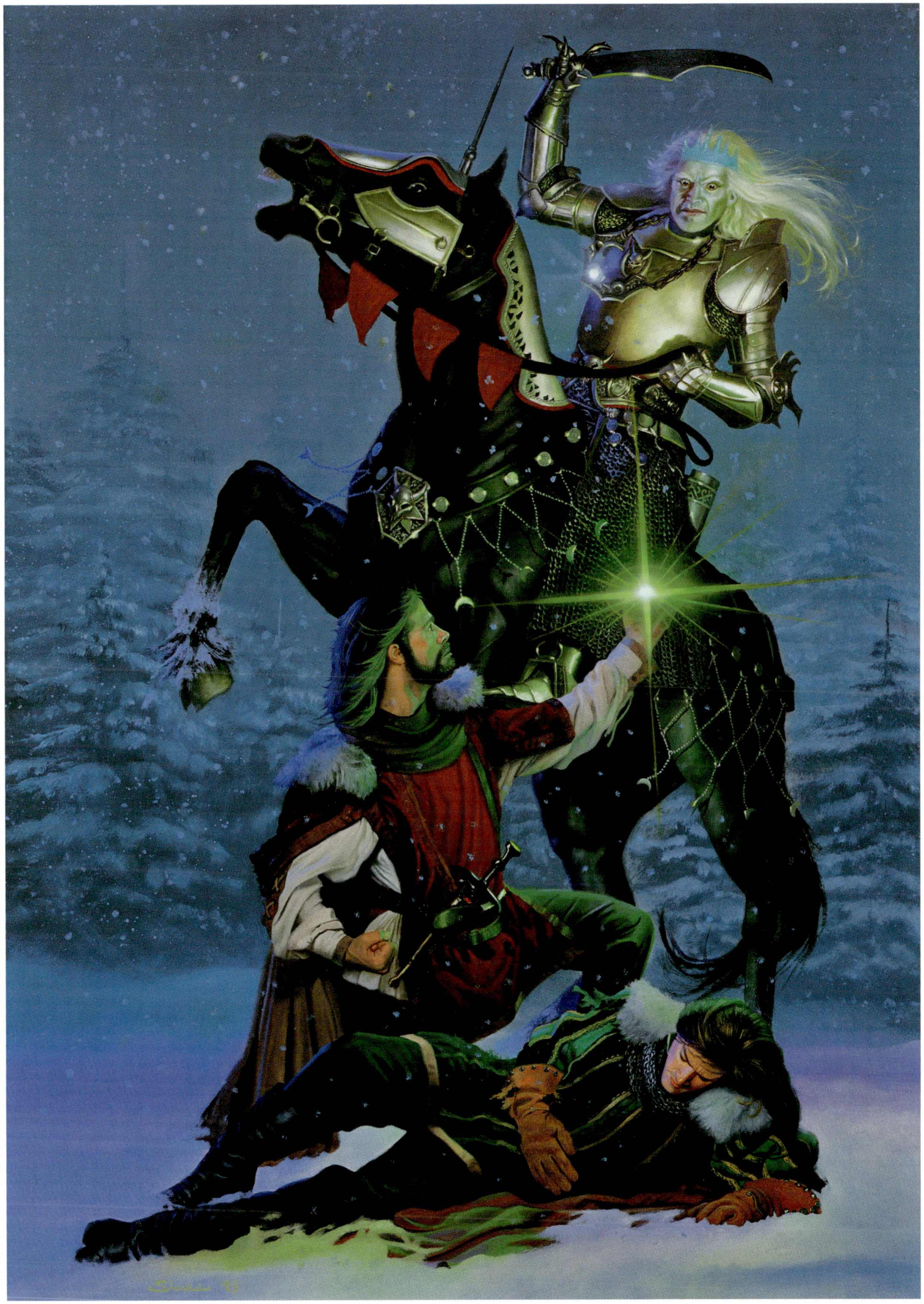

BEYOND THE PALE

MARK ANTHONY, BANTAM, 1998

OIL ON MASONITE, 22½ x 13¼in (57 x 34cm)

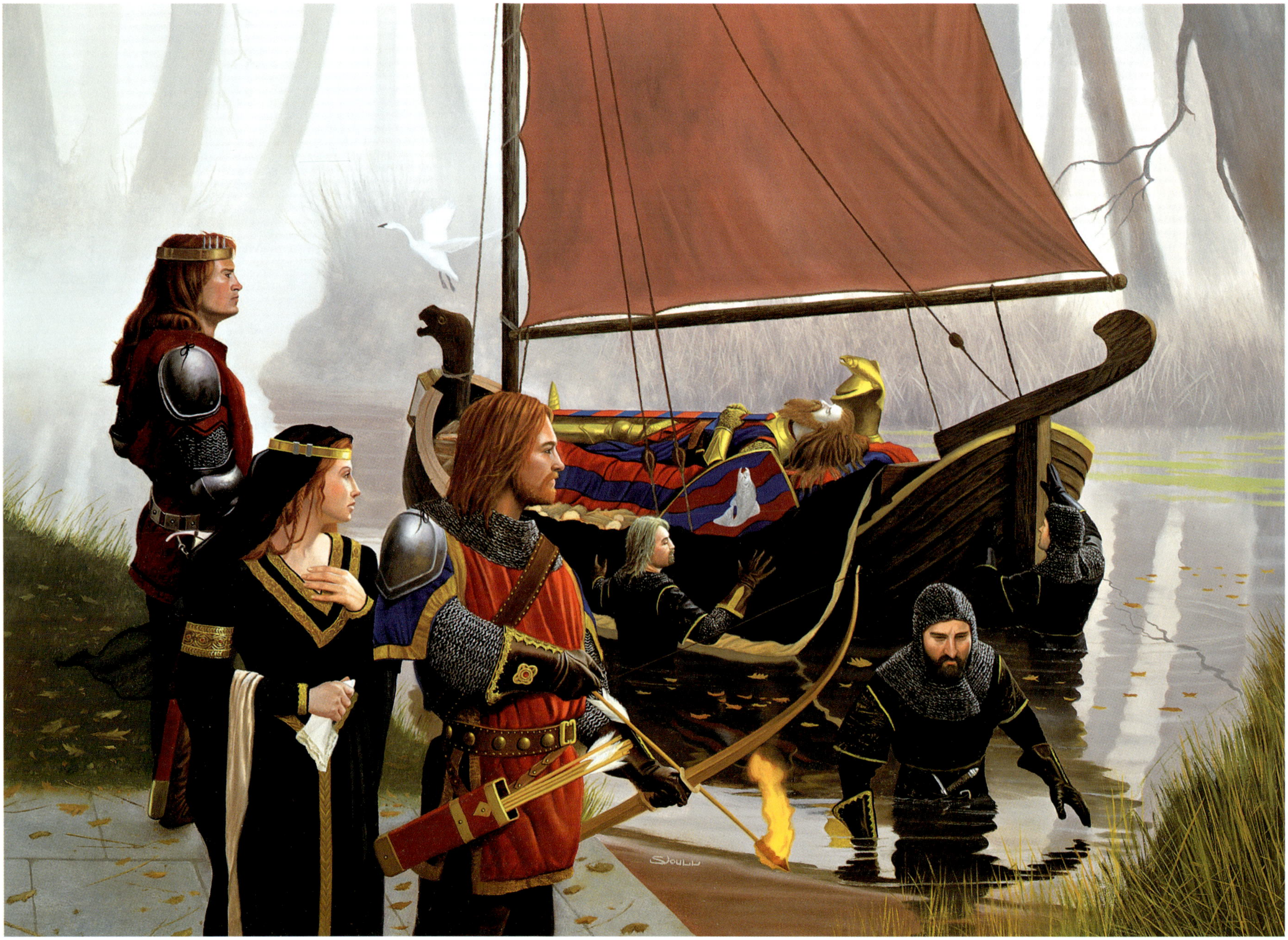

A STORM OF SWORDS
GEORGE R.R. MARTIN, BANTAM, 2000
OIL ON MASONITE, 17 x 24in (43 x 61cm)

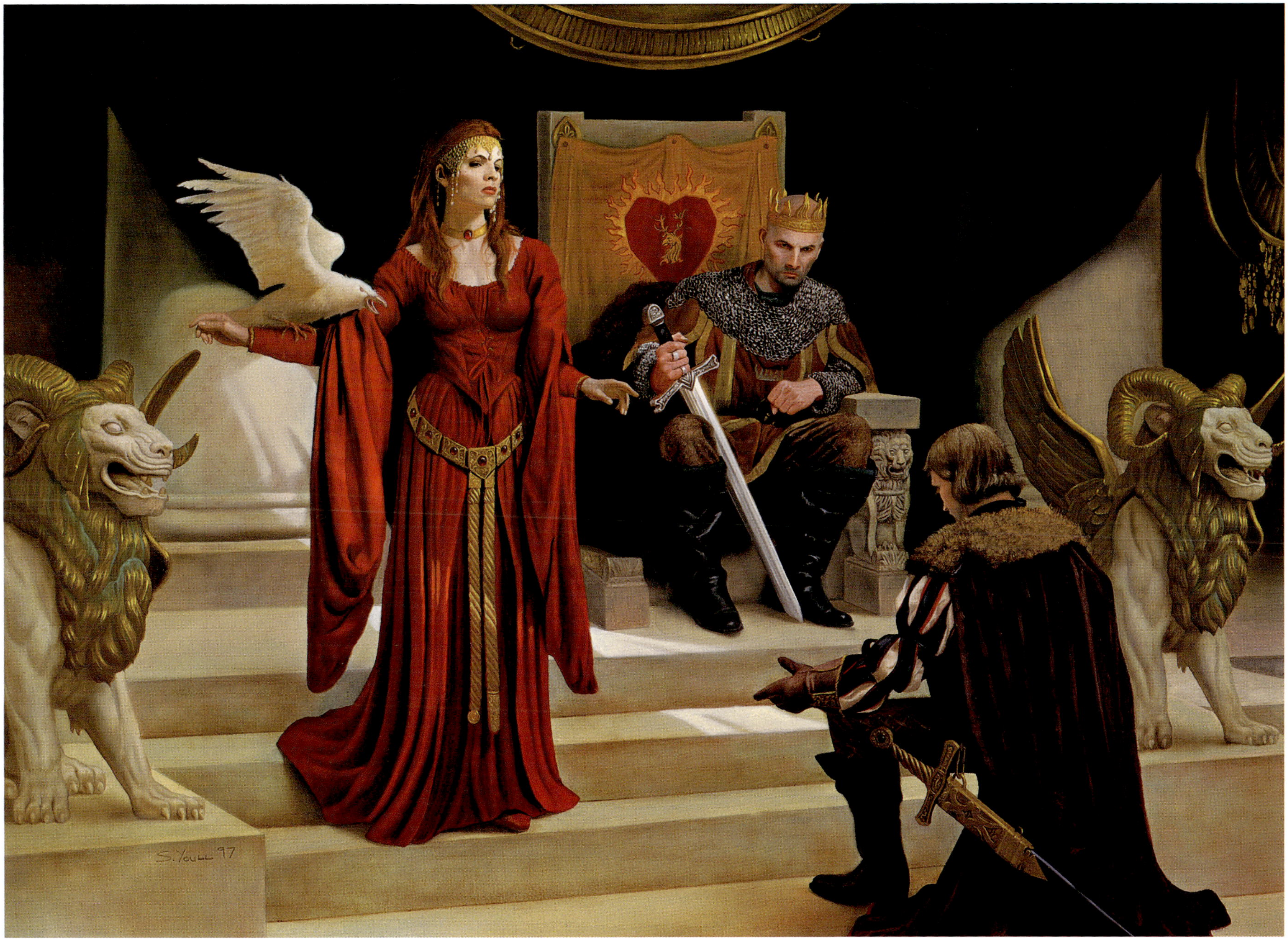

A CLASH OF KINGS

GEORGE R.R. MARTIN, BANTAM, 1997

OIL ON MASONITE, 16½ X 23½in (42 X 60cm)

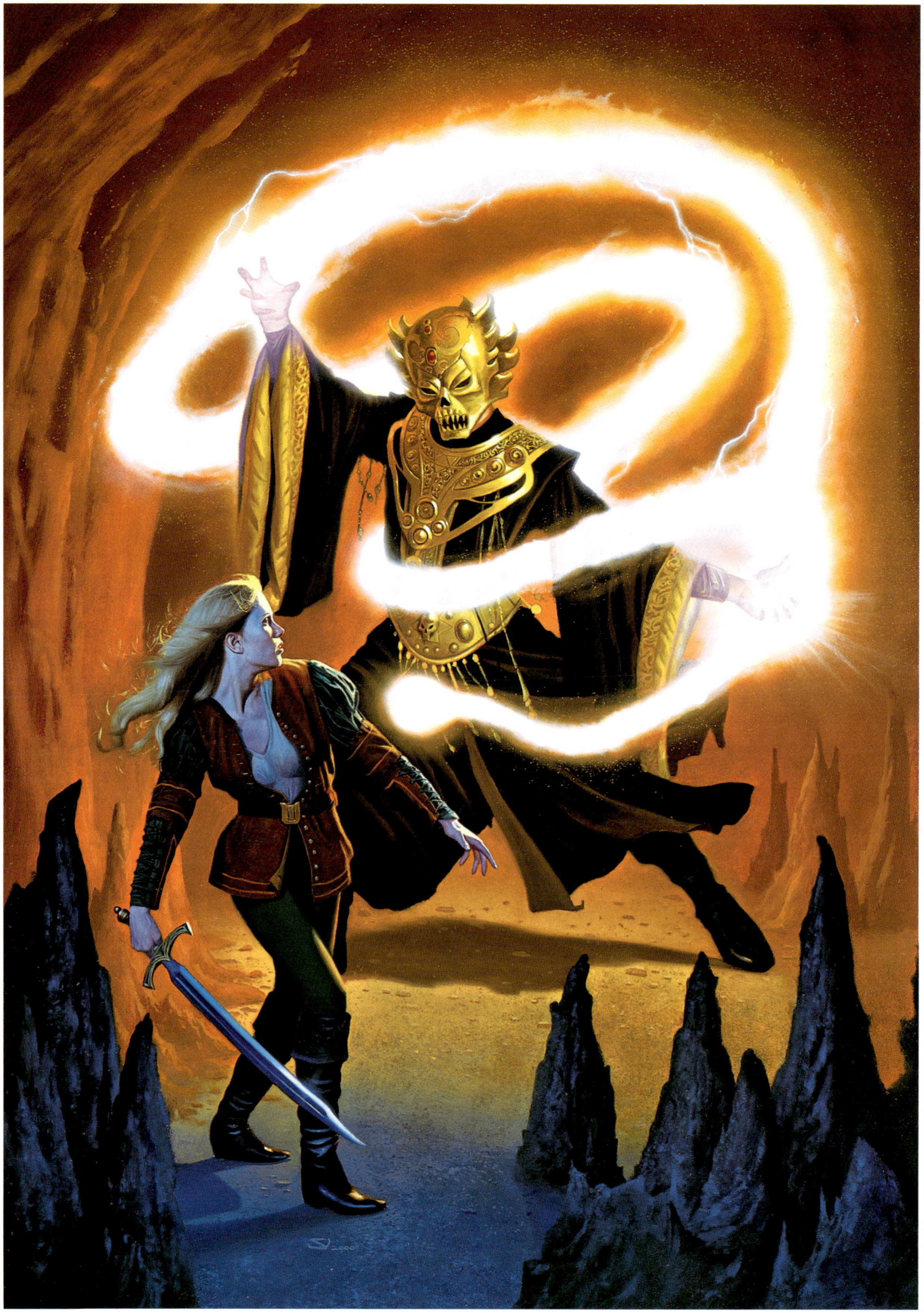

THE DARK REMAINS
MARK ANTHONY, BANTAM, 2000
OIL ON MASONITE, 25 x 16in (64 x 41cm)

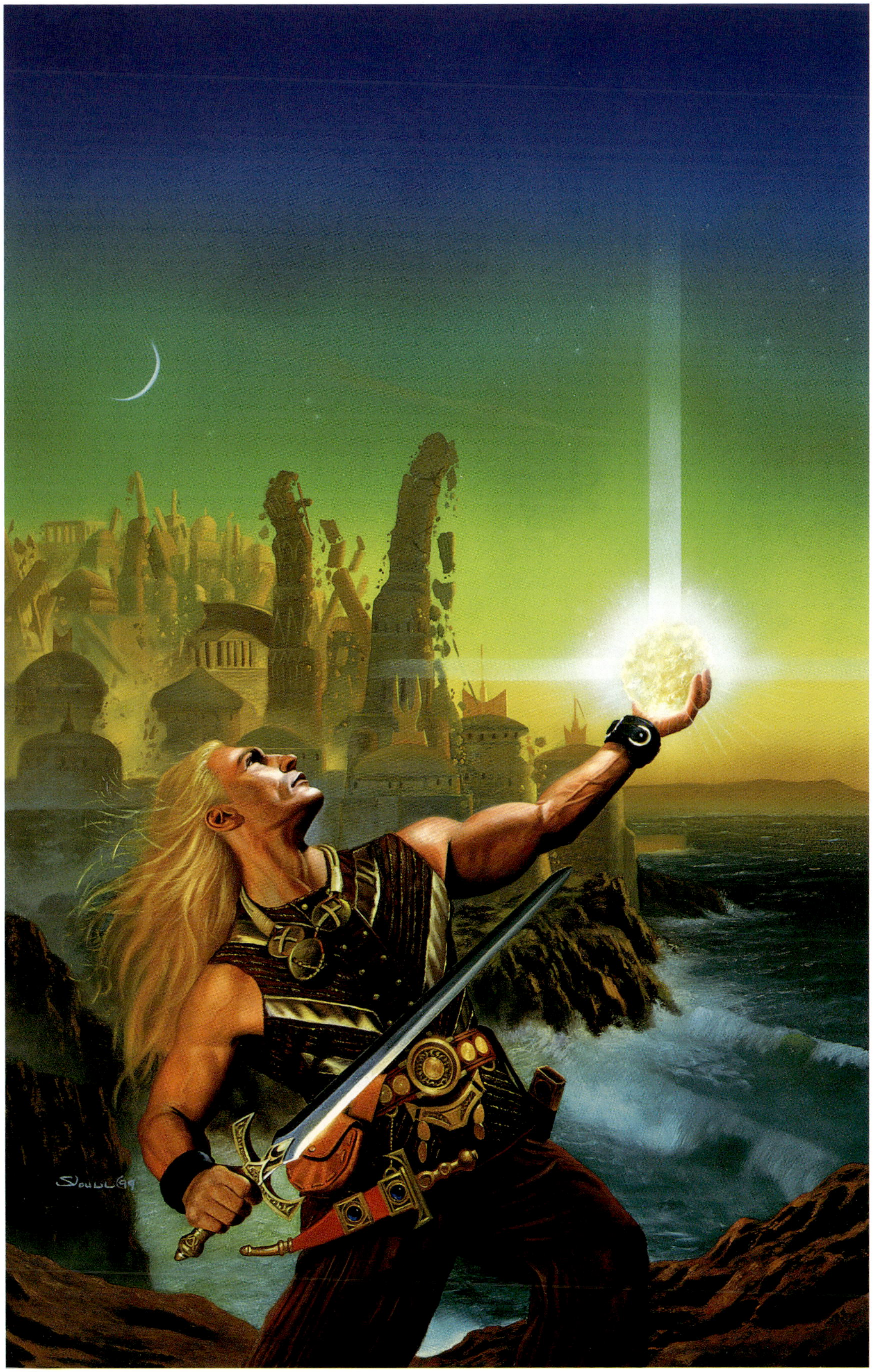

THE EMPIRE STONE

CHRIS BUNCH, WARNER, 1999

OIL ON MASONITE, 19 x 12in (48 x 30cm)

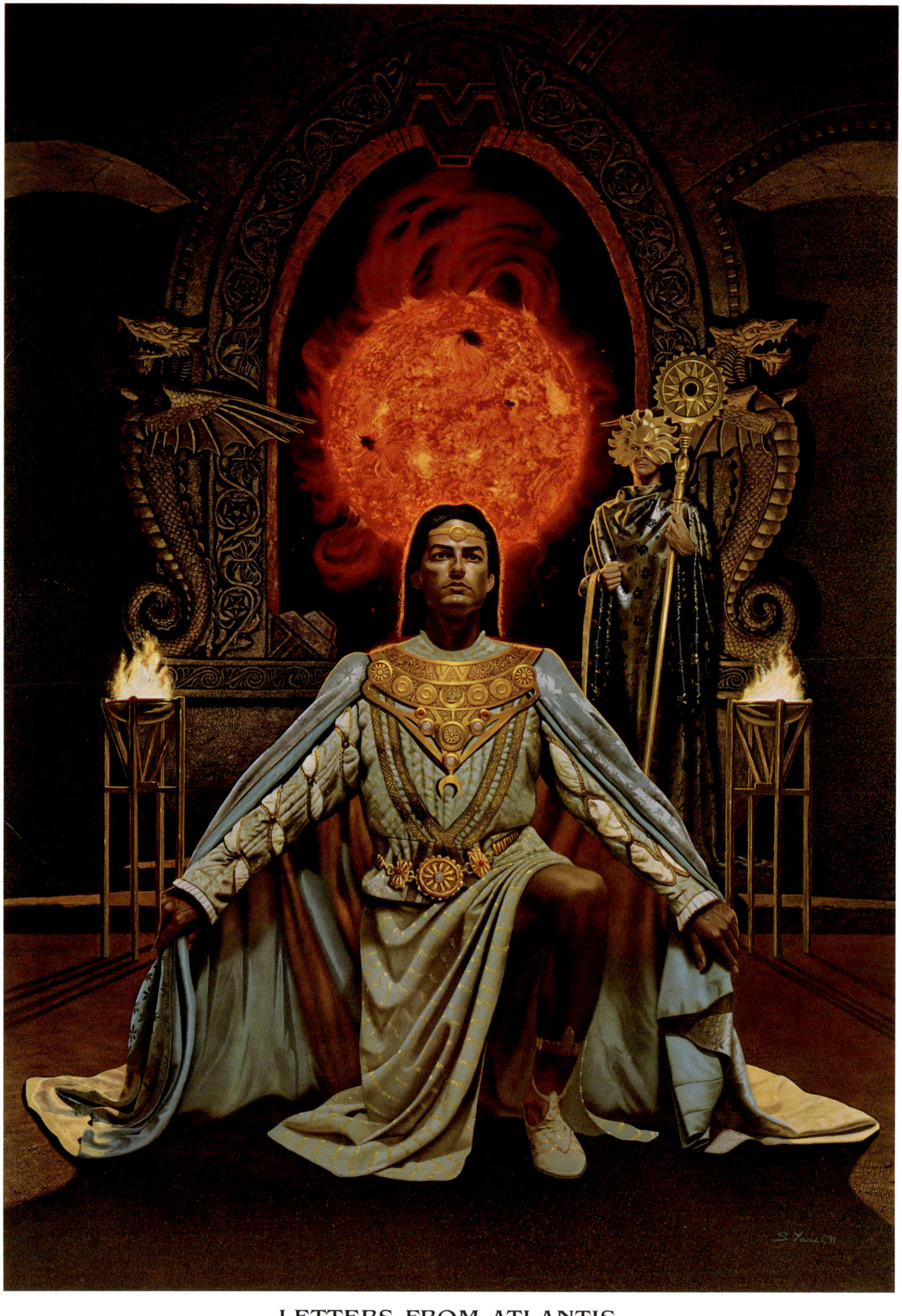

LETTERS FROM ATLANTIS
ROBERT SILVERBERG, WARNER, 1991
ACRYLIC ON MASONITE, 33 x 23in (84 x 58cm)

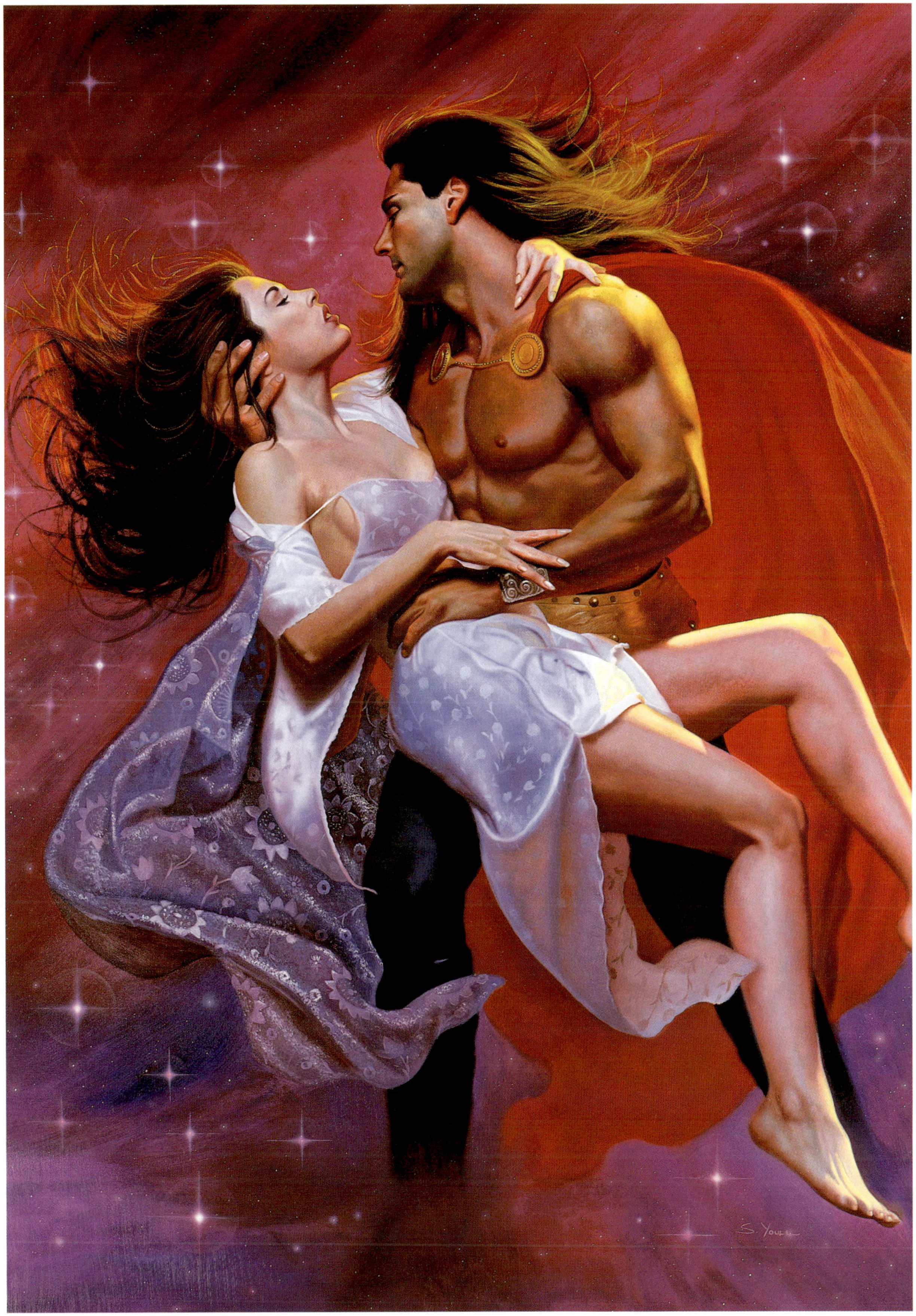

STAR CROSSED

SUSAN KRINARD, BANTAM, 1995

OIL ON ILLUSTRATION BOARD, 33 x 23in (84 x 58cm)

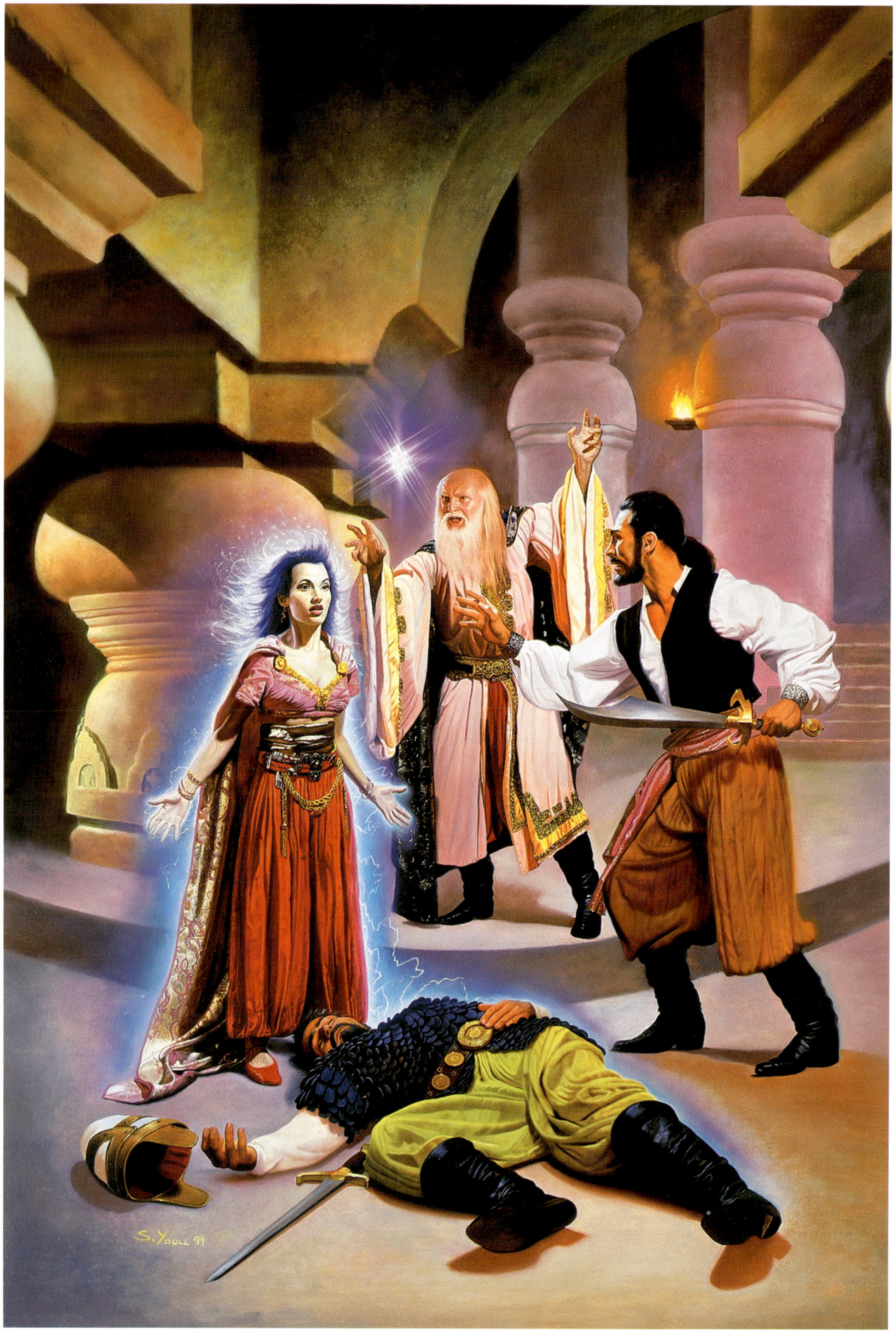

THE STOLEN THRONE
HARRY TURTLEDOVE, BALLANTINE, 1994
OIL ON ILLUSTRATION BOARD, 36 x 23½in (91 x 60cm)

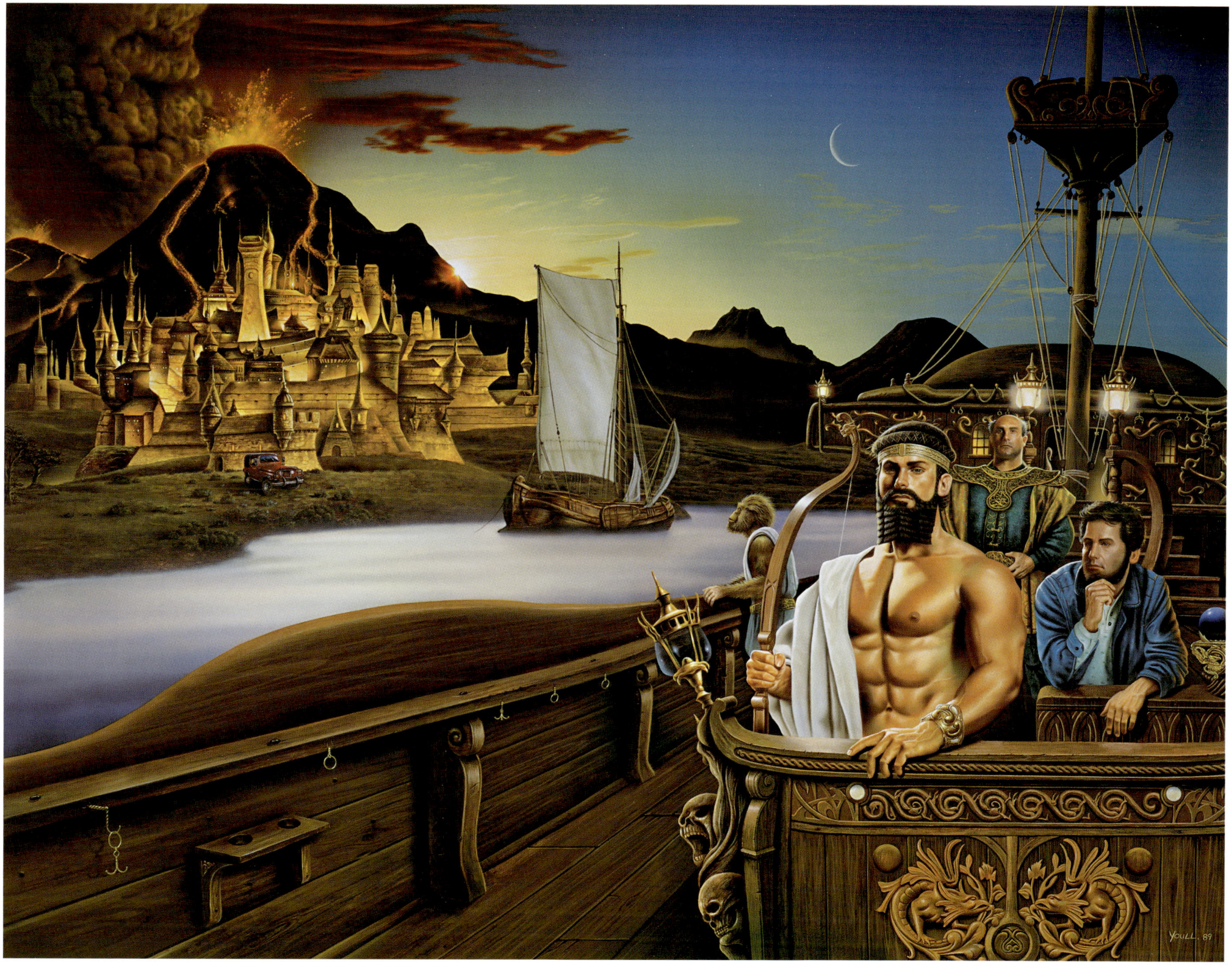

TO THE LAND OF THE LIVING
ROBERT SILVERBERG, WARNER, 1989
ACRYLIC ON ILLUSTRATION BOARD, 26 x 33½in (66 x 85cm)

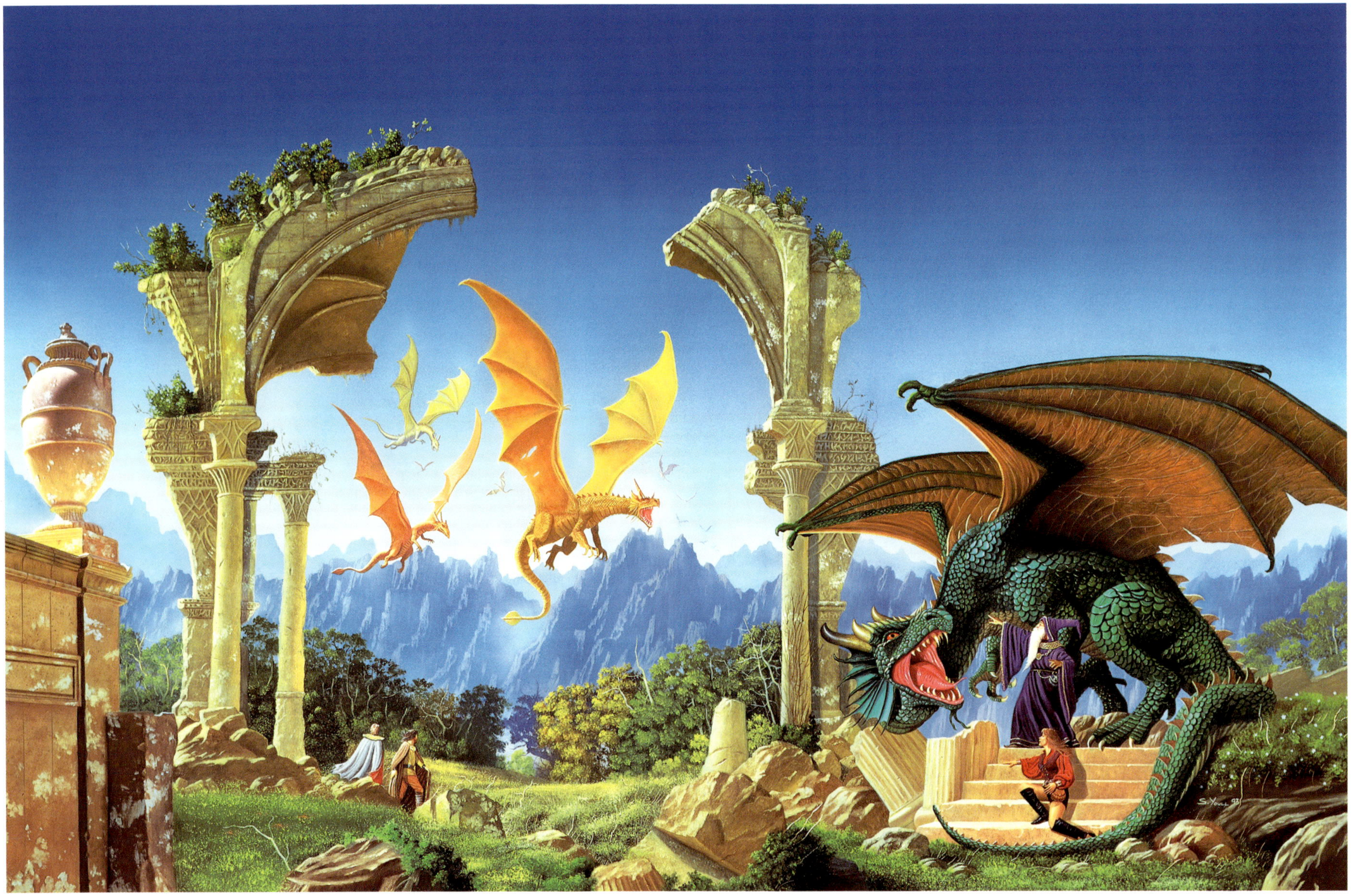

THE SEVENTH GATE
MARGARET WEIS AND TRACY HICKMAN, BANTAM, 1993
OIL ON ILLUSTRATION BOARD, 26 x 40in (66 x 102cm)

A CONTRADICTION OF REAL

One of my biggest influences as a boy was the movie *Jason and the Argonauts.* Its cavalcade of winged creatures, the scaled Hydra and the adventure-seeking warriors fighting living skeletons gave me much to daydream about. I would build plasticine models, complete with every little detail, and then draw them.

I still love creating creatures and just because they don't exist doesn't mean they shouldn't look real. One of my favourite paintings is *Speaking in Tongues* (page 48). I wanted the image not just to work as a book cover but as a piece of art allowing for speculation and thought. The initial idea was to convey a sense of communication between the two species; with a completely realistic and fully realized alien. I used photographic reference for the human, but had only my imagination for the alien. At the time I was painting in acrylics with the airbrush, but felt this medium was incapable of achieving the right results. I therefore experimented with oil paints, creating a variety of interesting effects. I used a pale acrylic underpainting for form, shape and shadows, and then, by splashing various thinning agents over still wet oil paint on top of the underpainting, I caused the oil paint to crack and break apart. After the oils had dried I applied more thin glazes, building up layers of colour to capture

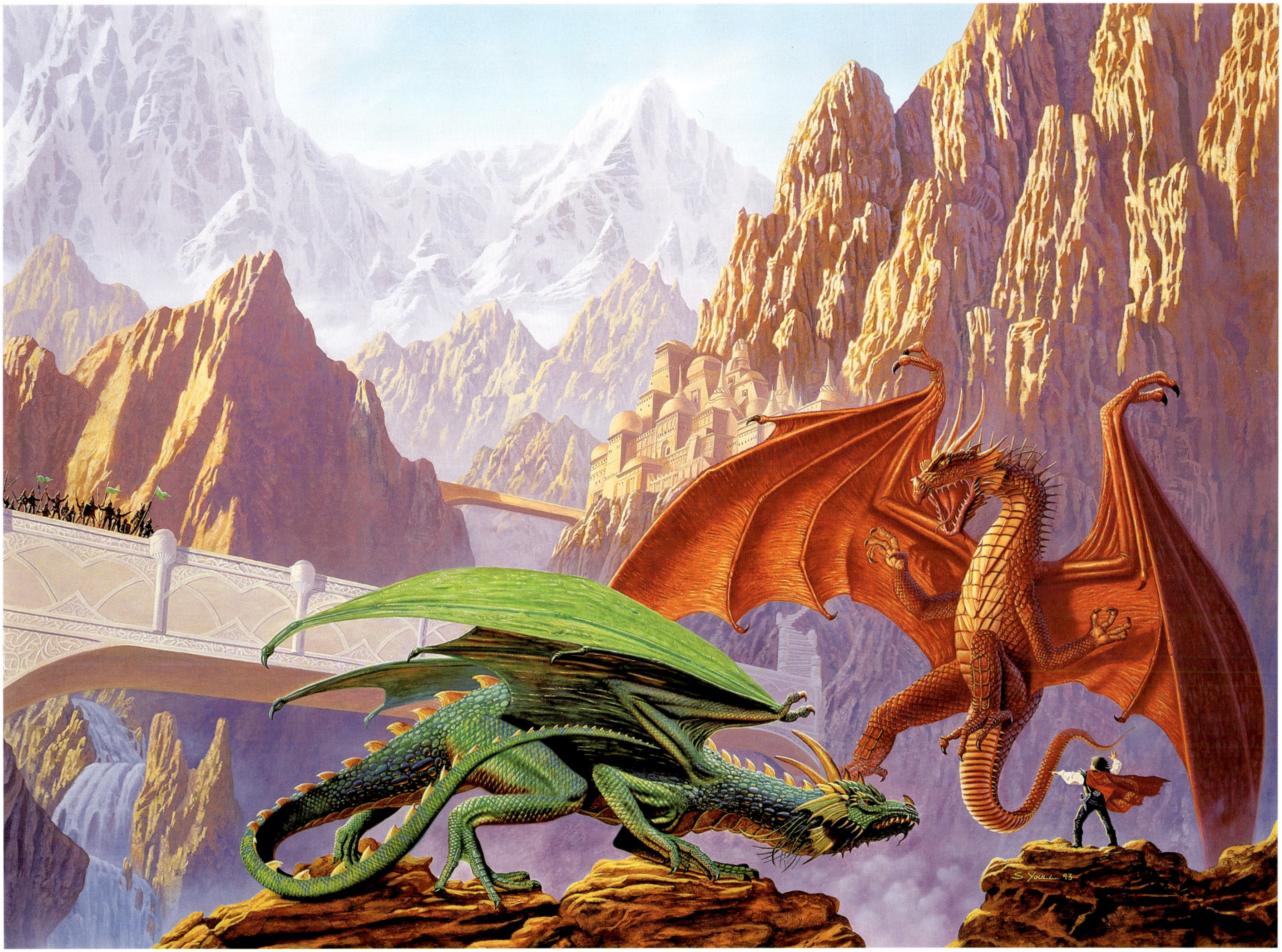

INTO THE LABYRINTH

MARGARET WEIS AND TRACY HICKMAN, BANTAM, 1993
OIL ON ILLUSTRATION BOARD, 28 x 38½in (71 x 98cm)

a wonderful luminosity, almost like stained glass. This oil-and-splash technique gave the work details that would have been impossible in acrylic. As I continued to paint the alien with a new confidence an amazing amount of ideas emerged… as if I had actually seen the creature and was rendering a subconscious memory.

The tiny gems encrusted in the alien's hand took hours and almost drove me mad! As a child I watched my mother create the most spectacular designs in crochet. She could sit for hours until her masterpiece was finished. I now value the virtue of that patience and have applied the same level of commitment to painting.

I believe *Speaking in Tongues,* painted in 1992, signalled a time of change in my artistic development. Every artist evolves; from our naive beginnings we change in response to what we see and what affects us. We have an innate sense, unclouded by logic, of the need to grow. Driven by our emotions and a will to better ourselves, this need is constant and sometimes overwhelming. It is the urge always to reach higher that allows us to evolve.

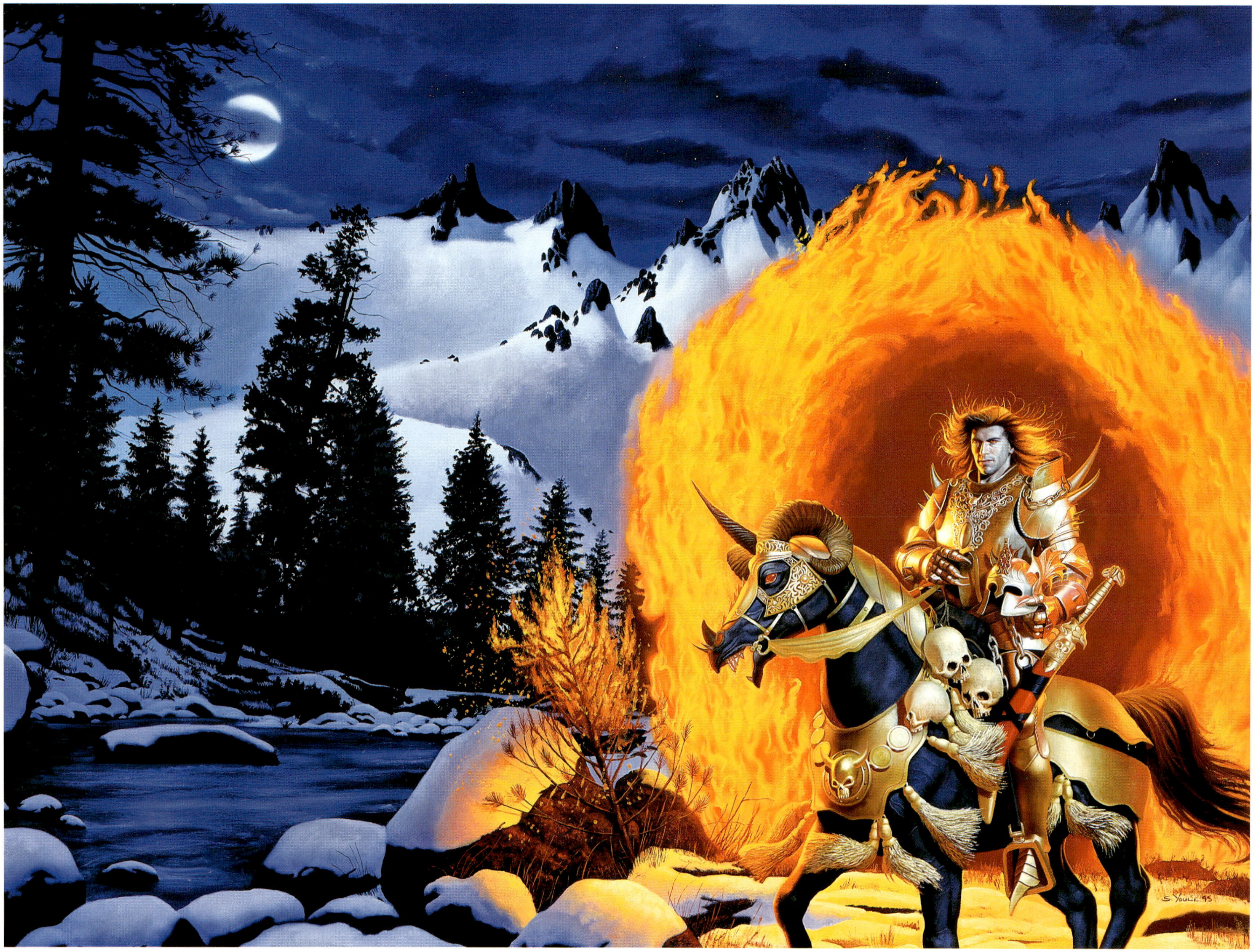

EXILE'S CHILDREN
ANGUS WELLS, BANTAM, 1995
OIL ON ILLUSTRATION BOARD, 29 x 40in (74 x 102cm)

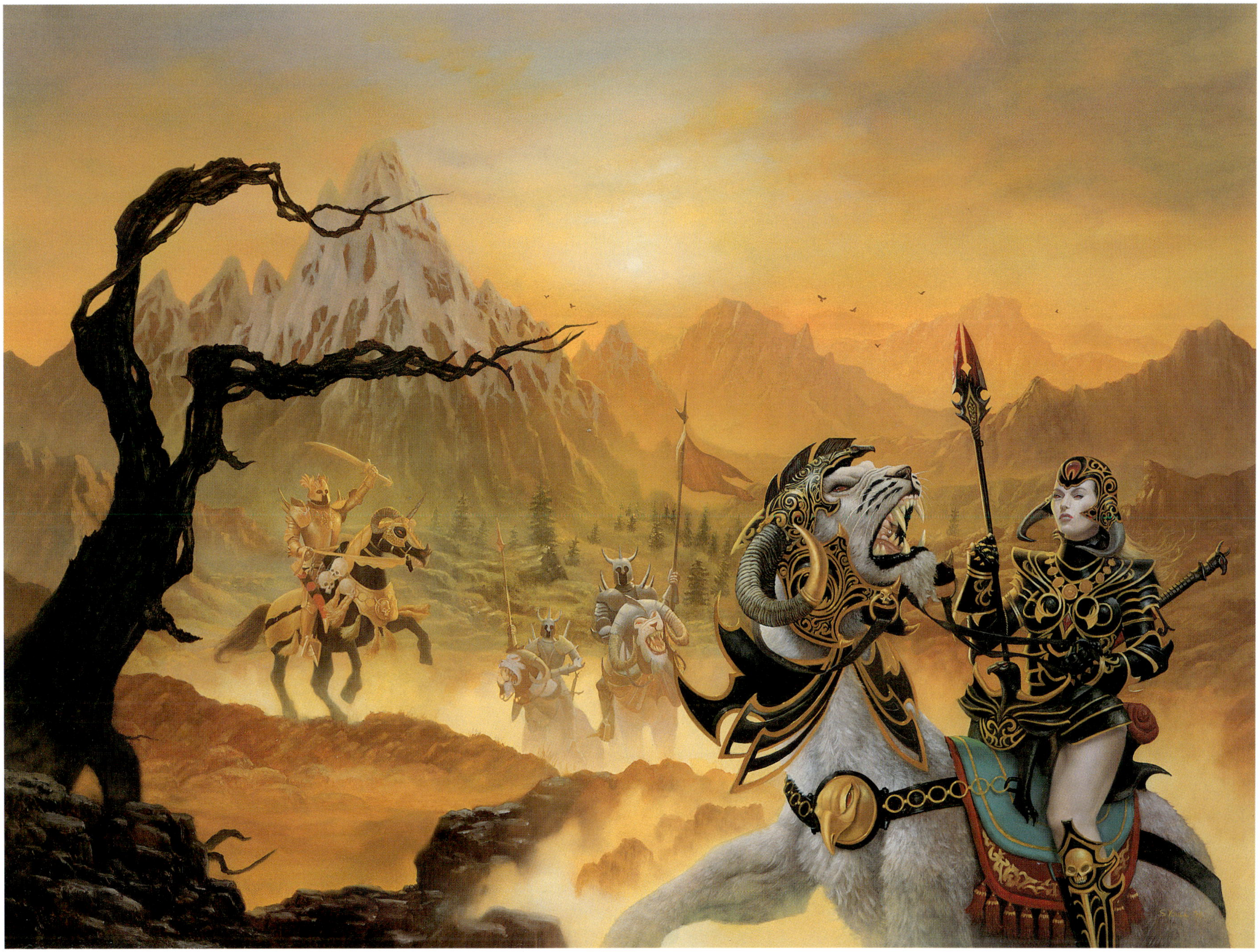

EXILE'S CHALLENGE
ANGUS WELLS, BANTAM, 1996
OIL ON MASONITE, 23½ x 33½in (60 x 85cm)

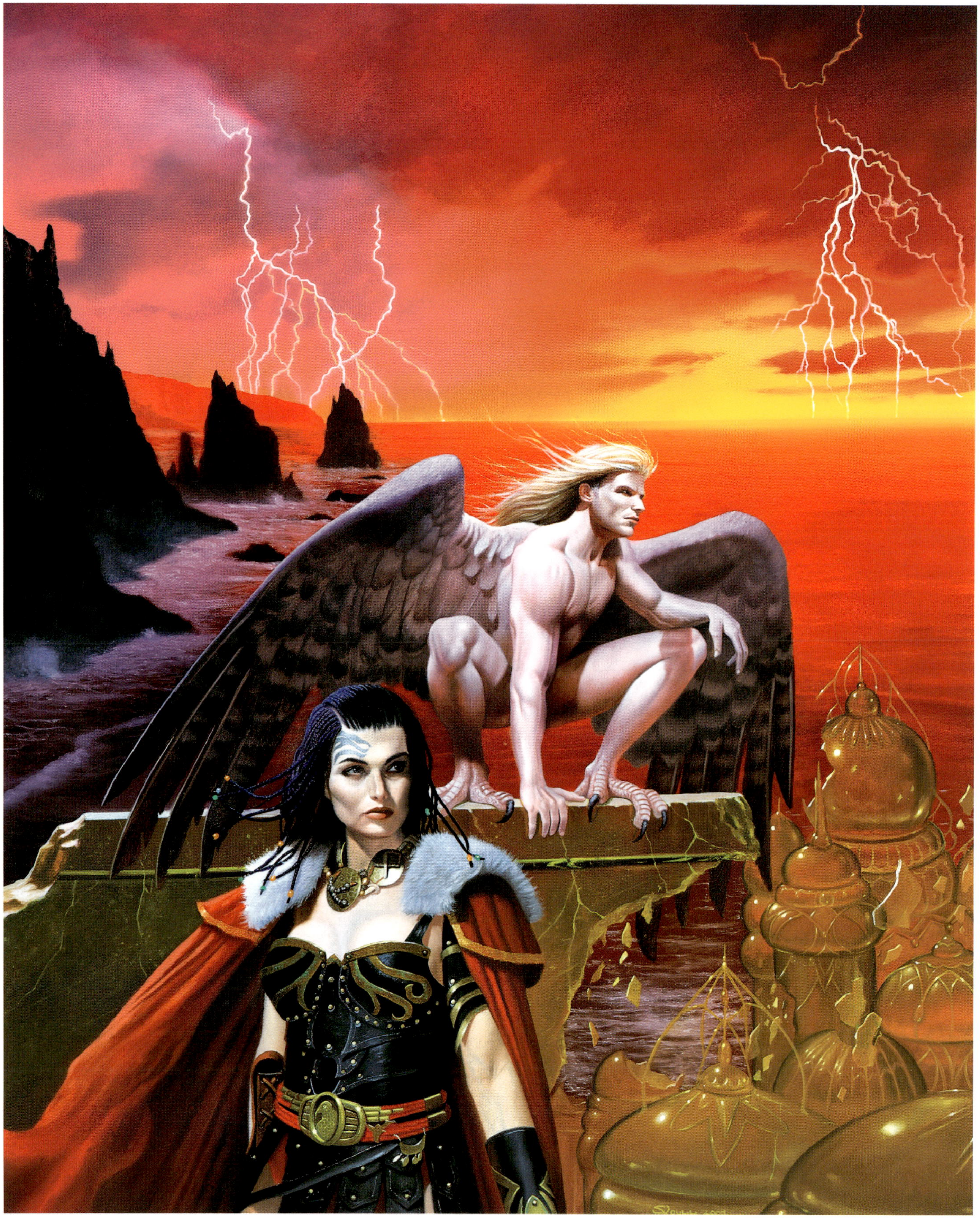

THE WAY OF THE ROSE

VALERY LEITH, BANTAM, 2001

OIL ON ILLUSTRATION BOARD, 20 x 16in (51 x 41cm)

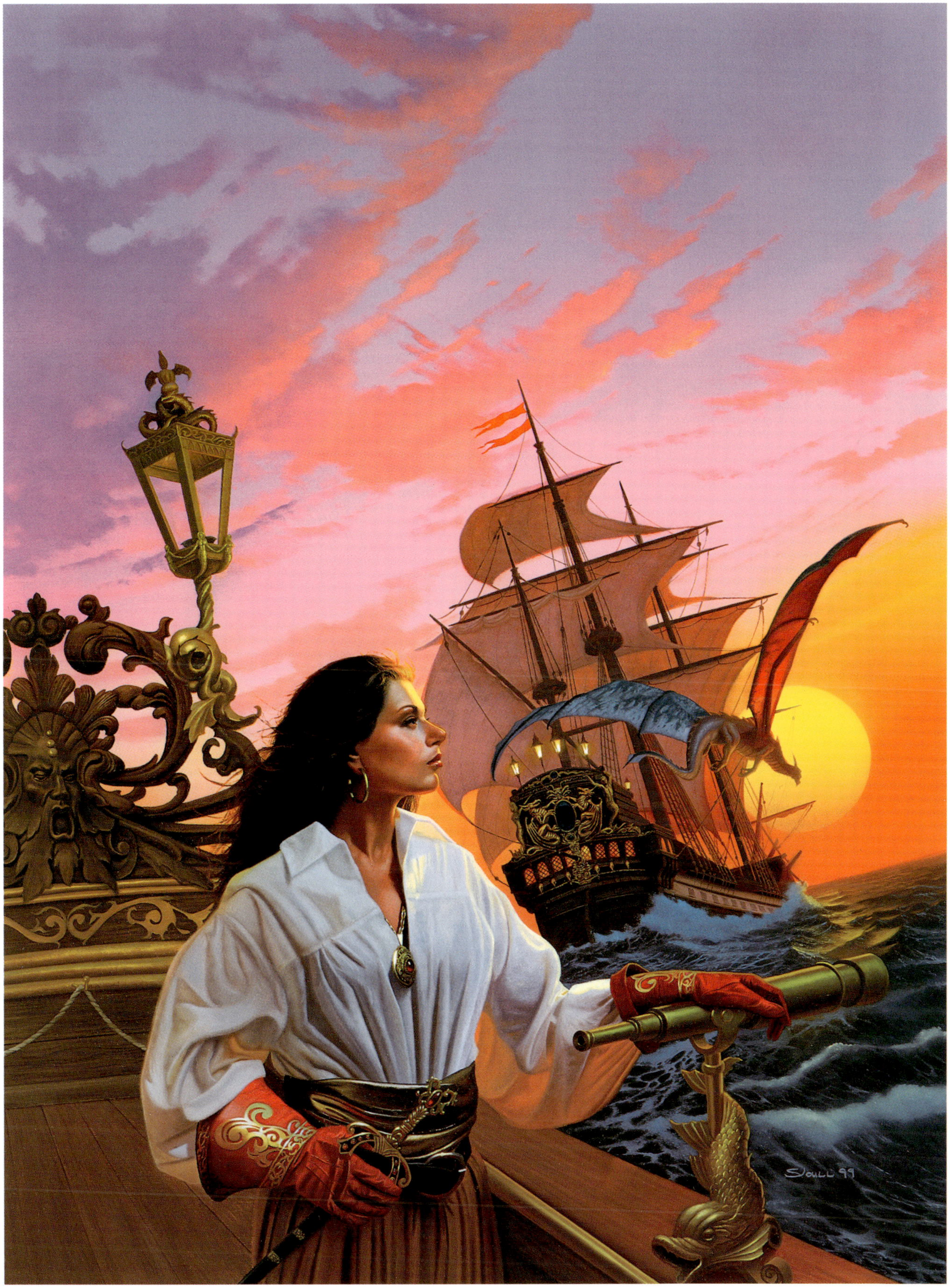

SHIP OF DESTINY

ROBIN HOBB, BANTAM, 1999
OIL ON ILLUSTRATION BOARD, 28 x 20in (71 x 51cm)

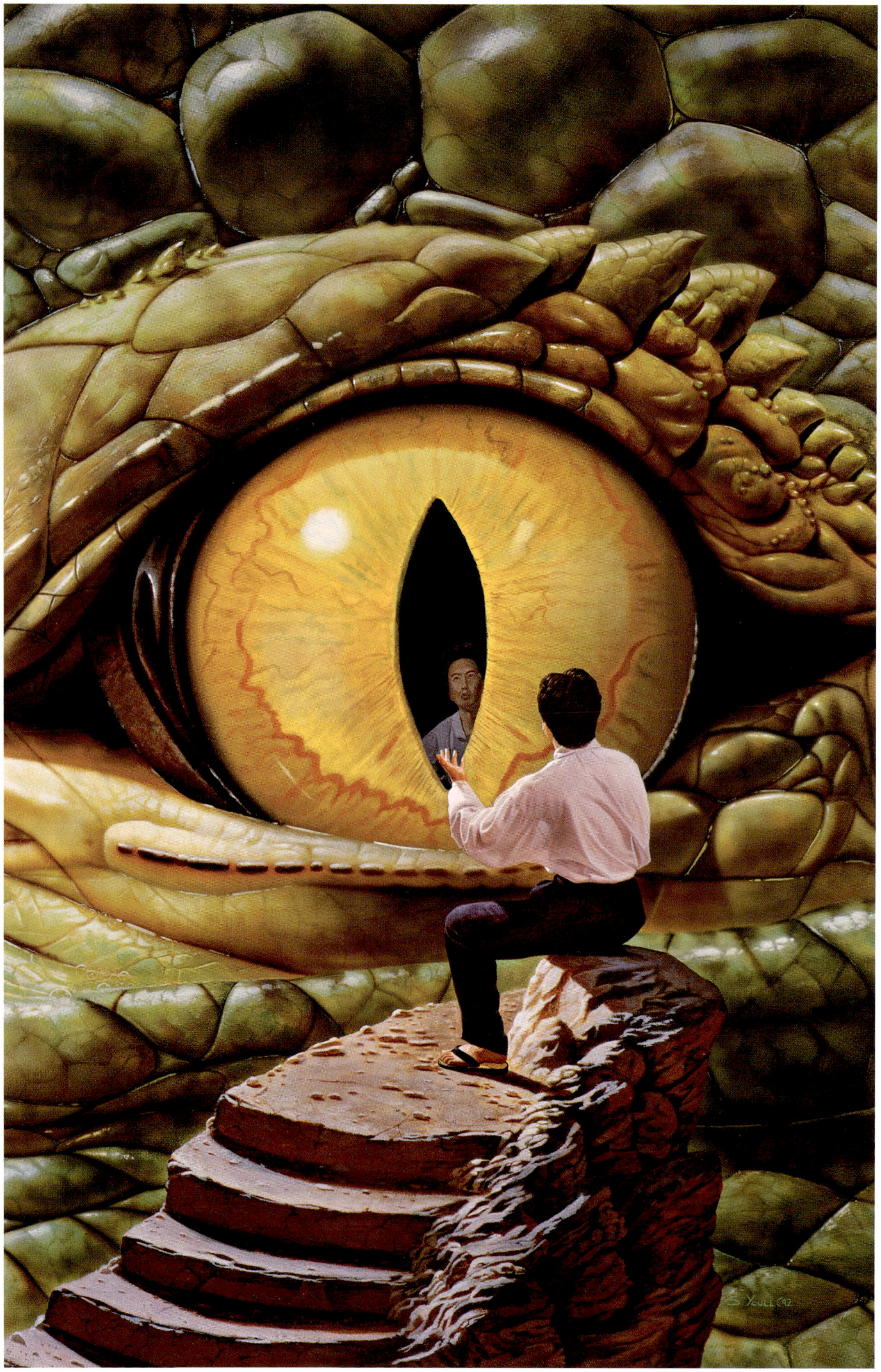

GOJIRO

MARK JACOBSON, BANTAM, 1992

OIL ON CANVAS BOARD, 24 x 15in (61 x 38cm)

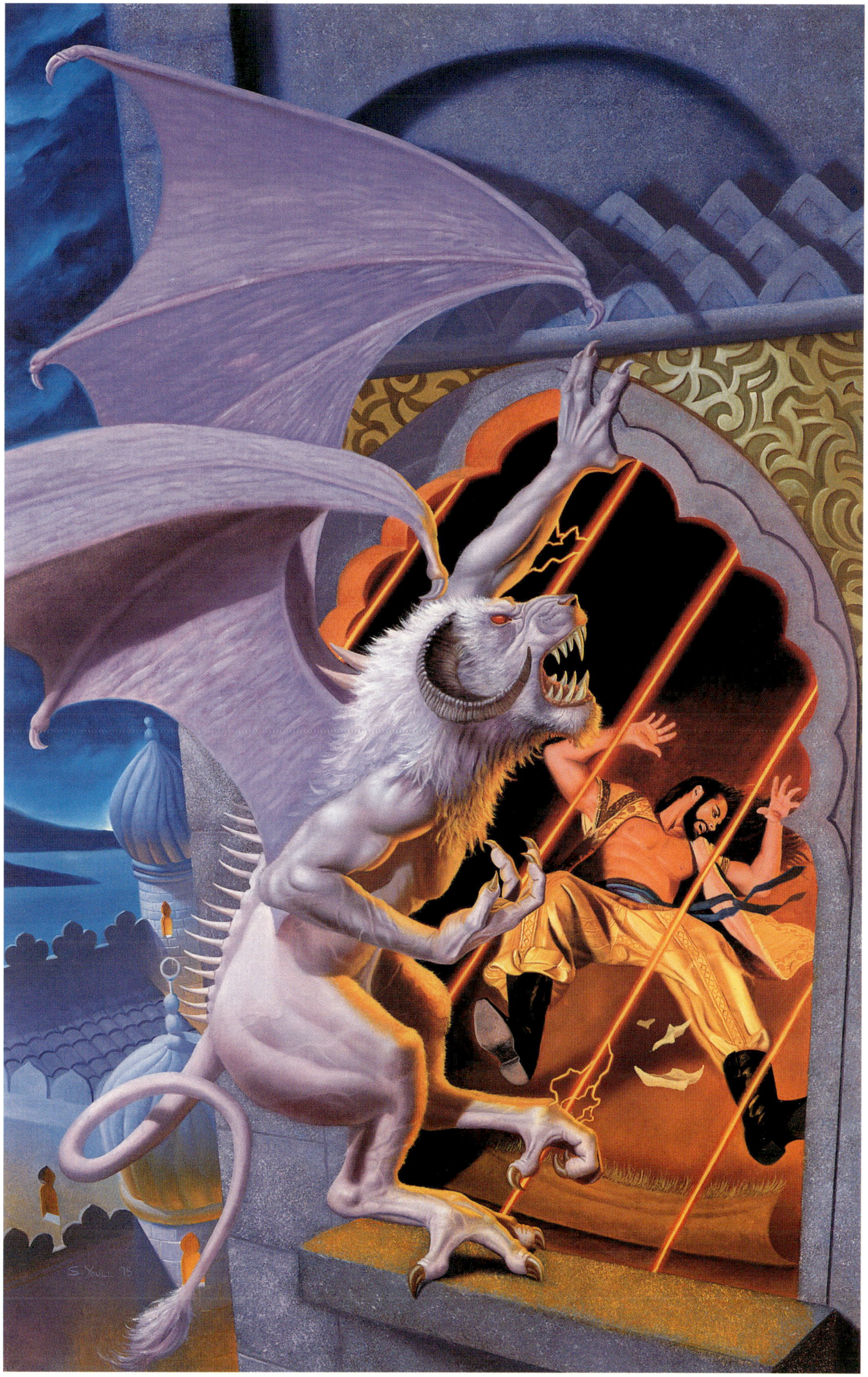

HAMMER AND ANVIL

HARRY TURTLEDOVE, BALLANTINE, 1995

OIL ON MASONITE, 30 x 17½in (76 x 44cm)

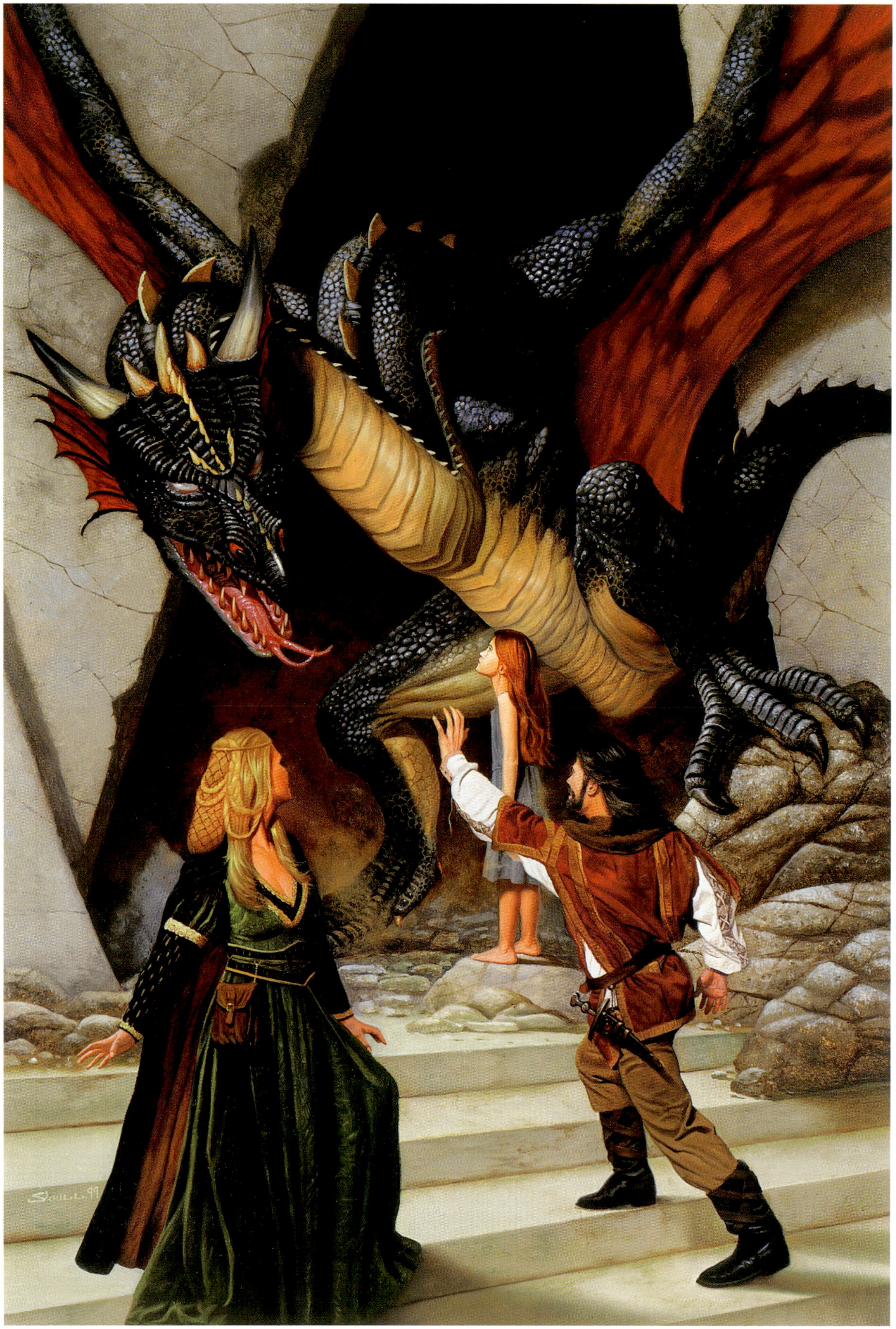

THE KEEP OF FIRE

MARK ANTHONY, BANTAM, 1999

OIL ON ILLUSTRATION BOARD, 19½ x 12½in (50 x 32cm)

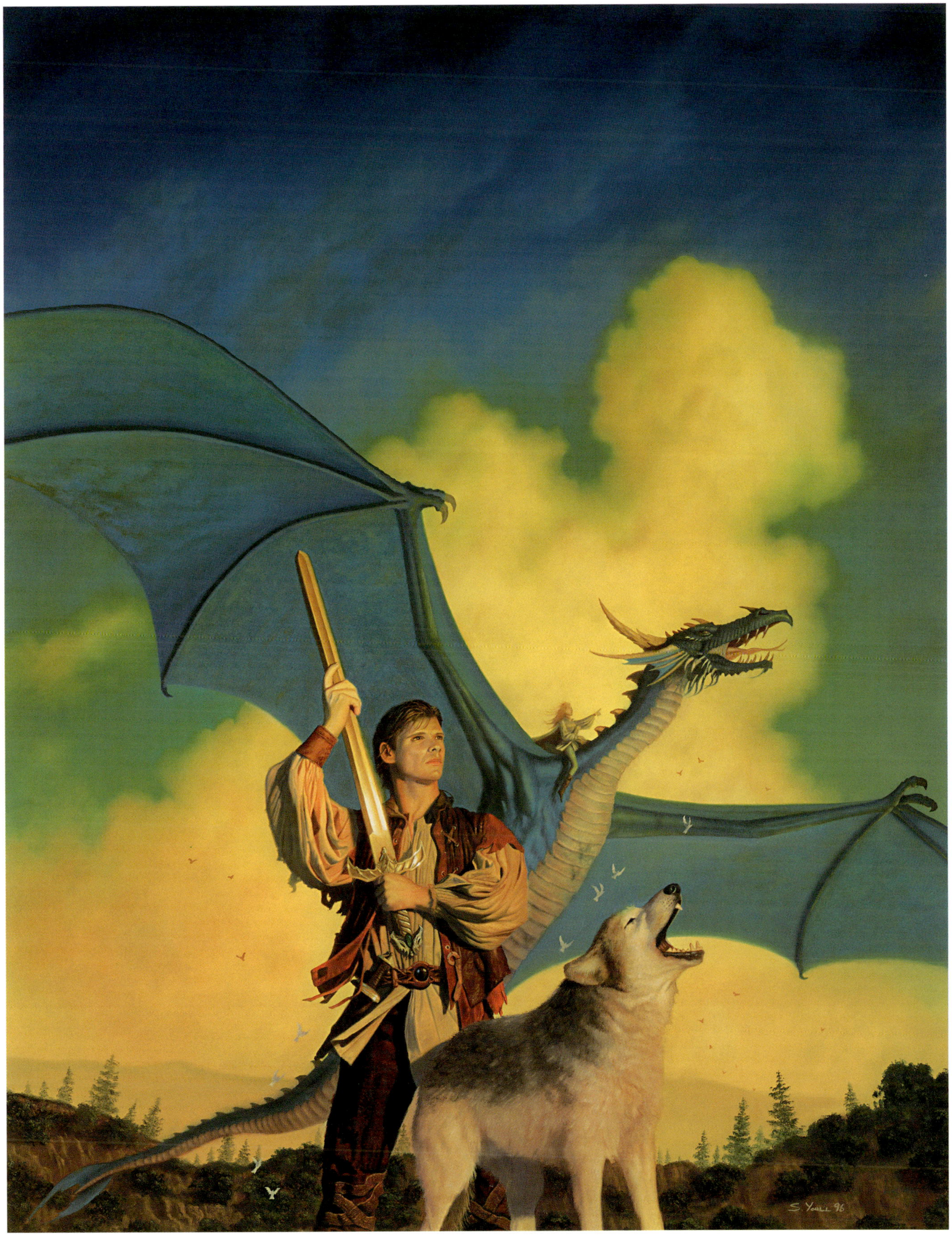

ASSASSIN'S QUEST

ROBIN HOBB, BANTAM, 1996

OIL ON ILLUSTRATION BOARD, 32½ x 24½in (83 x 62cm)

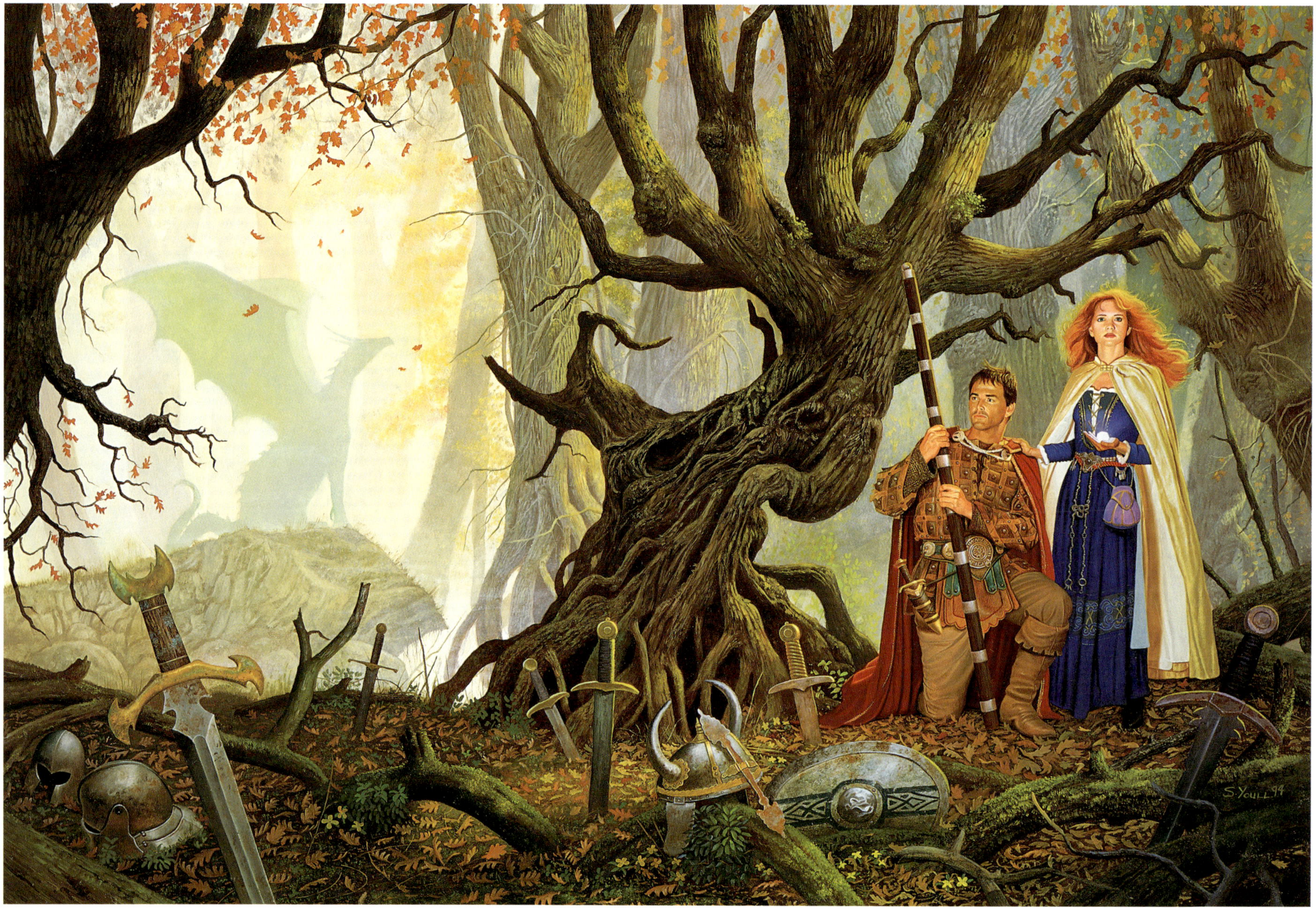

LORDS OF THE SKY
ANGUS WELLS, BANTAM, 1994
OIL ON MASONITE, 30 x 40in (76 x 102cm)

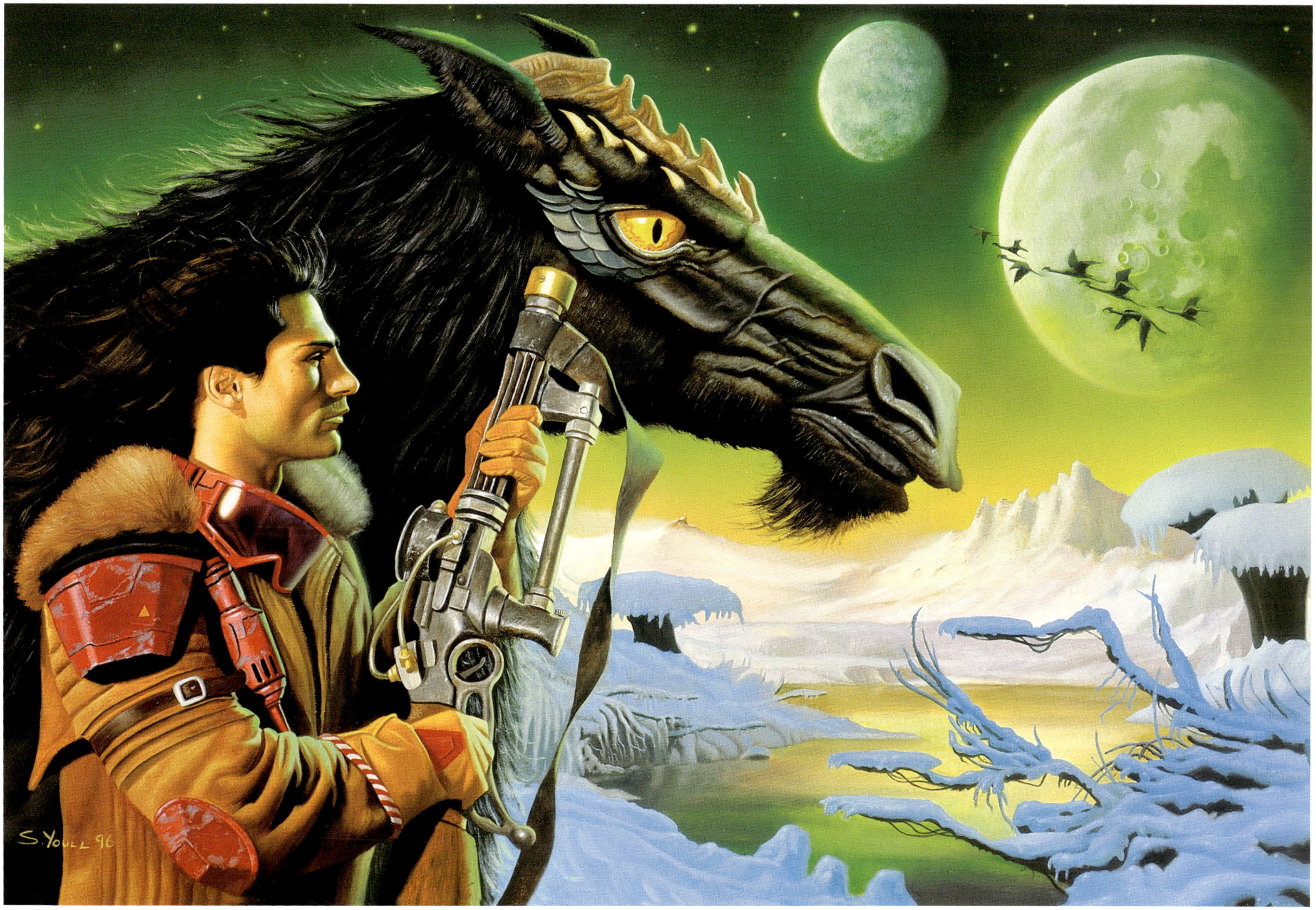

CLOUD'S RIDER

C. J. CHERRYH, WARNER, 1996

OIL ON MASONITE, 16 x 24in (41 x 61cm)

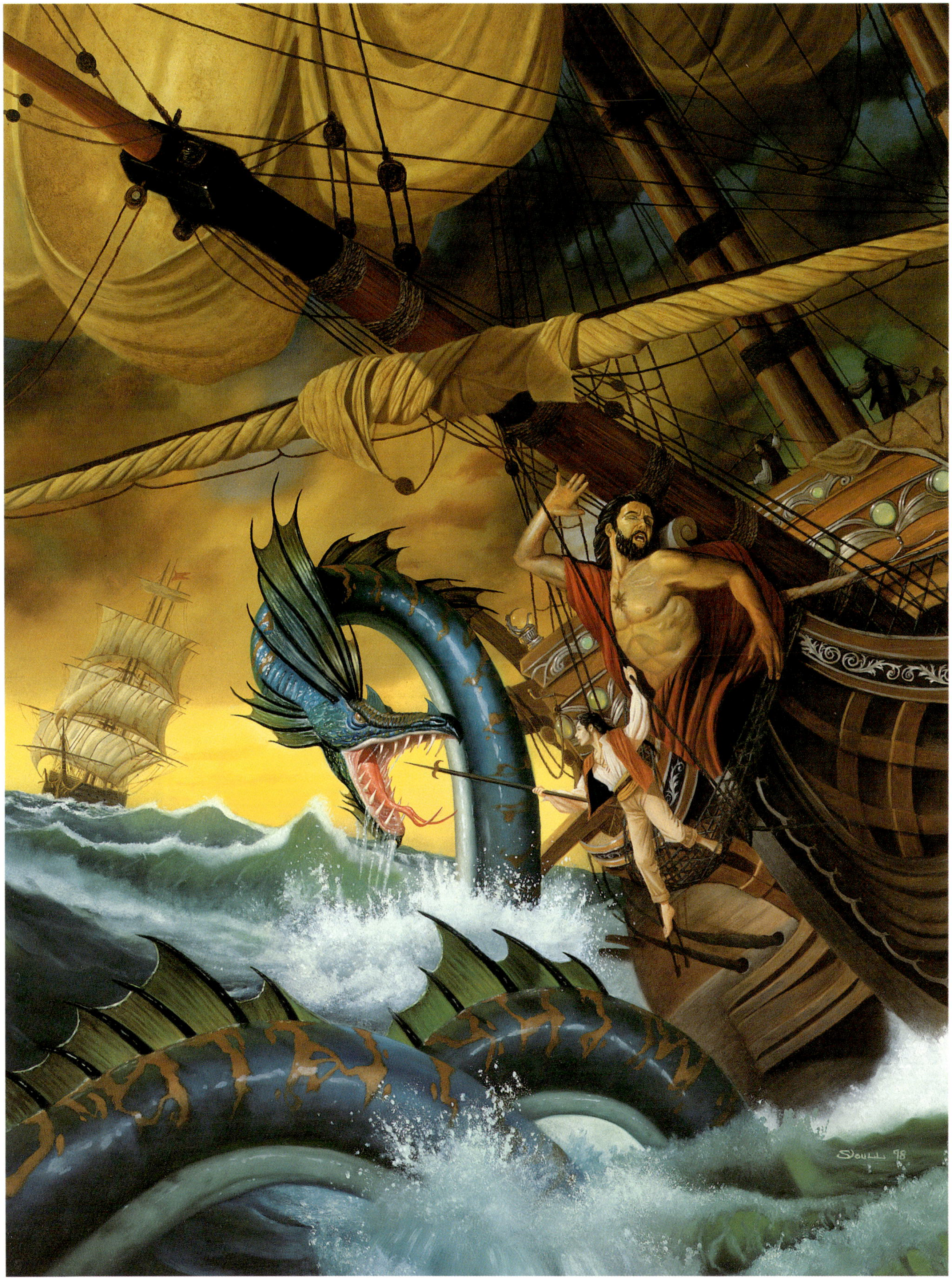

MAD SHIP

ROBIN HOBB, BANTAM, 1998

OIL ON MASONITE, 24 x 18in (61 x 46cm)

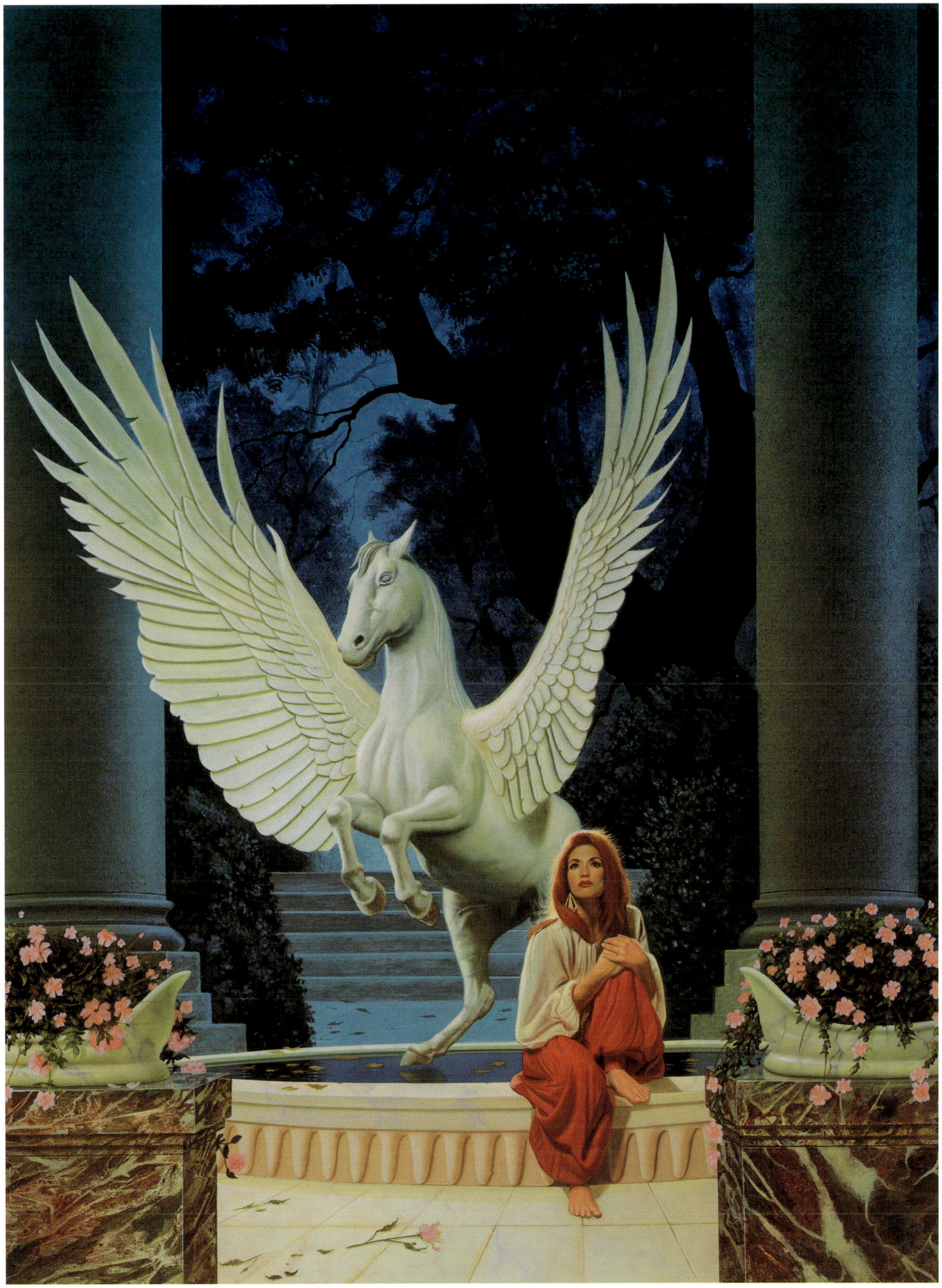

THE MAN WHO STAYED BEHIND

PAUL ASH, *ANALOG* COVER, 1993

OIL ON ILLUSTRATION BOARD, 25½ x 18½in (65 x 47cm)

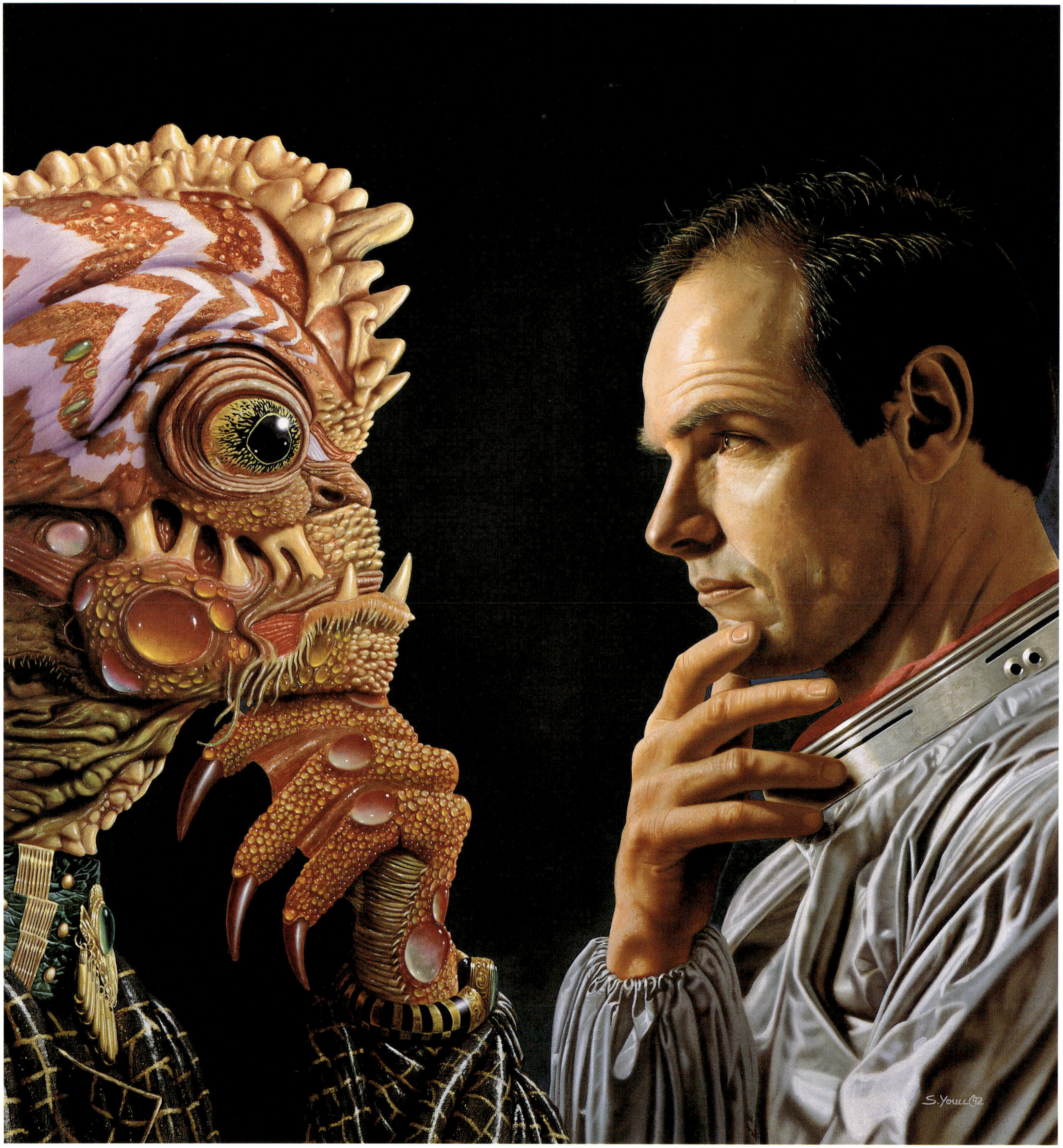

SPEAKING IN TONGUES
IAN McDONALD, BANTAM, 1992
OIL ON ILLUSTRATION BOARD, 26 x 16½in (66 x 42cm)

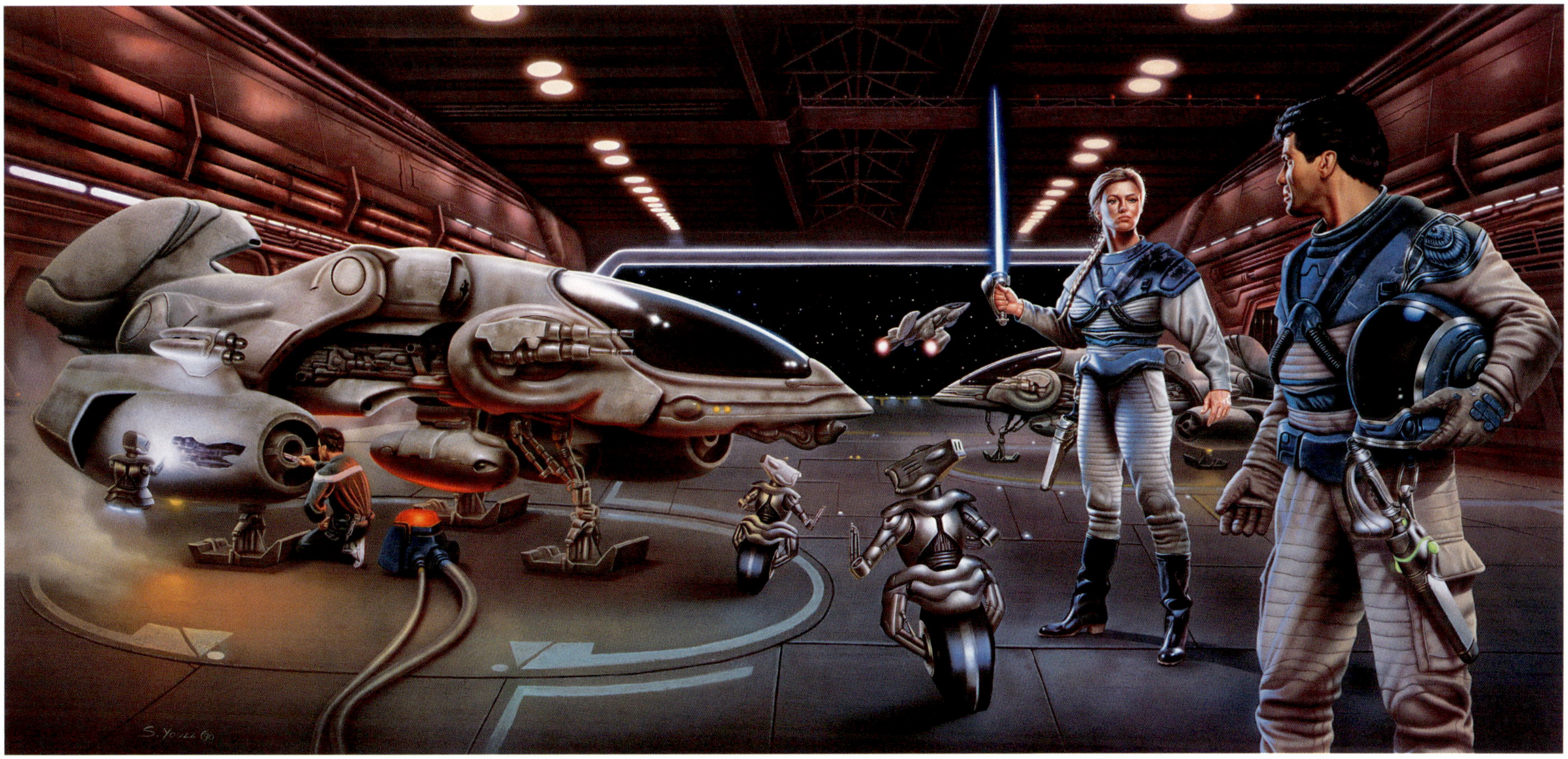

THE LOST KING
MARGARET WEIS, BANTAM, 1990
ACRYLIC ON ILLUSTRATION BOARD, 16 x 38in (41 x 97cm)

FASTER THAN LIGHT

When I was twelve my parents bought me a telescope for Christmas. The winter months are always the best times to look at the stars. As a child I would spend hours in the back yard in the freezing cold looking up and wondering if we would ever go there. I still do!

Today one of my favourite passions is depicting the spacecraft and starships that may one day be seen cruising through a triple star system, sailing by the Orion Nebula or zooming down a wormhole. I wish I could be around for that stage of human history. There's nothing so exciting as imagining a future where those spaceships could exist.

In my professional life as an artist I have always tried to render the various spacecraft and vehicles of the future in as three-dimensional a way as possible, using various lighting effects to bring out form and scale. I love to get into detail: chipped paint, rust, polished steel, reflections and exhaust stains all serve to give the spaceships personality and character. Although my technical background comes in very useful when I'm drawing these creations, a lot of their design style shows the influence of my youthful love of watching television. Those wonderful spacecraft from the great Gerry Anderson's *Thunderbirds, Captain Scarlet* and *Stingray* captivated me, generating a sense of amazement and stimulating my imagination.

Imagination has always caused change: without it we couldn't grow as a society, and it affects every aspect of our culture – science, medicine, ecology, etc. It's our capacity to dream that allows us to grow. I dreamed of being an artist and became one. So I have faith that we will one day reach the stars.

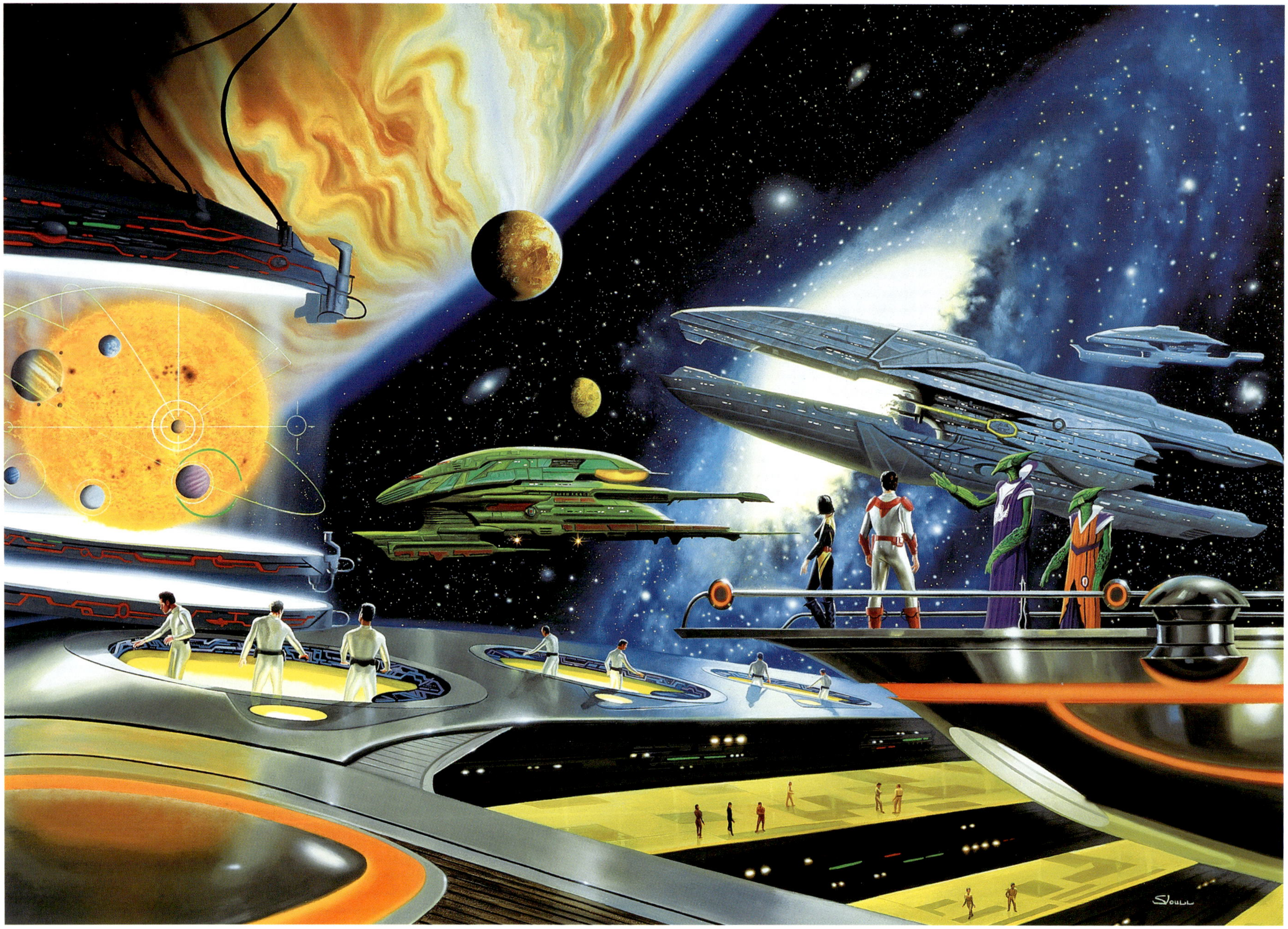

ETERNITY'S END

JEFFREY A. CARVER, TOR, 2000

OIL ON ILLUSTRATION BOARD, 21 x 26in (53 x 66cm)

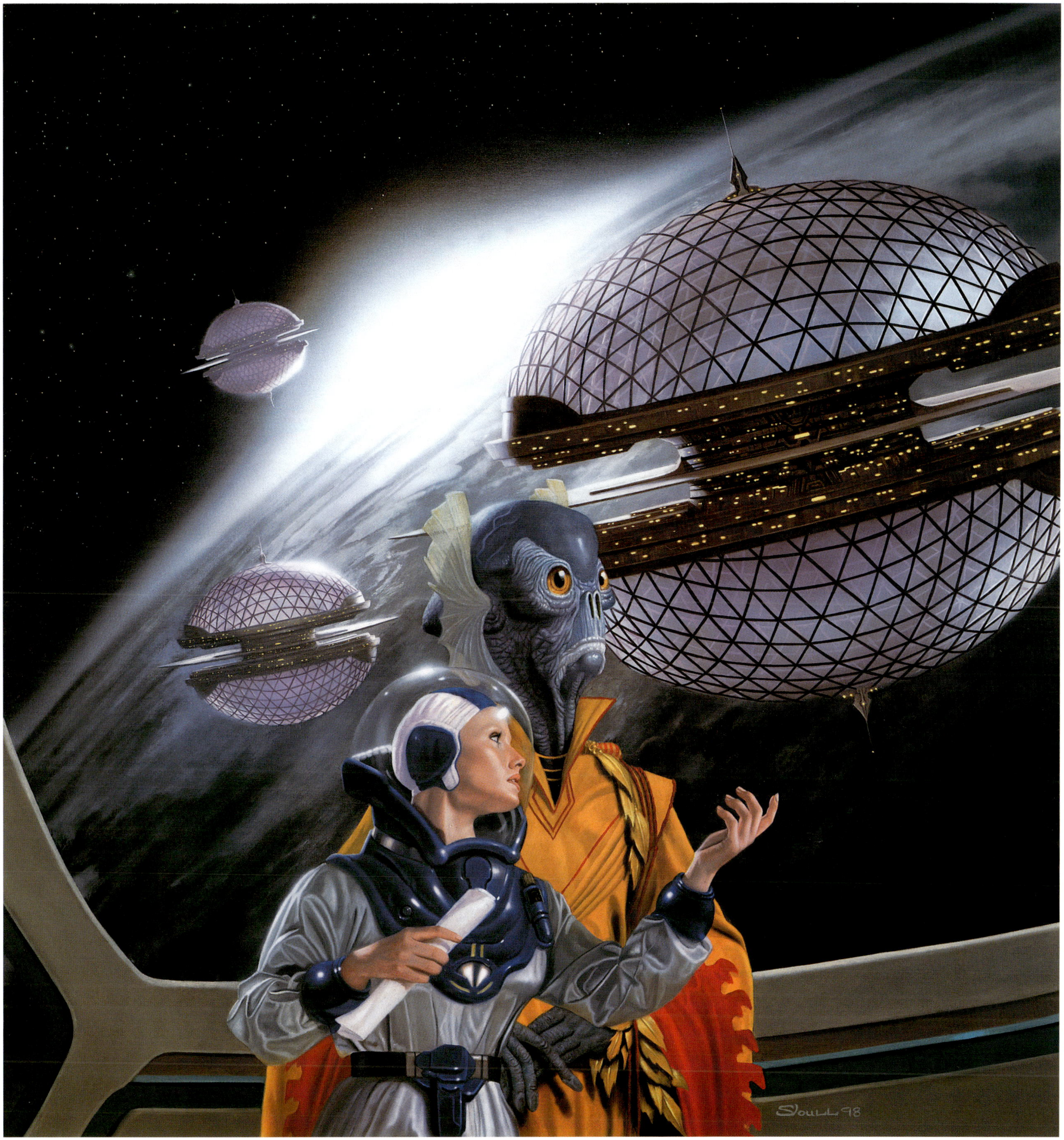

PLAYING GOD

SARAH ZETTEL, WARNER, 1998

OIL ON ILLUSTRATION BOARD, 23½ x 17in (60 x 43cm)

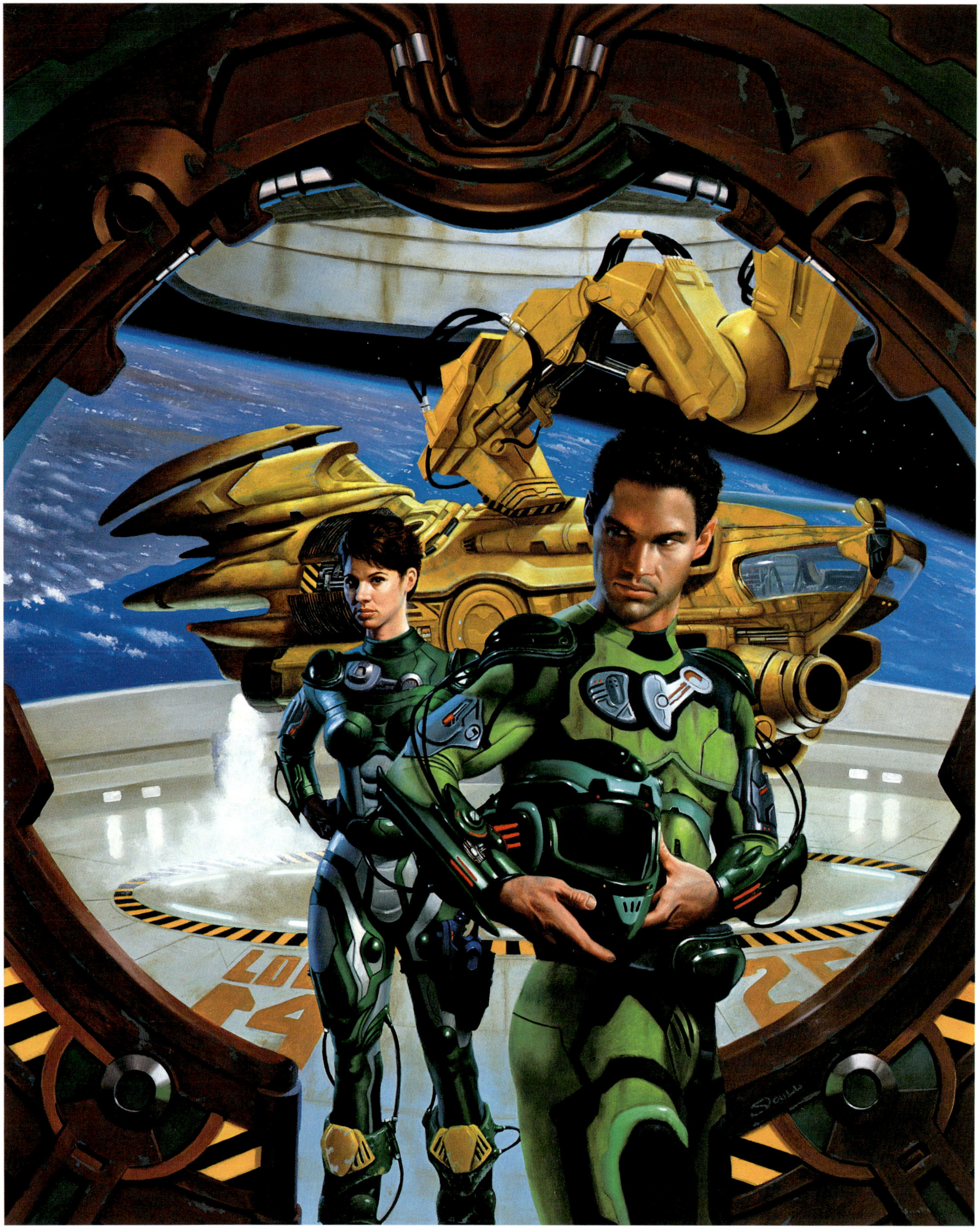

GRAVITY DREAMS

L.E. MODESITT, JR, TOR, 1998

OIL ON MASONITE, 19½ x 15¼in (50 x 39cm)

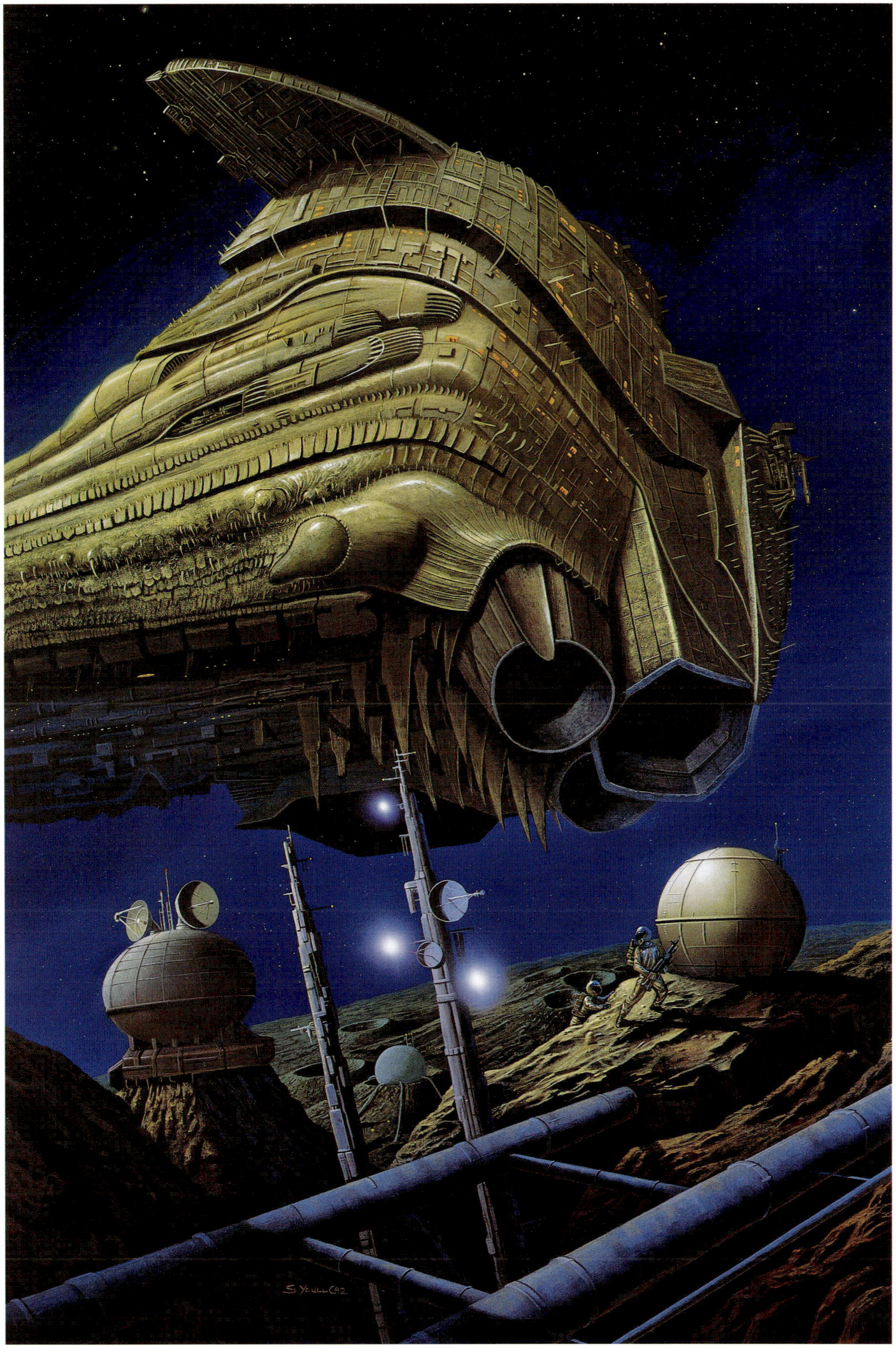

A DARK AND HUNGRY GOD ARISES

STEPHEN R. DONALDSON, BANTAM, 1992

ACRYLIC ON ILLUSTRATION BOARD, 28 x 18¼in (71 x 46cm)

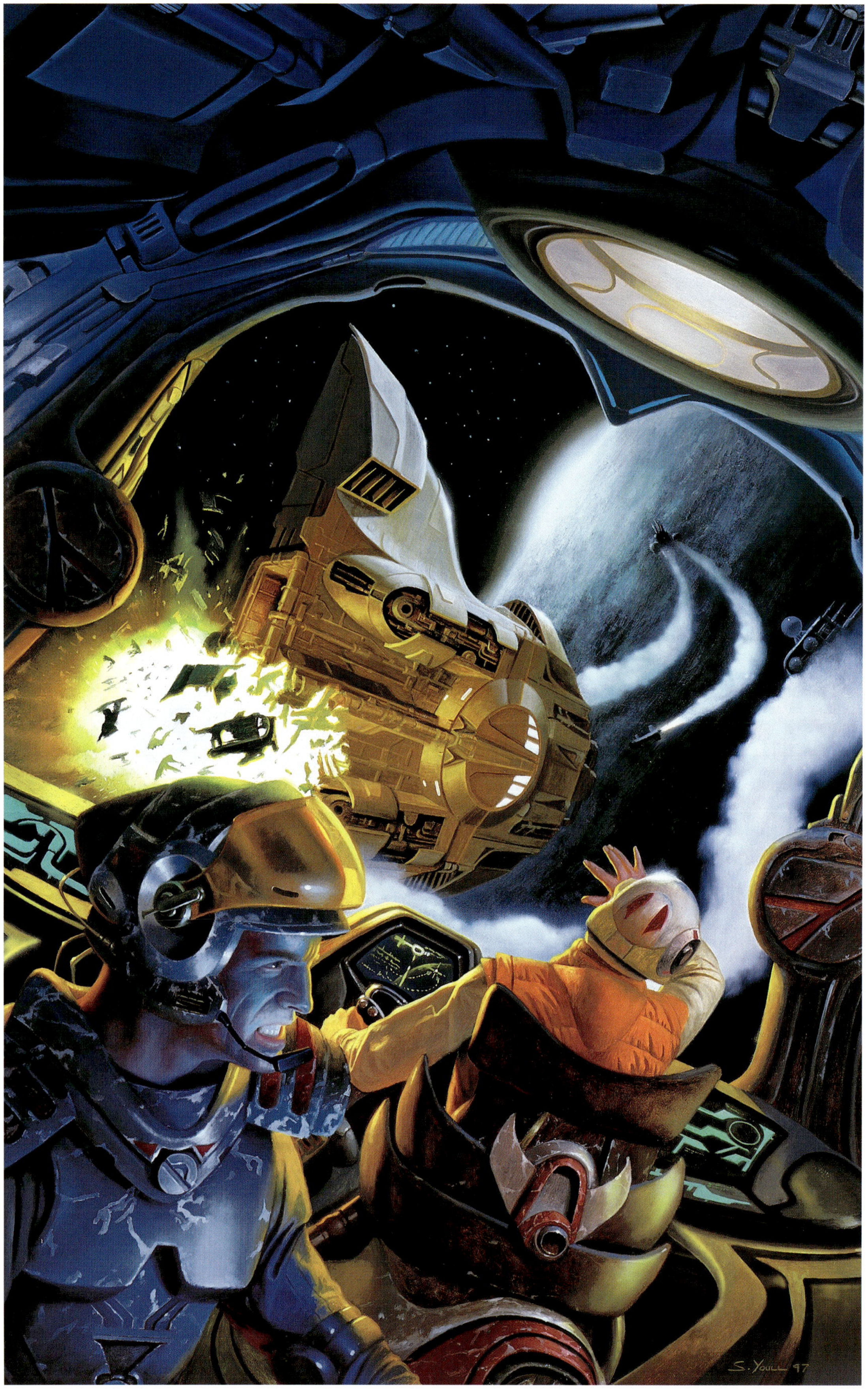

HUNG OUT

MARGARET WEIS AND DON PERRIN, PENGUIN USA, 1997

OIL ON MASONITE, 21 x 13in (53 x 33cm)

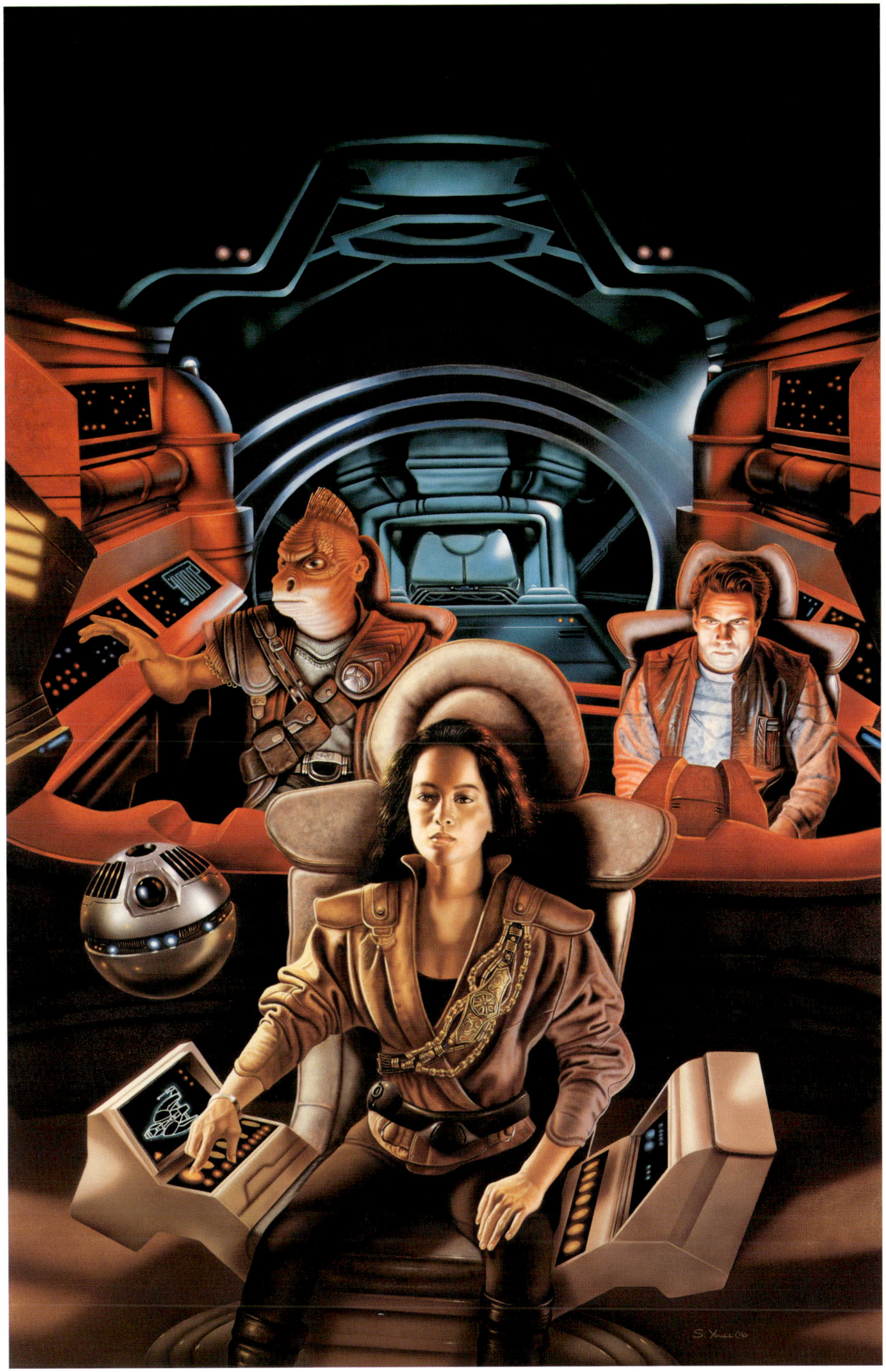

THE PRICE OF RANSOM
ALIS A. RASMUSSEN, BANTAM, 1990
ACRYLIC ON ILLUSTRATION BOARD, 26 x 16¼in (66 x 41cm)

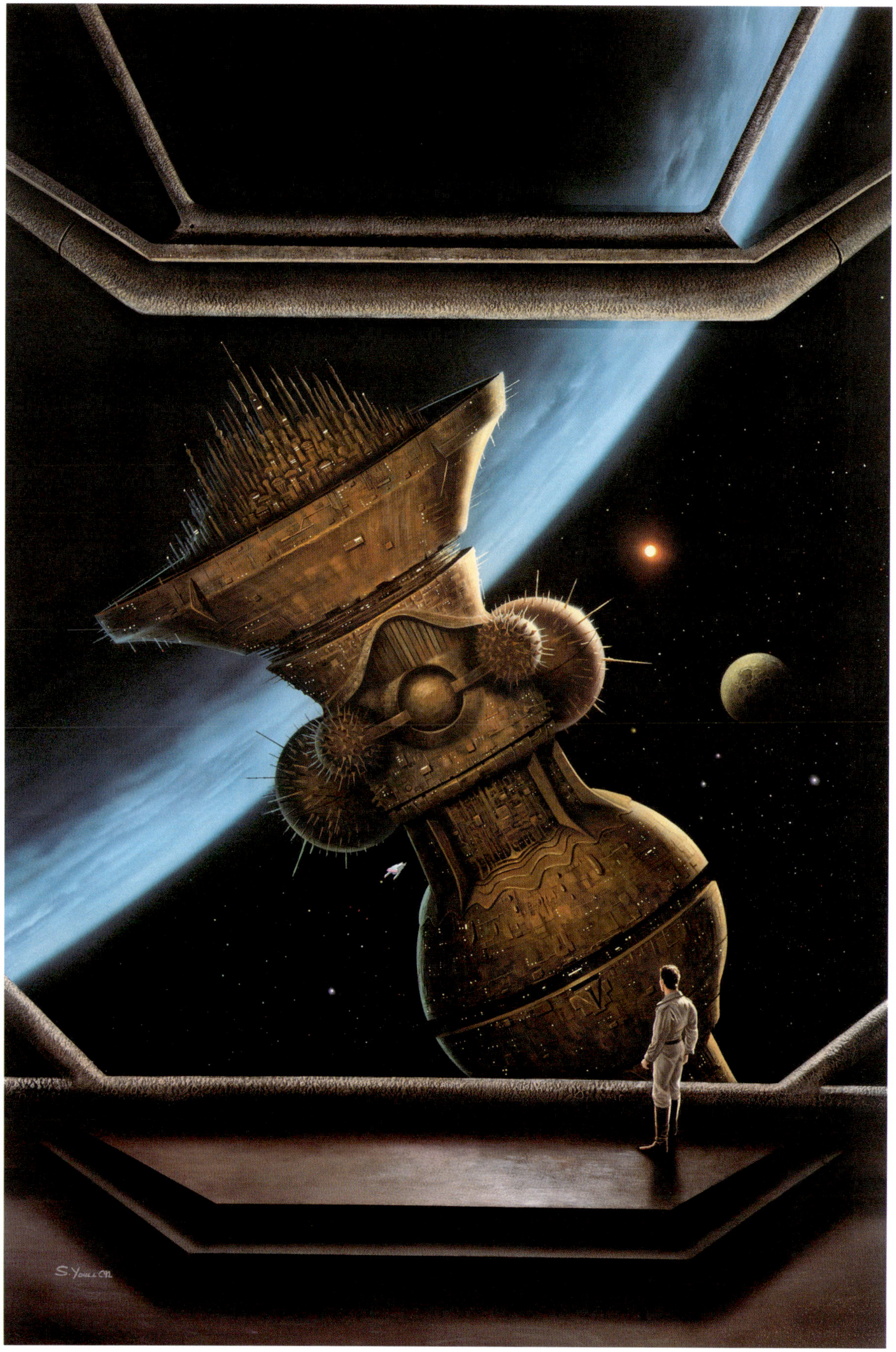

FORBIDDEN KNOWLEDGE

STEPHEN R. DONALDSON, BANTAM, 1992

ACRYLIC ON ILLUSTRATION BOARD, 27½ x 18¼in (70 x 46cm)

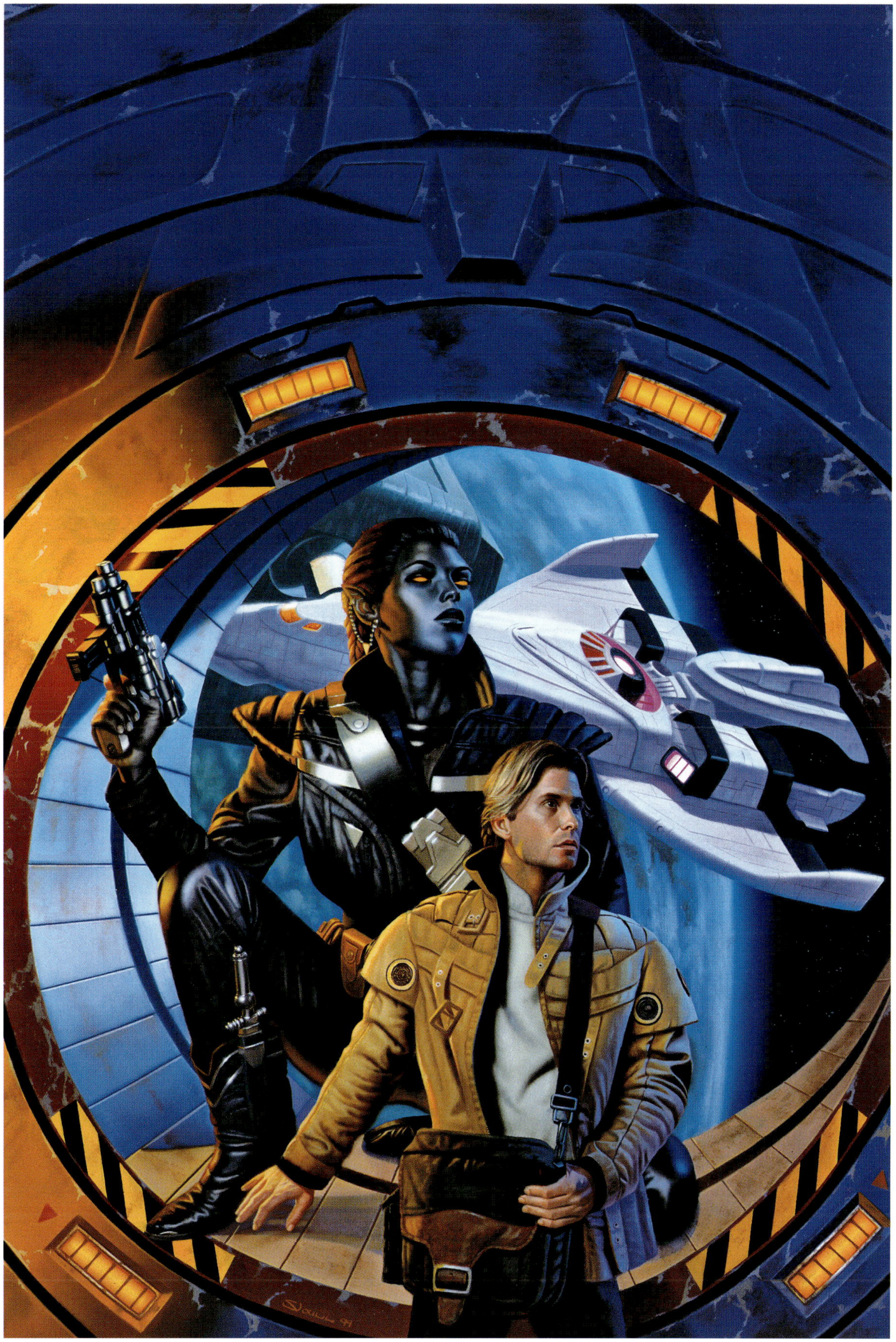

PRECURSOR

C.J. CHERRYH, DAW, 1999

OIL ON ILLUSTRATION BOARD, 25 x 15in (64 x 38cm)

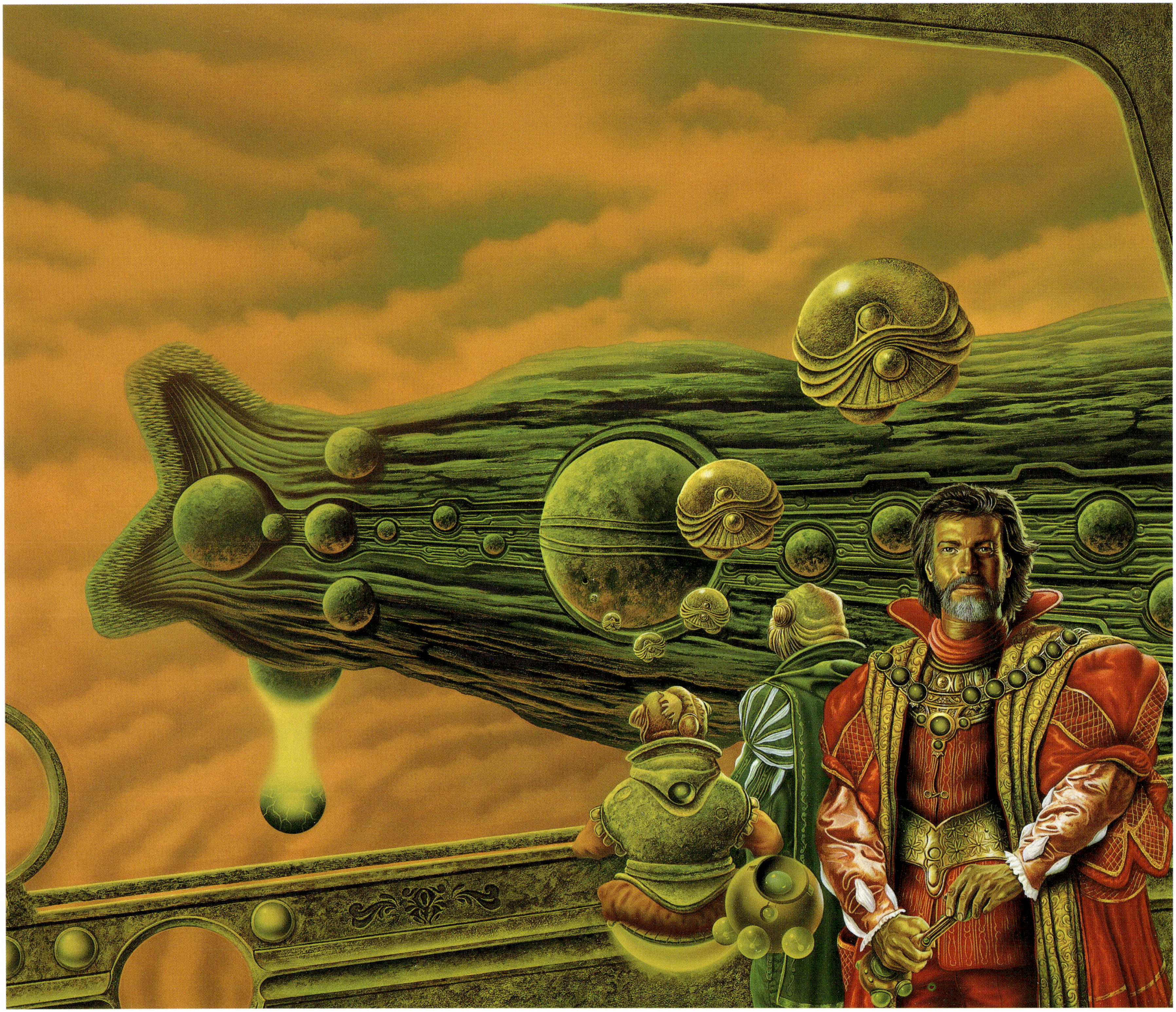

THE AMBASSADOR
SELF-PROMOTION, 1987
ACRYLIC ON ILLUSTRATION BOARD, 16½ x 20½in (42 x 52cm)

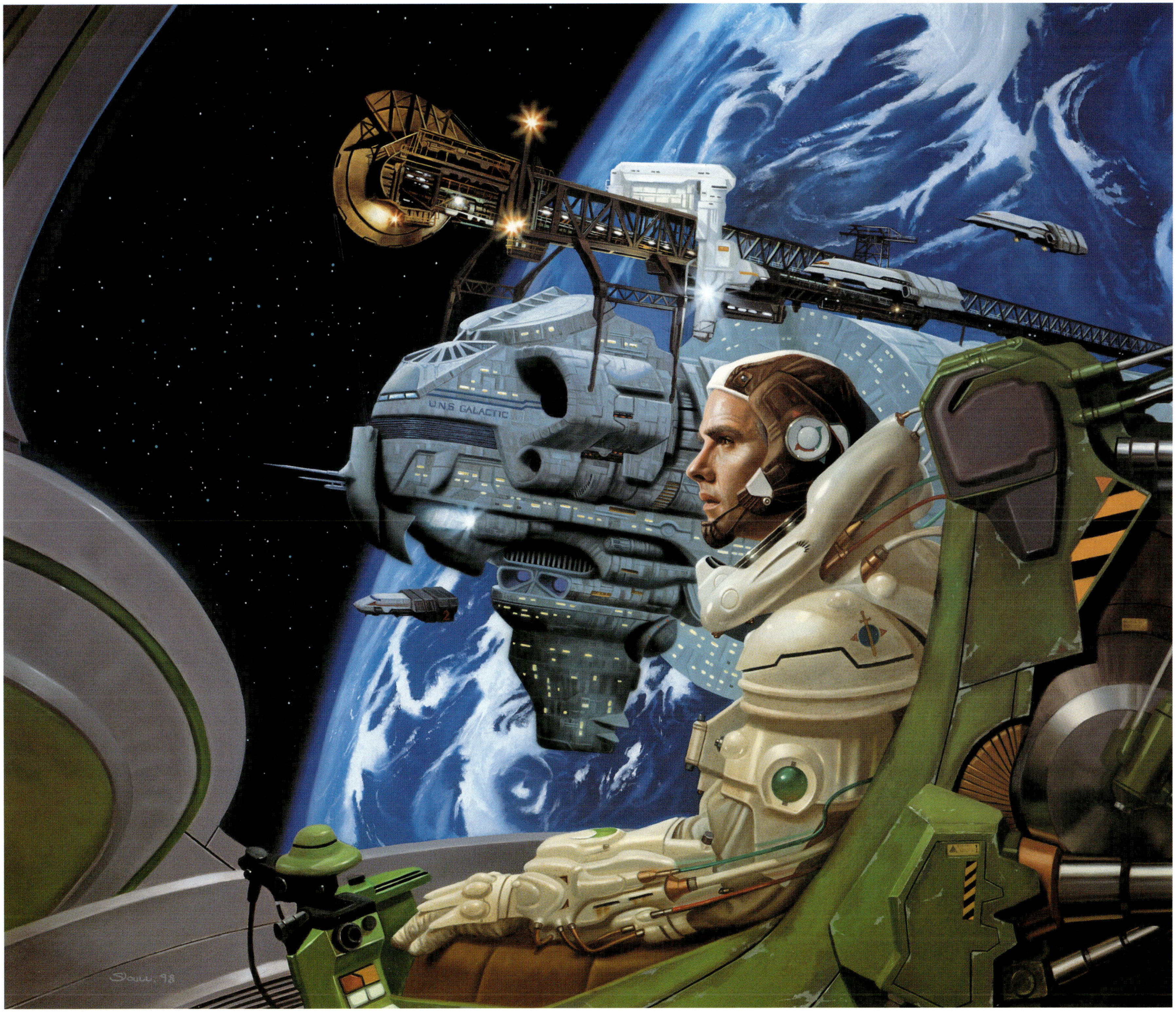

PATRIARCH'S HOPE

DAVID FEINTUCH, WARNER, 1998

OIL ON MASONITE, 24 x 34in (61 x 86cm)

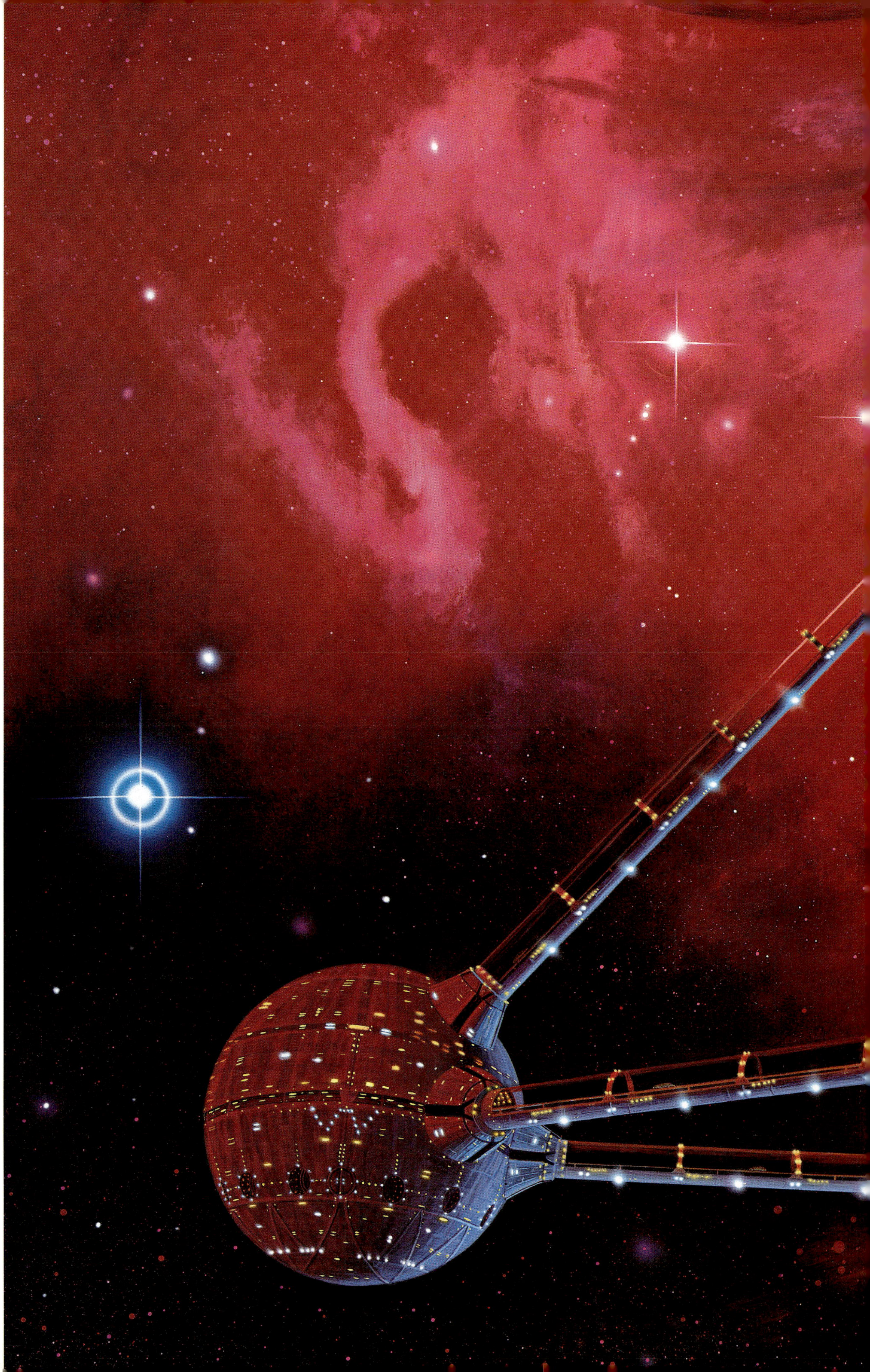

RAMA REVEALED
ARTHUR C. CLARKE AND GENTRY LEE,
BANTAM, 1993
OIL ON ILLUSTRATION BOARD
26 x 34in (66 x 86cm)

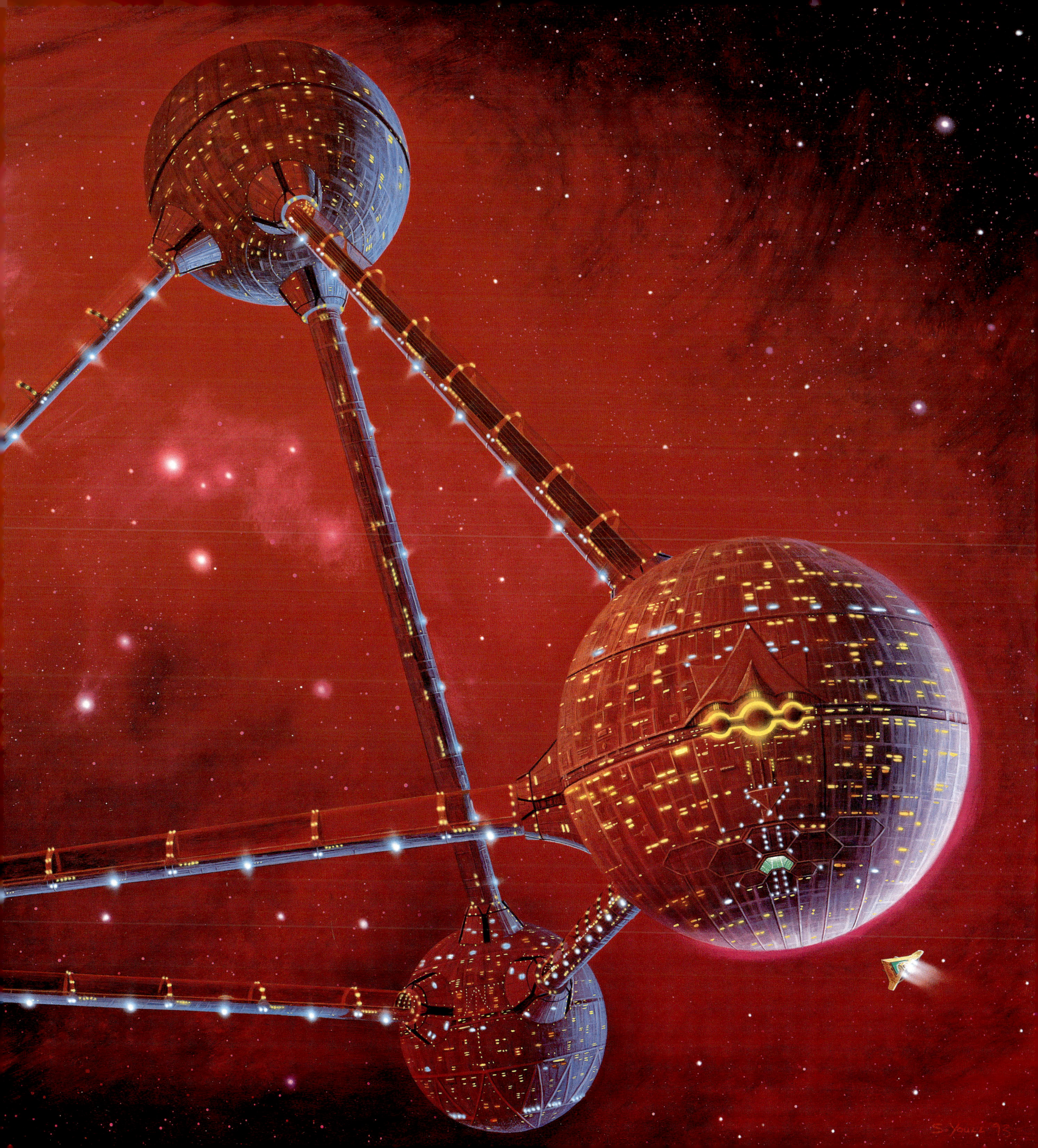

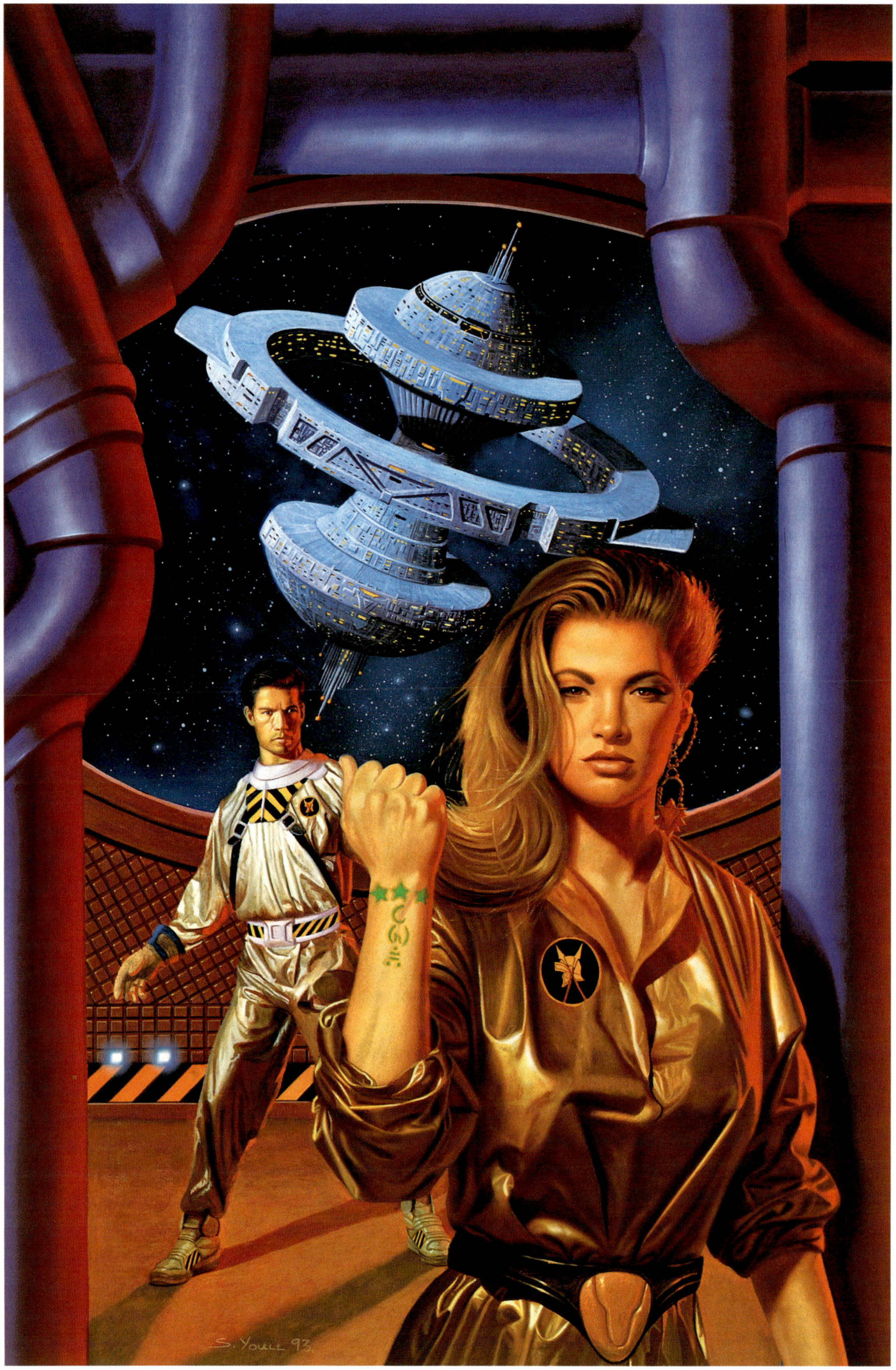

TRIPOINT

C.J. CHERRYH, WARNER, 1993

OIL ON MASONITE, 20 x 13in (51 x 33cm)

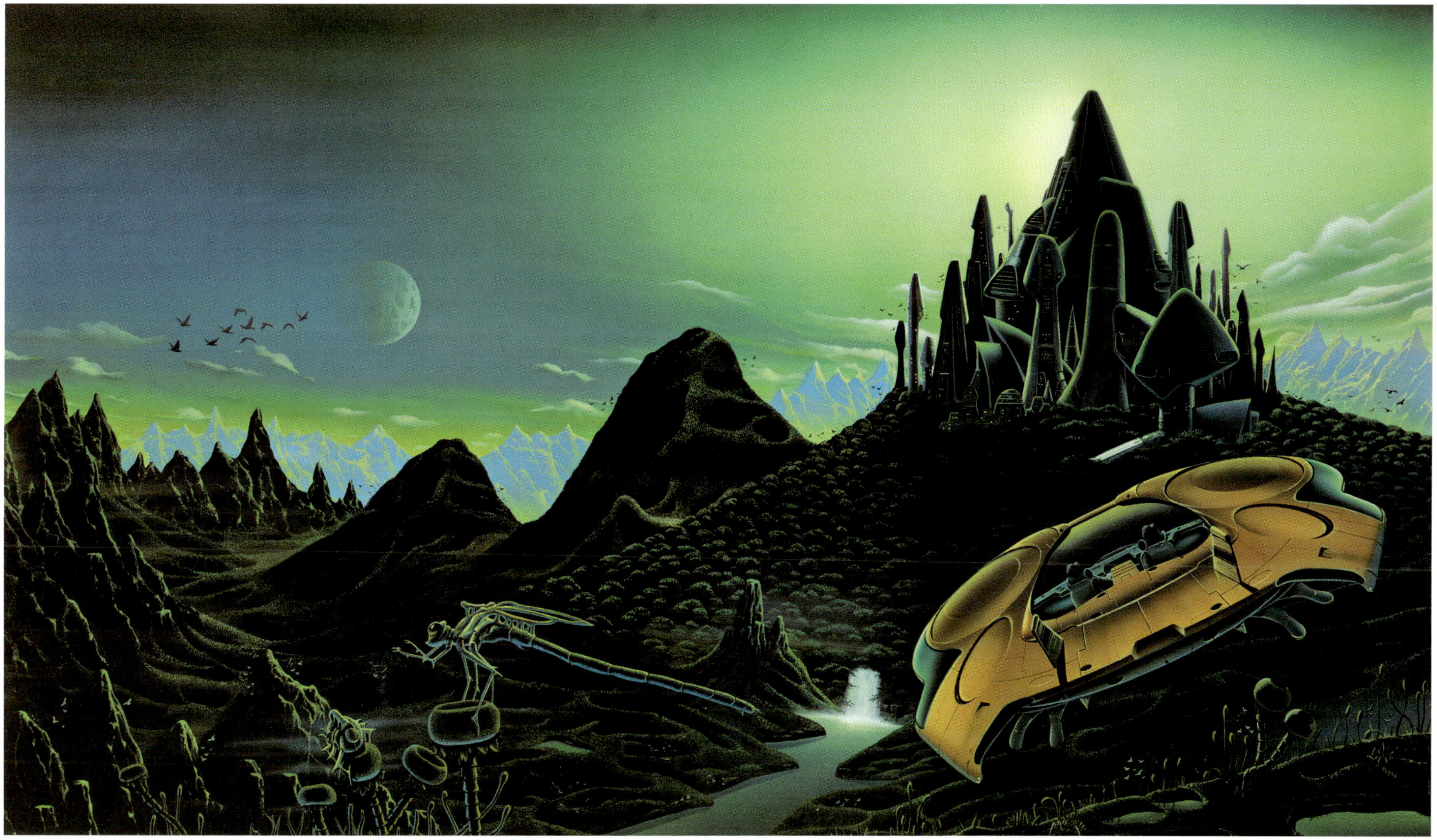

RETURN TO SYPHER

FIRST SCIENCE FICTION STUDY AT COLLEGE, 1985
GOUACHE ON ILLUSTRATION BOARD, 15 x 25in (38 x 64cm)

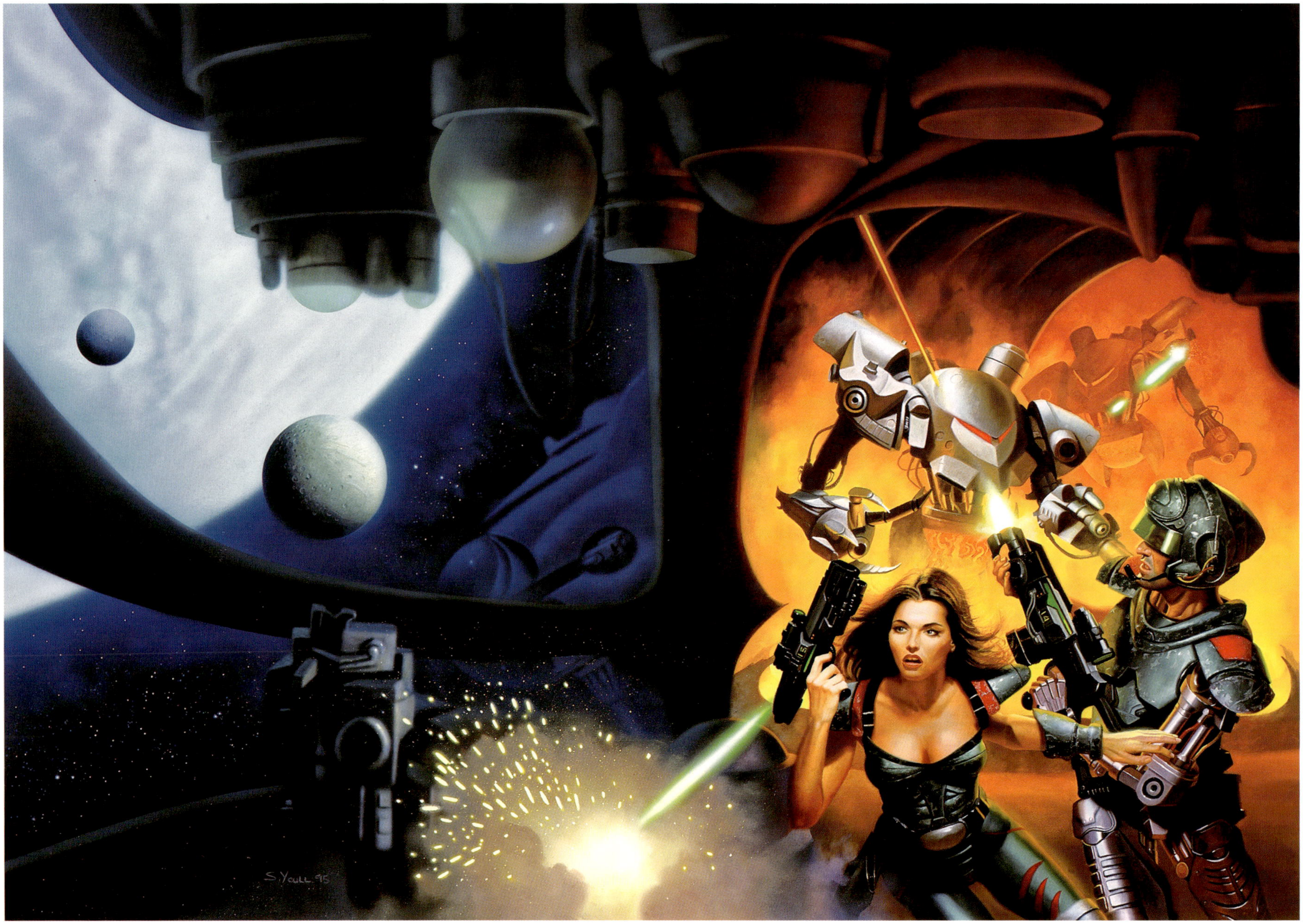

ROBOT BLUES

MARGARET WEIS AND DON PERRIN, PENGUIN USA, 1995

OIL ON MASONITE, 21 x 28½in (53 x 72cm)

NOTHING UNREAL EXISTS

One of the most interesting topics explored in SF is artificial intelligence. I've always been fascinated by robots and cybernetic life forms. My memories of childhood are awash with gleamingly polished robots from movies like *Forbidden Planet, The Day the Earth Stood Still* and *Star Wars*. Ever since I saw Robby the Robot in a TV screening of *Forbidden Planet* when I was about seven years old, I've had a compulsion to paint and draw robots. As an illustrator I've painted the robots that feature in some of the most beloved and revered SF novels, from Isaac Asimov's own *I, Robot* and *Robots of Dawn* to his and Robert Silverberg's *The Positronic Man*. These cover illustrations (pages 66, 68 and 72) are still great favourites of mine. We are inundated with stories on the effect of the computer; it has more profoundly influenced our society than any other invention in our short history. It has become part of our evolution, but also a major way we create art.

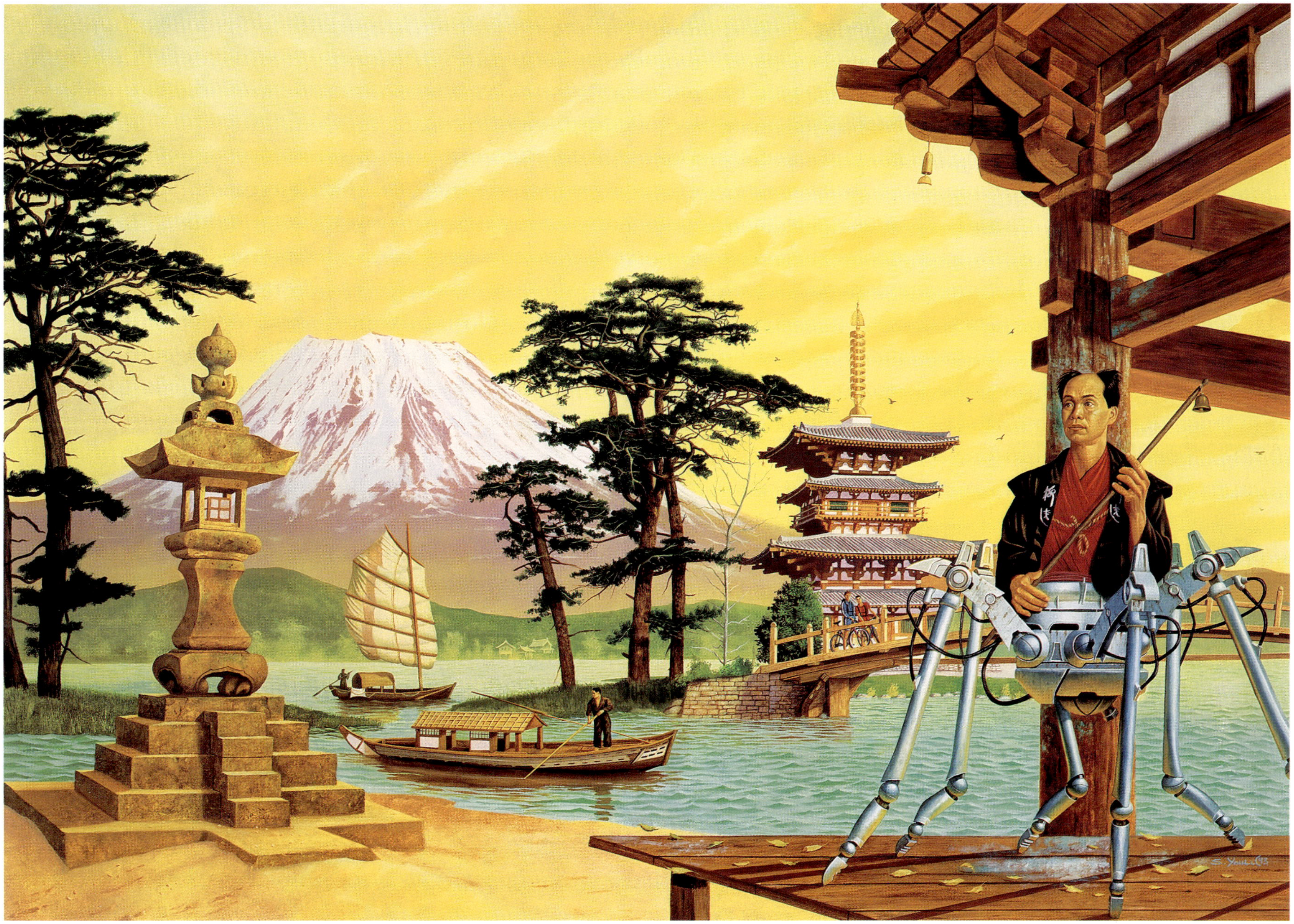

SCISSORS CUT PAPER WRAP STONE

IAN McDONALD, BANTAM, 1995
OIL ON MASONITE, 27 x 36½in (69 x 93cm)

In 1997 IBM commissioned me to paint three images depicting a new communication software called WOM; after careful consideration, I and their art director decided that a single painting would be better. I had also been struck by IBM's seeming lack of enthusiasm regarding a digital approach, and their preference for more traditional media. Once I realized the sheer scope of the project, however, I decided digital work was required to cut down the amount of time it would take to produce such a complicated image. Naturally, I assured the art director that the end result would be a perfect blending of print and paint! This was the first and so far only time I've combined computer art with painting. The goal was to portray as many aspects of the software's capability as was possible through symbolic imagery which people could easily relate to. At the same time, the illustration had to look alive, in motion, with everything working together.

The illustration (pages 70–71) took long enough to paint – three months – but a full year to design, and it remains the most challenging and rewarding piece I've created. I still don't know what WOM actually means.

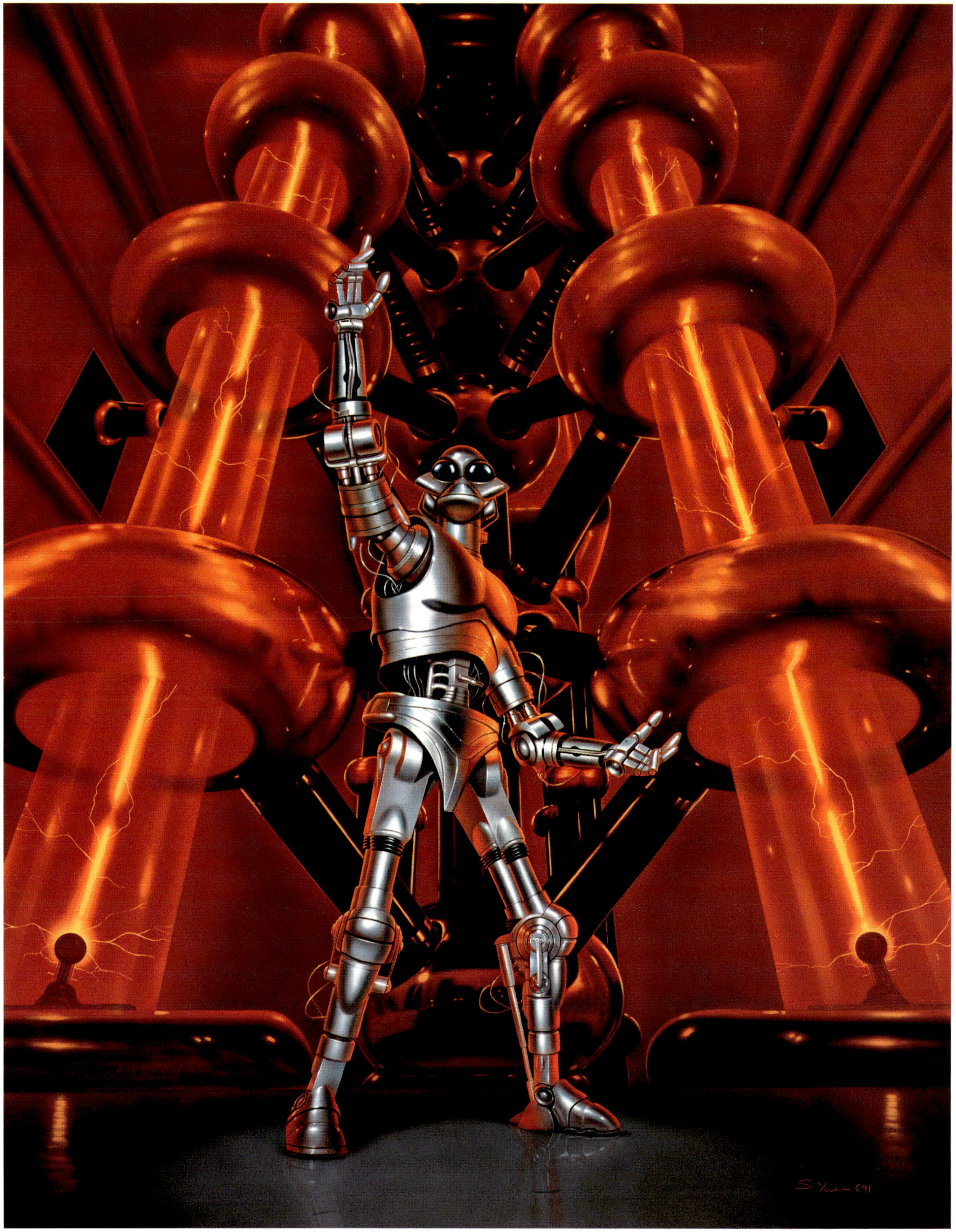

I, ROBOT

ISAAC ASIMOV, BANTAM, 1991

ACRYLIC ON ILLUSTRATION BOARD, 26½ x 21in (67 x 53cm)

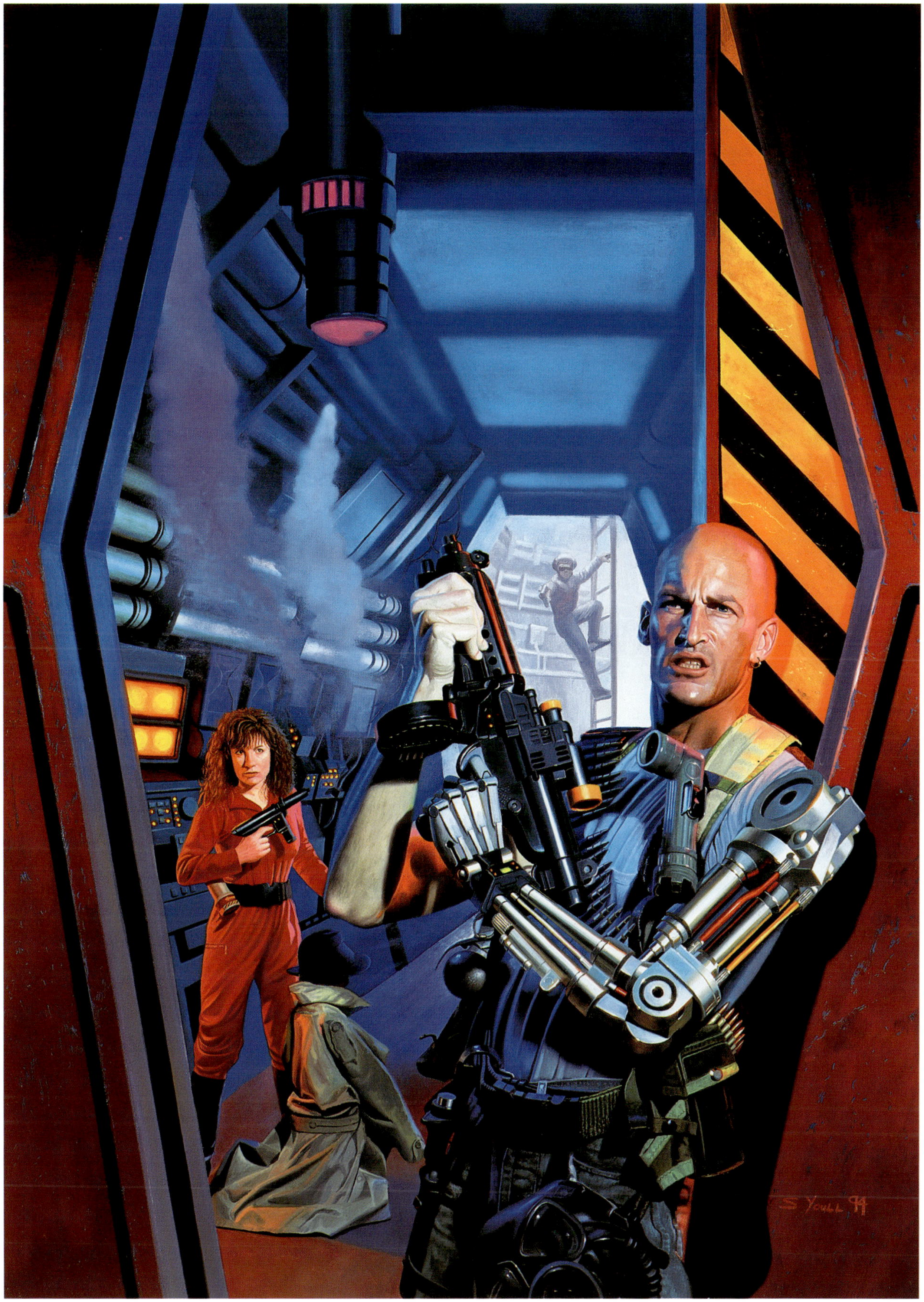

KNIGHTS OF THE BLACK EARTH
MARGARET WEIS AND DON PERRIN, PENGUIN USA, 1994
OIL ON ILLUSTRATION BOARD, 26 x 16in (66 x 41cm)

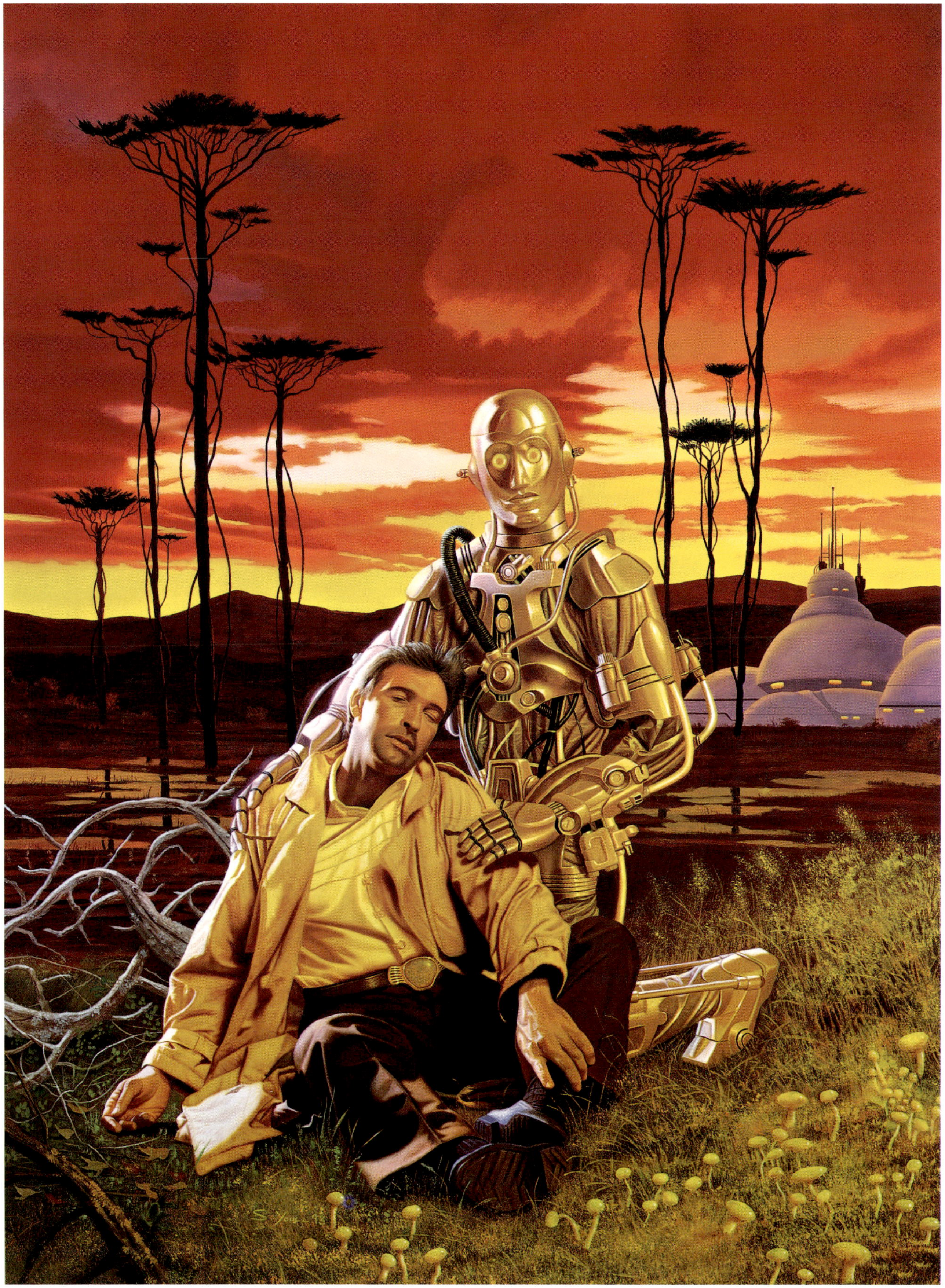

THE ROBOTS OF DAWN
ISAAC ASIMOV, BANTAM, 1993
OIL ON MASONITE, 30 x 21in (76 x 53cm)

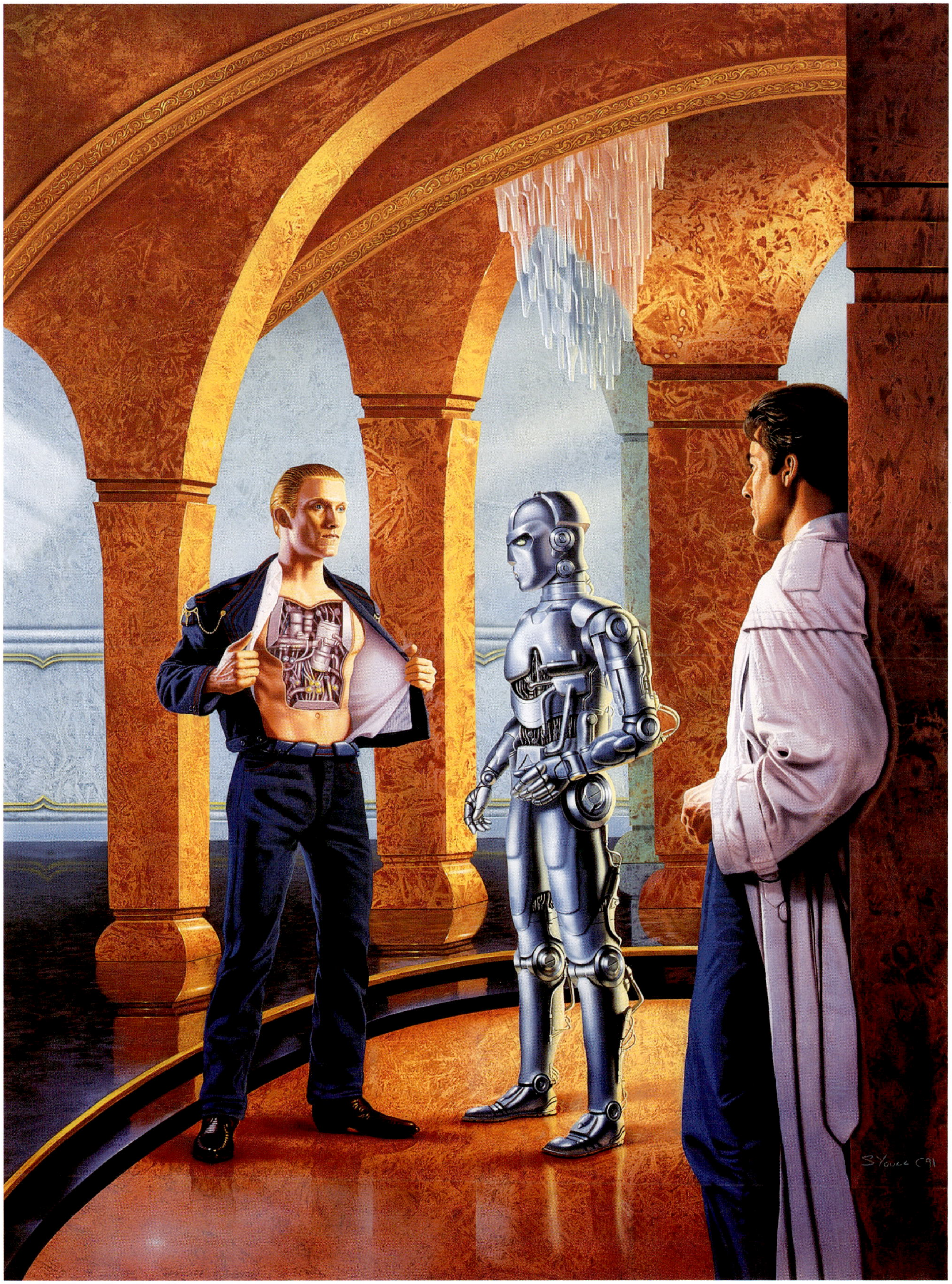

THE NAKED SUN

ISAAC ASIMOV, BANTAM, 1991

ACRYLIC ON MASONITE, 26½ x 21in (67 x 53cm)

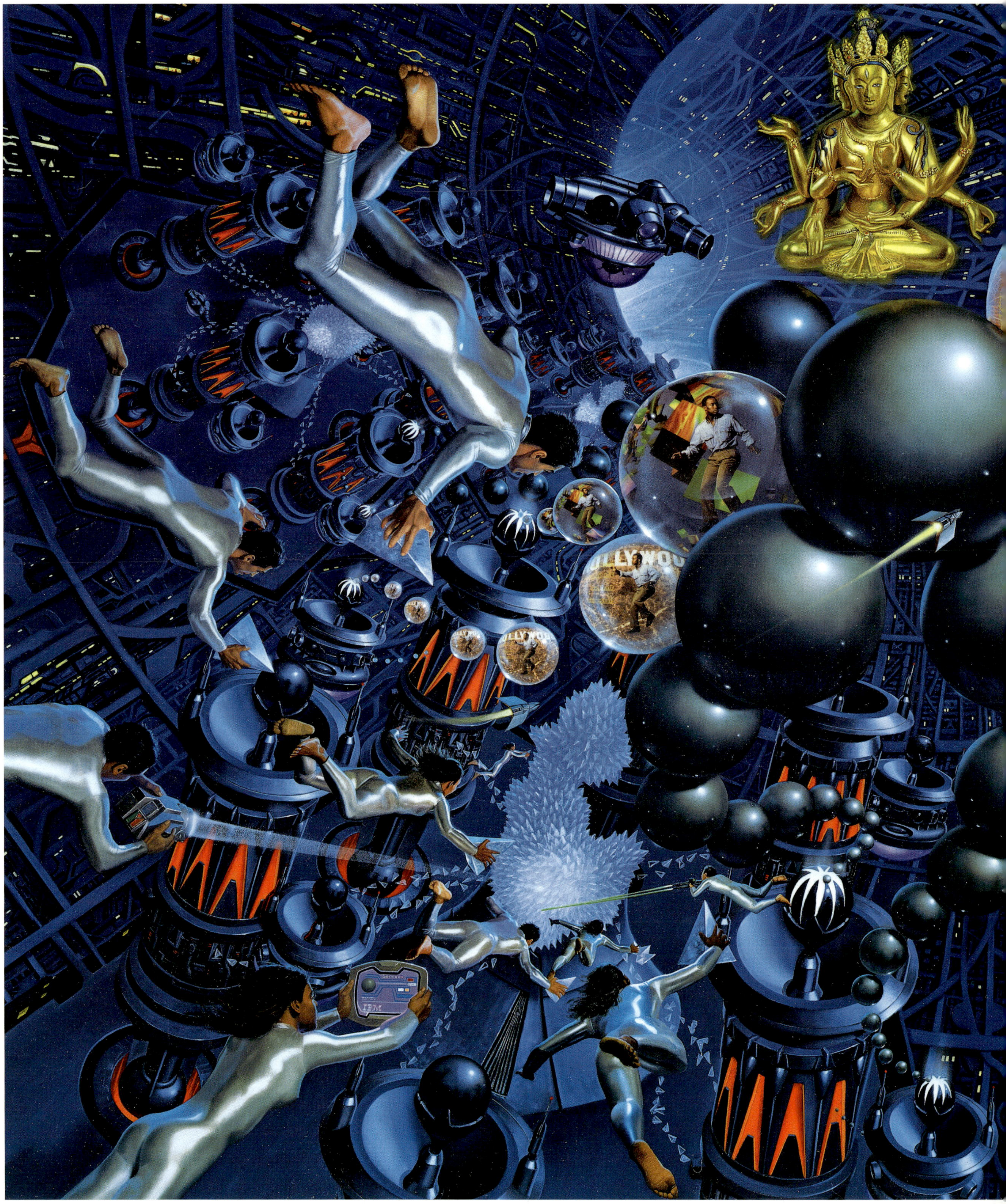
IBM

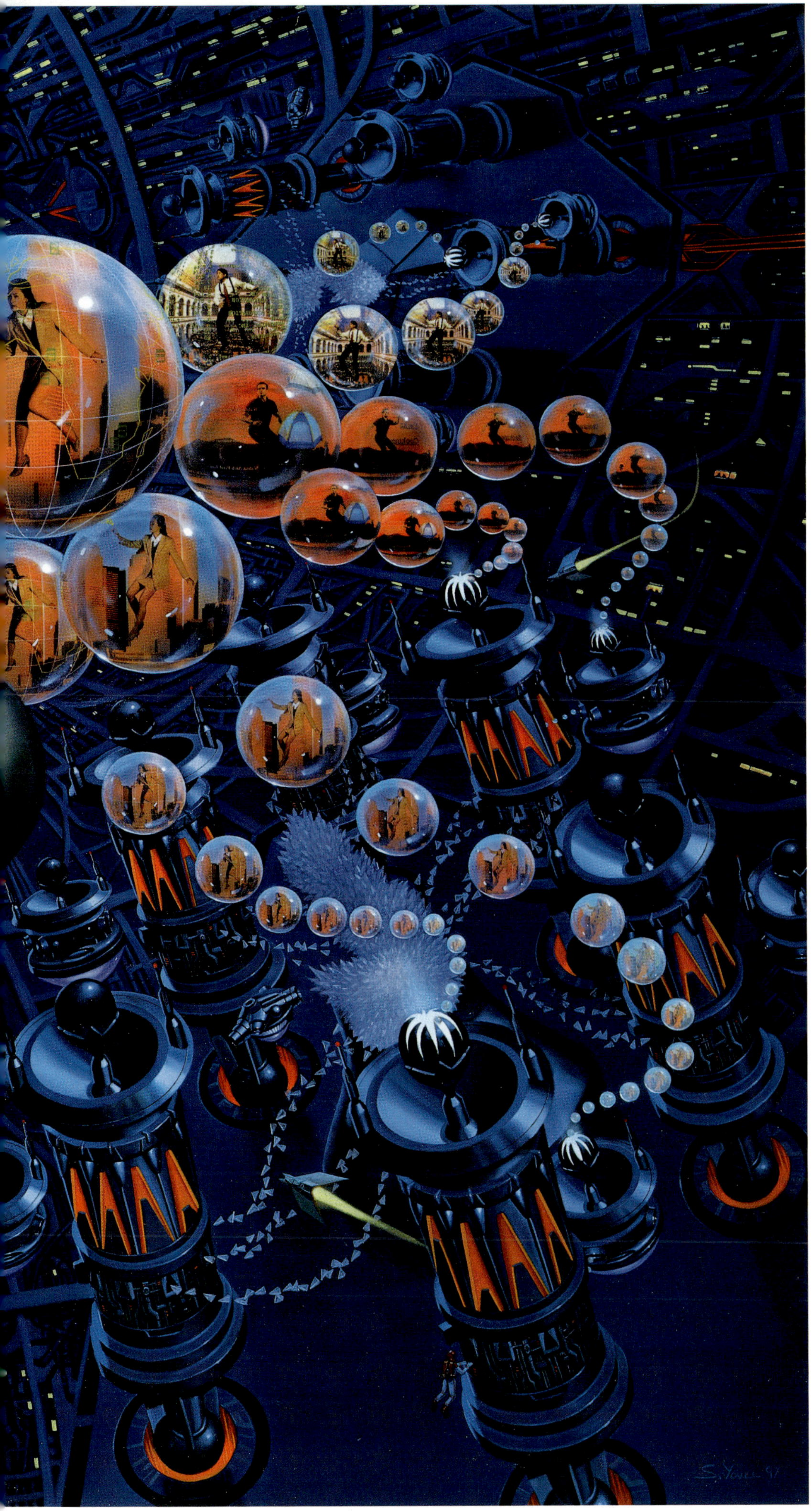

WOM PLANET
IBM CORPORATION, 1997
OIL AND DIGITAL ON WATERCOLOUR PAPER
24 x 35in (61 x 89cm)

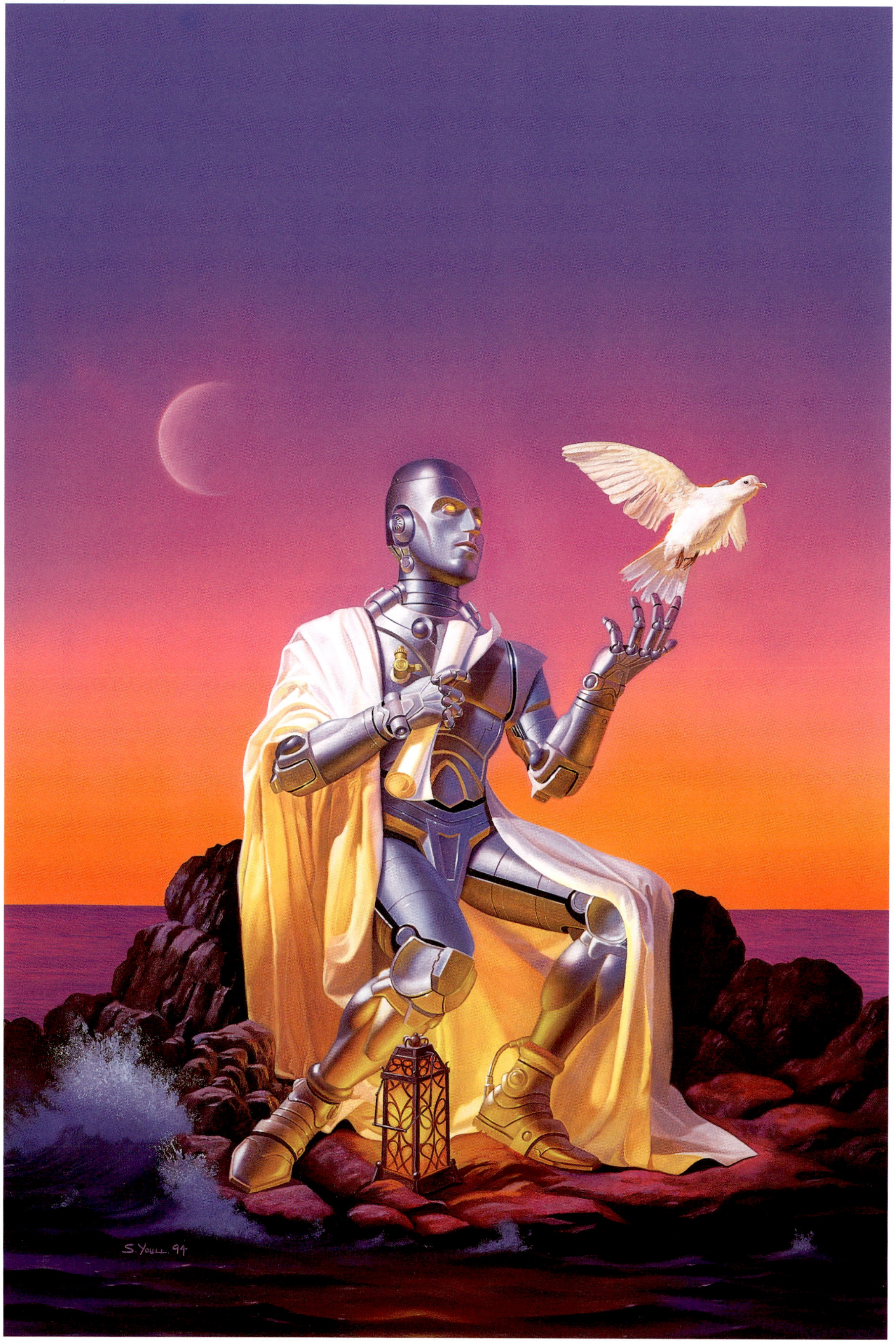

THE POSITRONIC MAN

ISAAC ASIMOV AND ROBERT SILVERBERG, BANTAM, 1994
OIL ON MASONITE, 32 x 19½in (81 x 50cm)

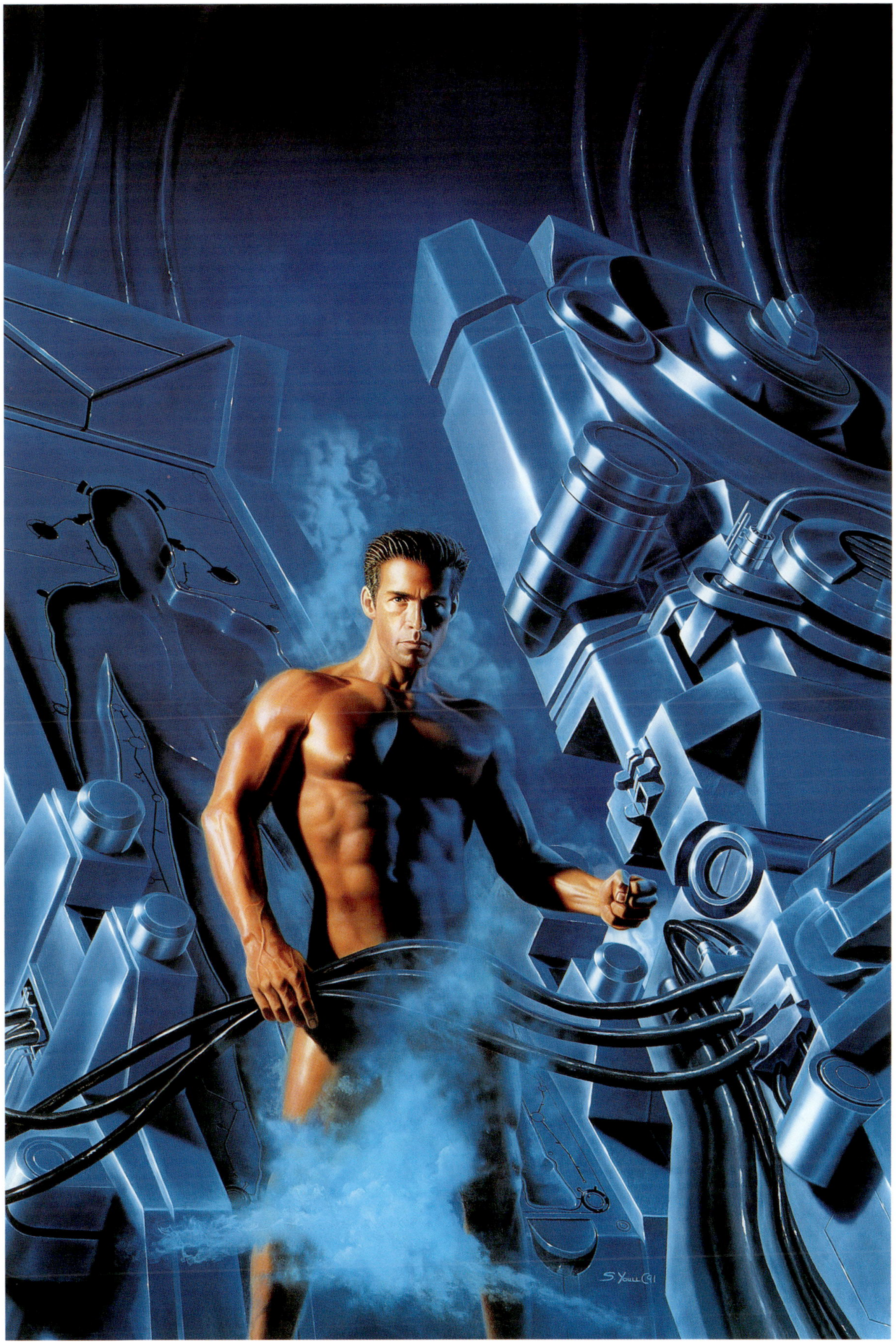

DARK SKY LEGION

WILLIAM BARTON, BANTAM, 1991

ACRYLIC AND OIL ON ILLUSTRATION BOARD, 28 x 17½in (71 x 44cm)

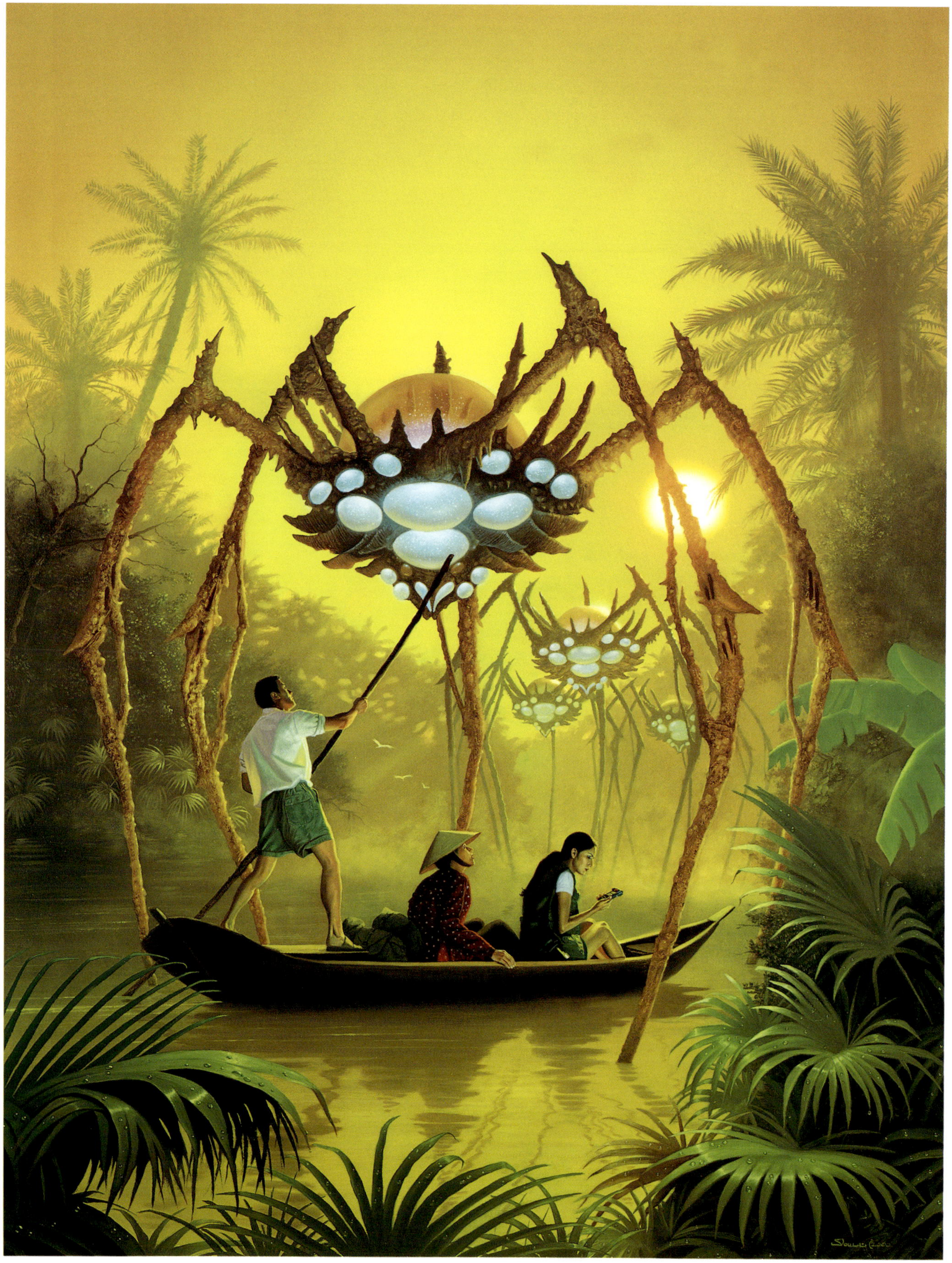

LIMIT OF VISION

LINDA NAGATA, TOR, 2000

OIL ON MASONITE, 28 x 19½in (71 x 50cm)

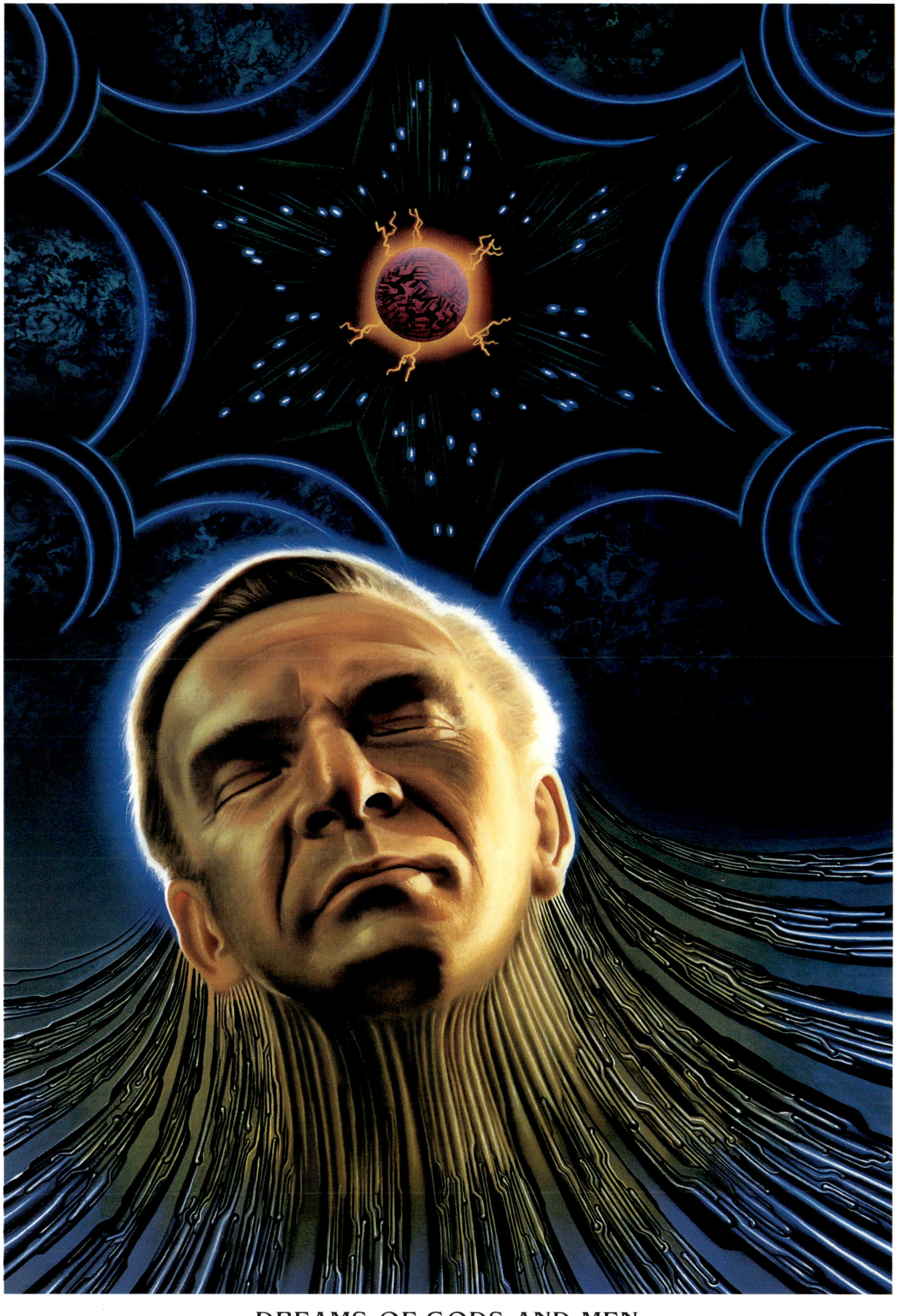

DREAMS OF GODS AND MEN

W.T. QUICK, FUTURA, 1988

ACRYLIC ON MASONITE, 17 x 11in (43 x 28cm)

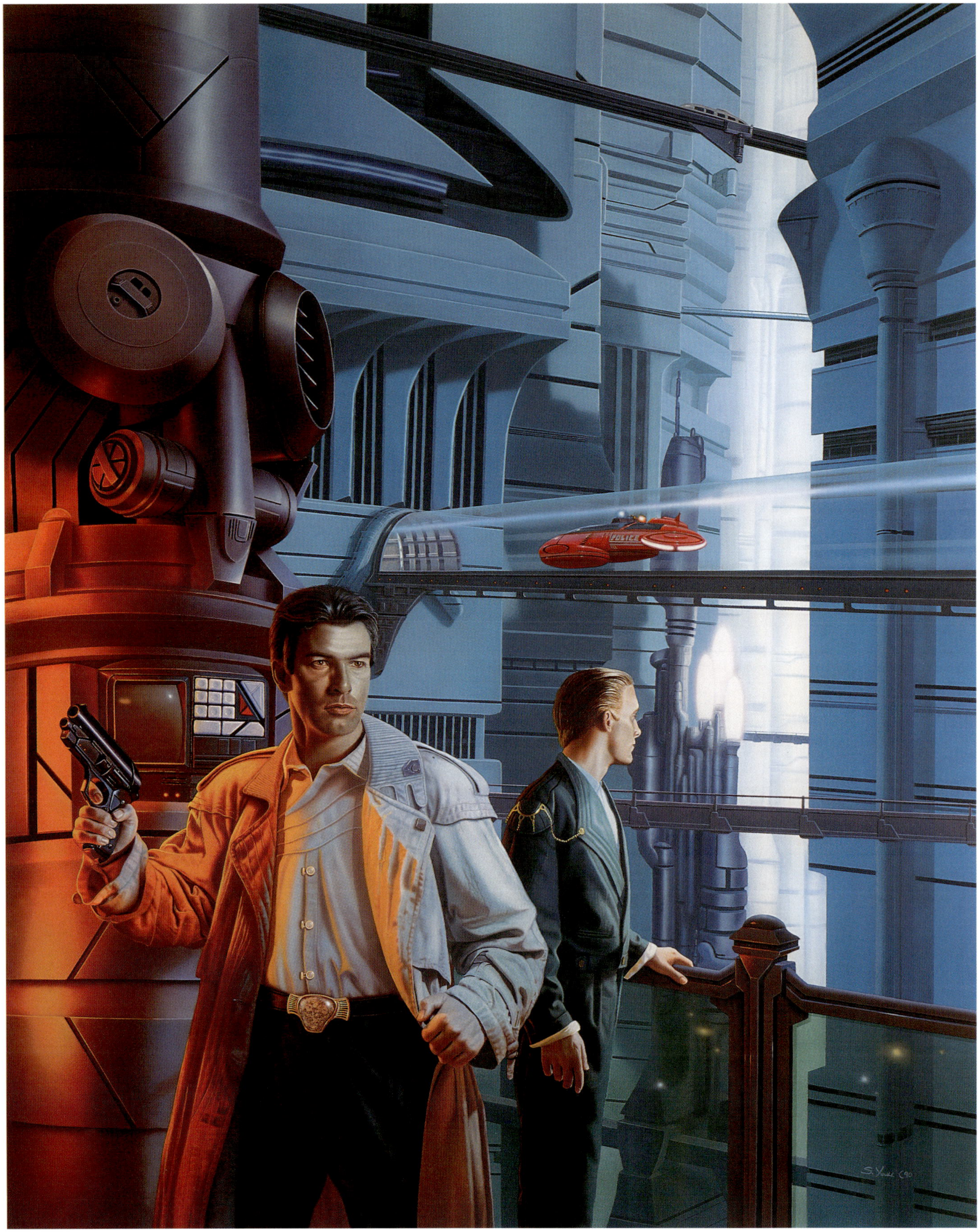

THE CAVES OF STEEL

ISAAC ASIMOV, BANTAM, 1990

ACRYLIC AND OIL ON MASONITE, 26½ x 21in (67 x 53cm)

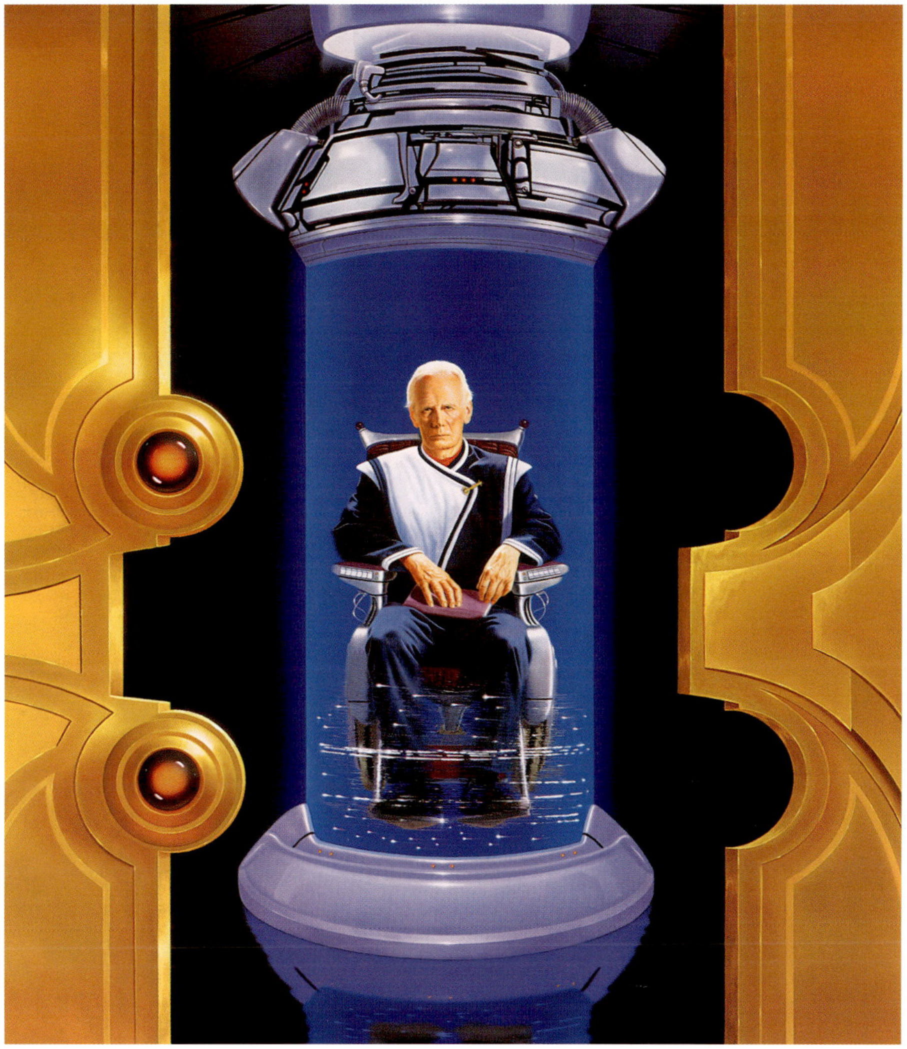

FOUNDATION
ISAAC ASIMOV, BANTAM, 1991
ACRYLIC AND OIL ON ILLUSTRATION BOARD, 26½ x 21in (67 x 53cm)

PSYCHOHISTORIC

In 1990 Bantam asked I and several other artists to submit portfolios to be sent to Isaac Asimov. Bantam was repackaging many of his classic novels, and wanted to involve the author in the selection of cover artists. I was a relatively new artist in the field at the time, so I was nervous, to say the least. A week later, however, I got the news that Asimov had seen something special in my work and that I was one of the three artists chosen to illustrate these new editions of his novels.

When I was offered the commission my first reaction was to turn it down: it was a pretty daunting assignment, being for eleven books – the *Robot*, *Empire* and *Foundation* novels. Eleven covers would take me about a year to complete, which was a long time. However, I was persuaded by the editors that this was the chance of a lifetime, and so it proved to be. I got into the habit of reading the novels while travelling on the subway to and from my studio, and became so engrossed in the stories that often I missed my stop. (Sometimes reading the books is one of the major perks of the job!)

The editors had decided that, since the previous covers had all been illustrated symbolically, this time what was wanted instead were scenes from the stories. The books had on the one hand to look like a series but the individual covers should also be able to stand alone. This dual requirement was both frustrating and demanding. If I had had my own way I would have followed my original inclinations and given the novels covers that were more symbolic. Nevertheless, several of the paintings I did for those books remain among my favourites.

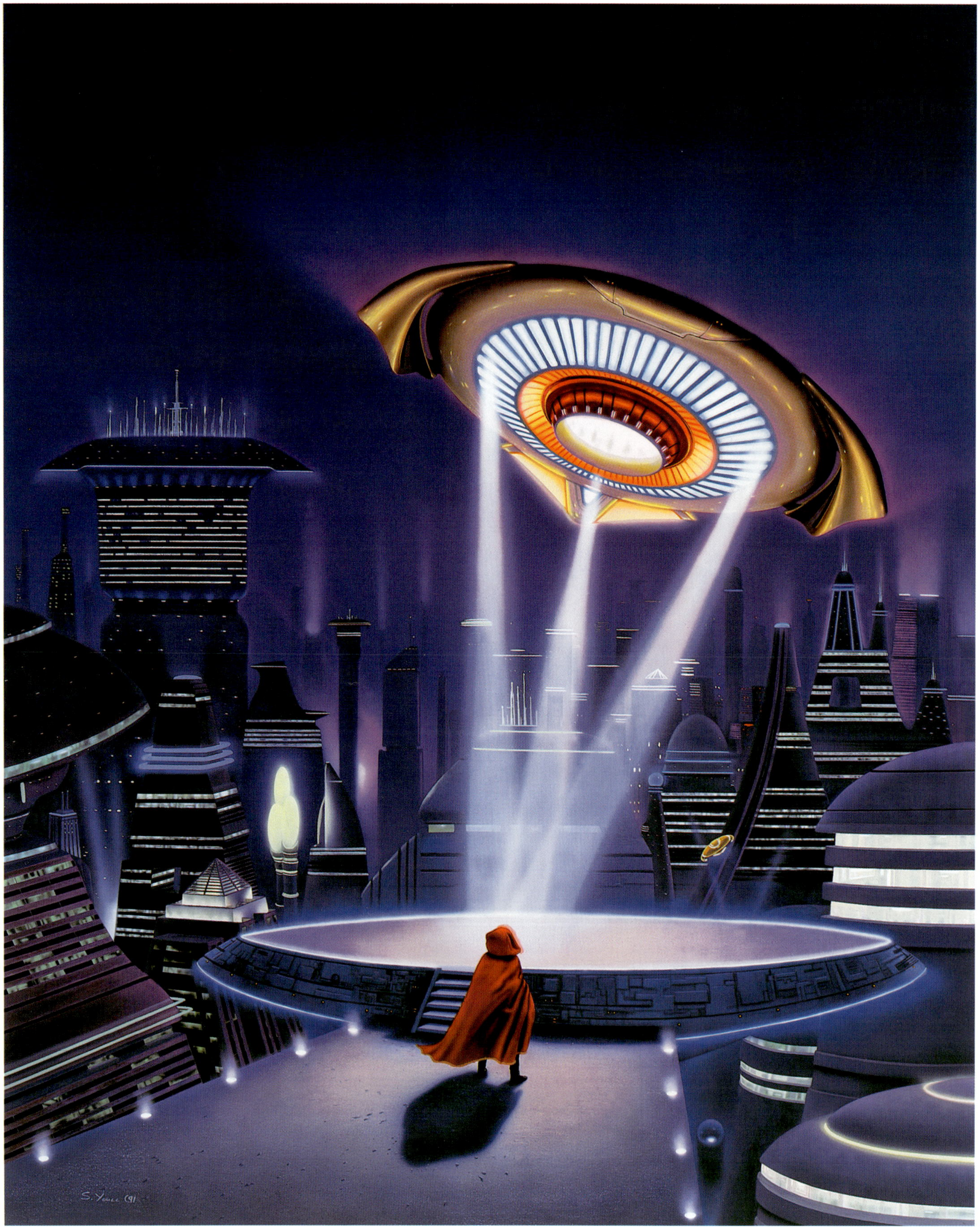

SECOND FOUNDATION

ISAAC ASIMOV, BANTAM, 1991

ACRYLIC ON ILLUSTRATION BOARD, 26½ x 21in (67 x 53cm)

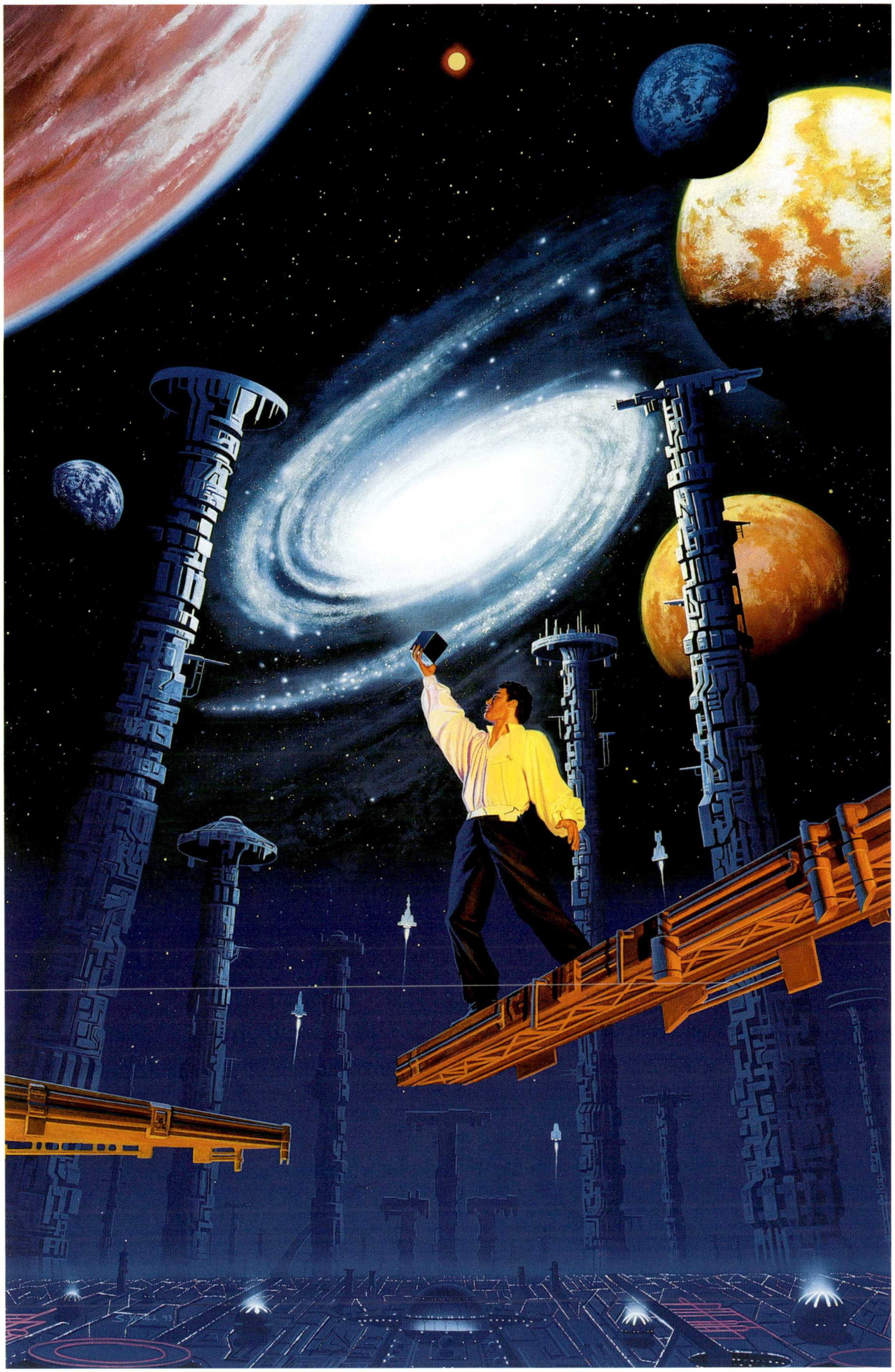

FORWARD THE FOUNDATION
ISAAC ASIMOV, BANTAM, 1993
ACRYLIC AND OIL ON CANVAS, 29 x 18½in (74 x 47cm)

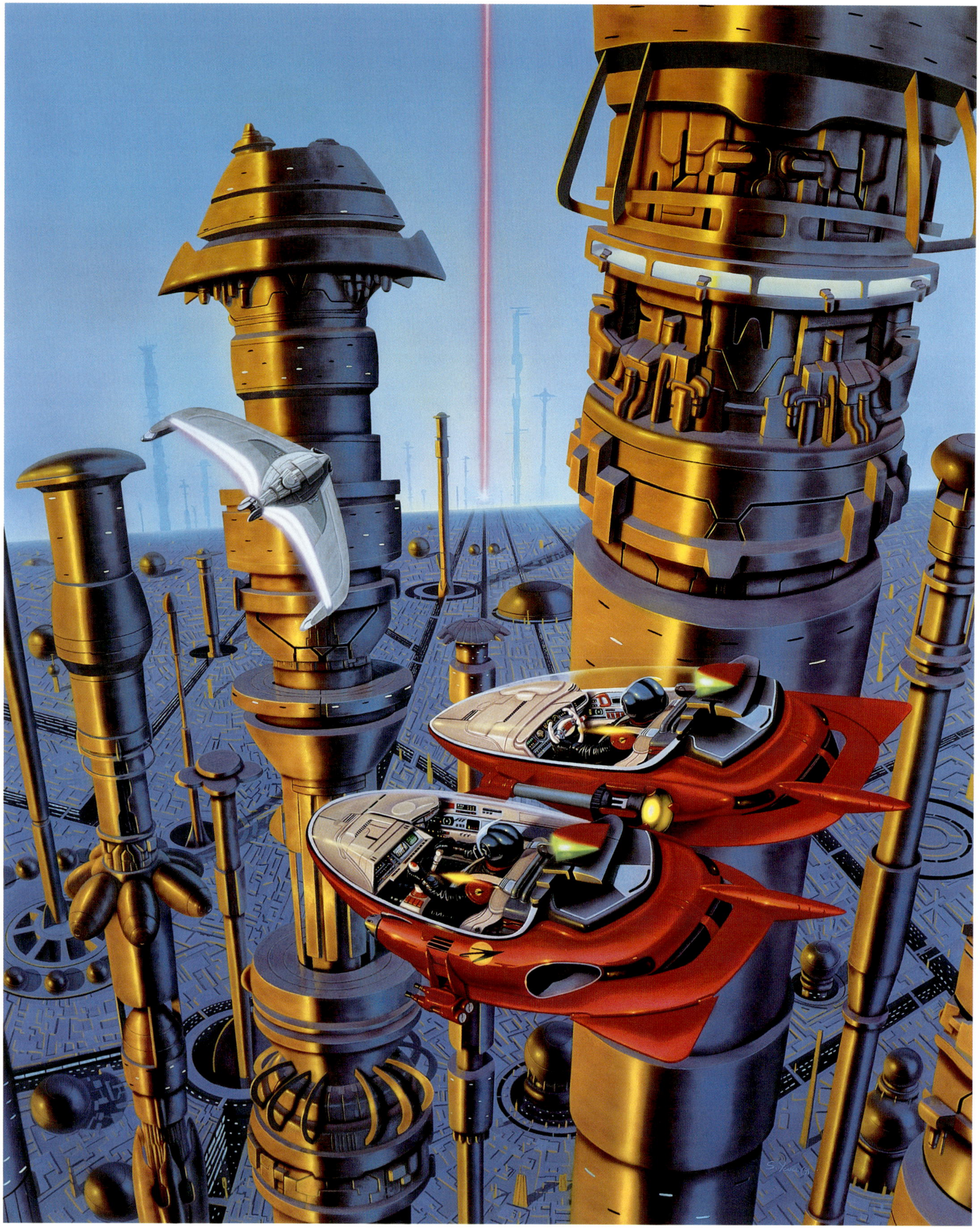

FOUNDATION AND EMPIRE

ISAAC ASIMOV, BANTAM, 1991

ACRYLIC ON MASONITE, 26½ x 21in (67 x 53cm)

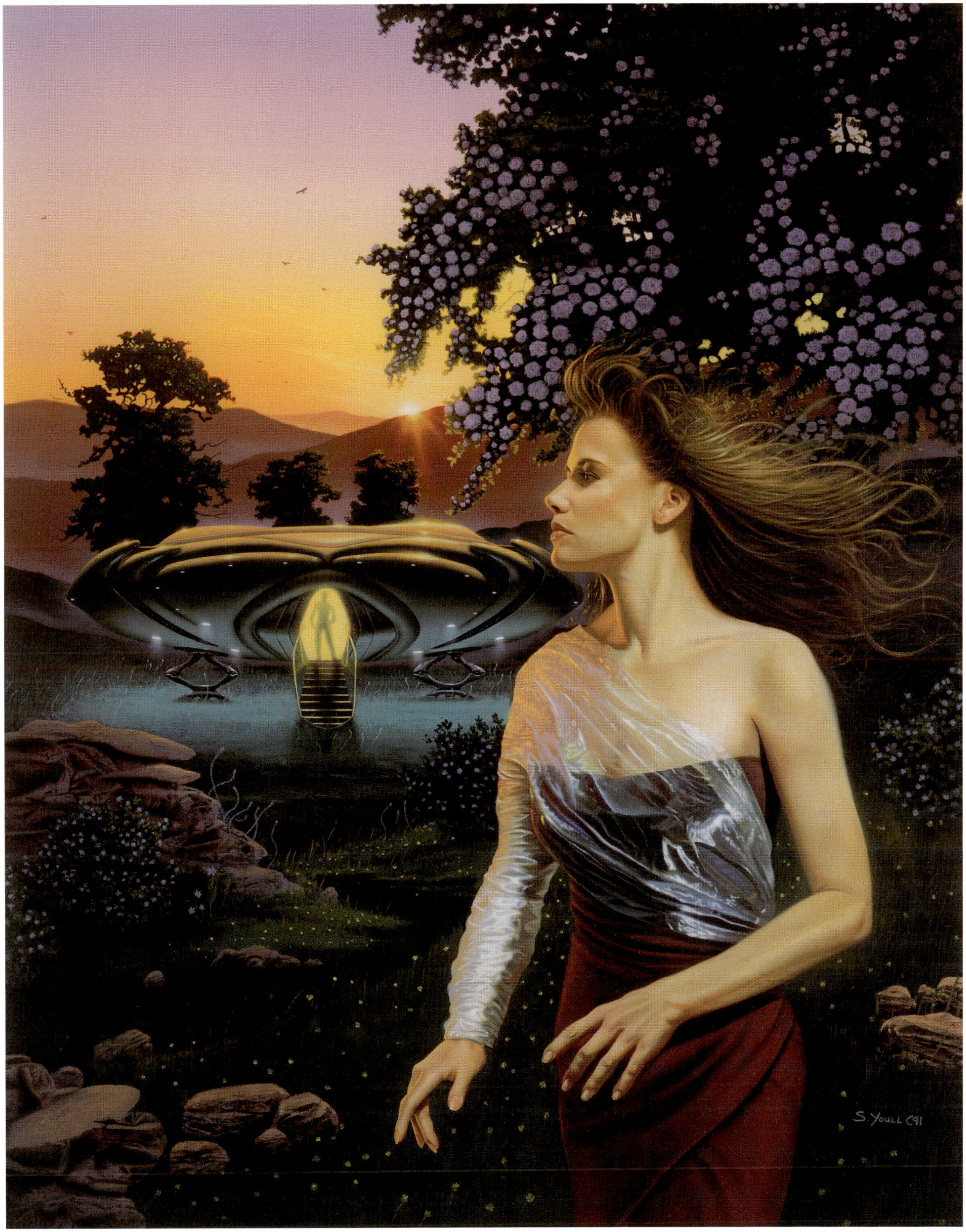

FOUNDATION'S EDGE

ISAAC ASIMOV, BANTAM, 1991

ACRYLIC AND OIL ON ILLUSTRATION BOARD, 23½ x 18in (60 x 46cm)

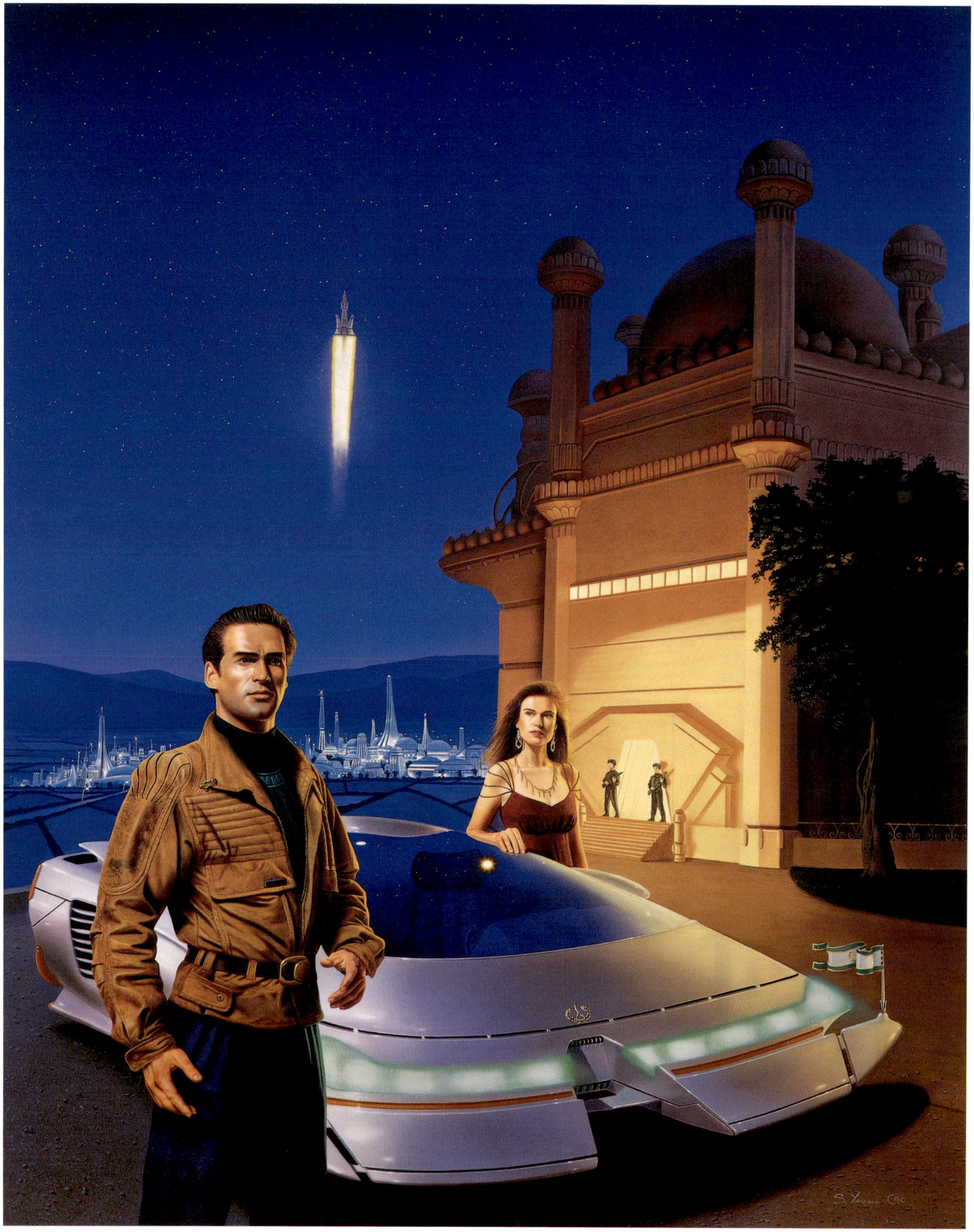

PEBBLE IN THE SKY

ISAAC ASIMOV, BANTAM, 1990

ACRYLIC ON MASONITE, 26½ x 21in (67 x 53cm)

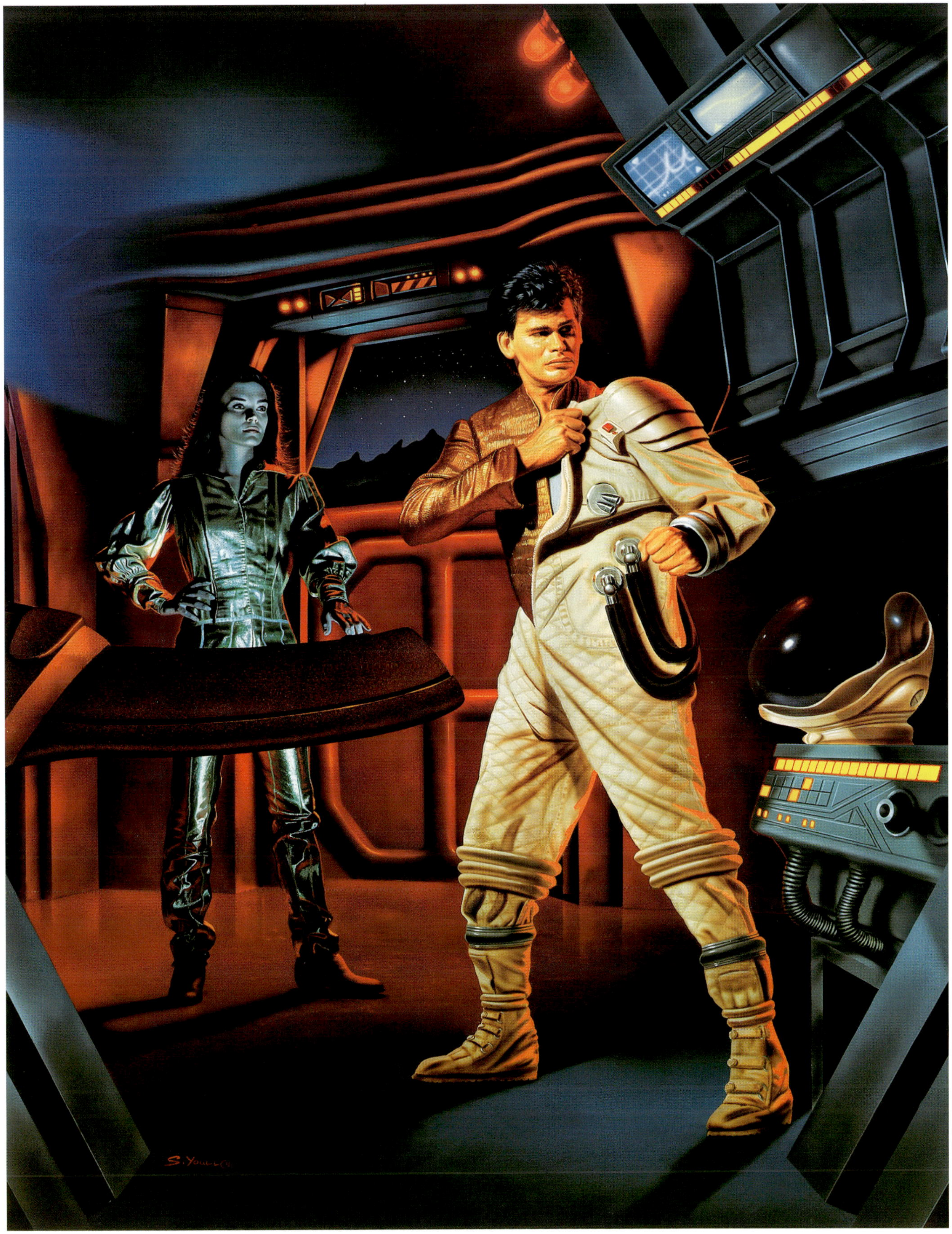

THE STARS, LIKE DUST

ISAAC ASIMOV, BANTAM, 1991

ACRYLIC AND OIL ON MASONITE, 26½ x 21in (67 x 53cm)

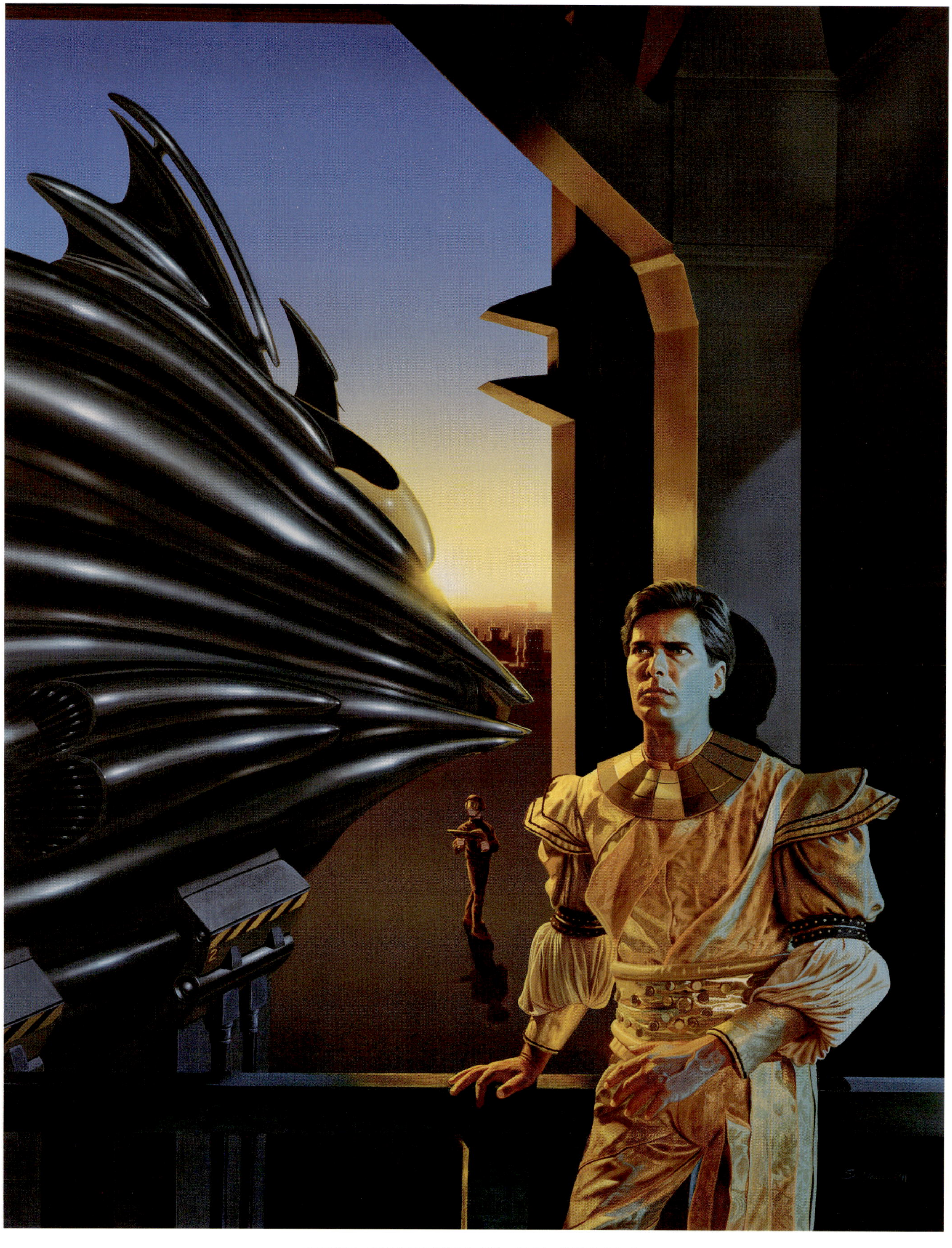

THE CURRENTS OF SPACE
ISAAC ASIMOV, BANTAM, 1991
ACRYLIC ON MASONITE, 26½ x 21in (67 x 53cm)

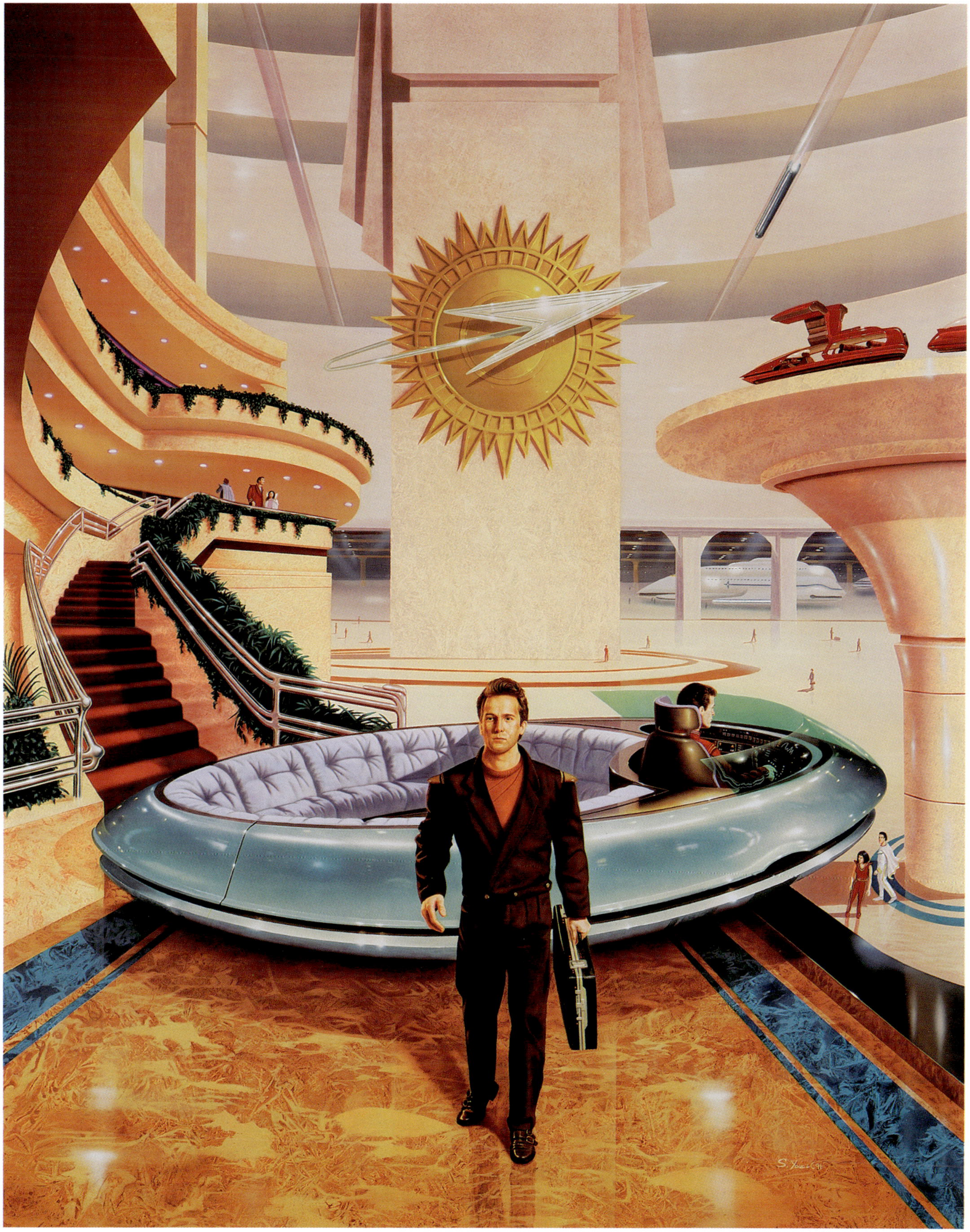

PRELUDE TO FOUNDATION

ISAAC ASIMOV, BANTAM, 1991

ACRYLIC ON ILLUSTRATION BOARD, 26½ x 21in (67 x 53cm)

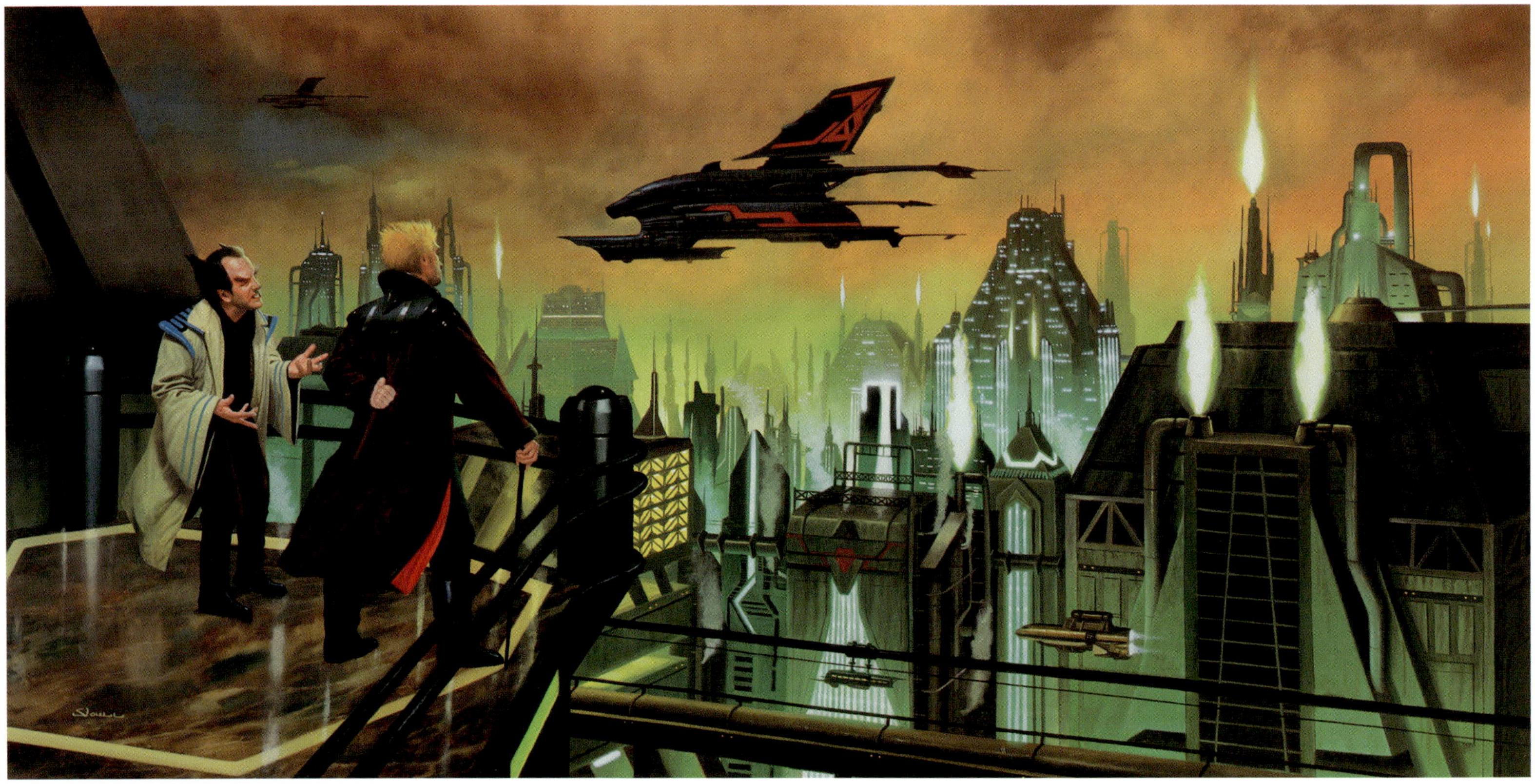

DUNE: HOUSE HARKONNEN
BRIAN HERBERT AND KEVIN J. ANDERSON, BANTAM, 2000
OIL ON ILLUSTRATION BOARD, 13½ x 25in (34 x 64cm)

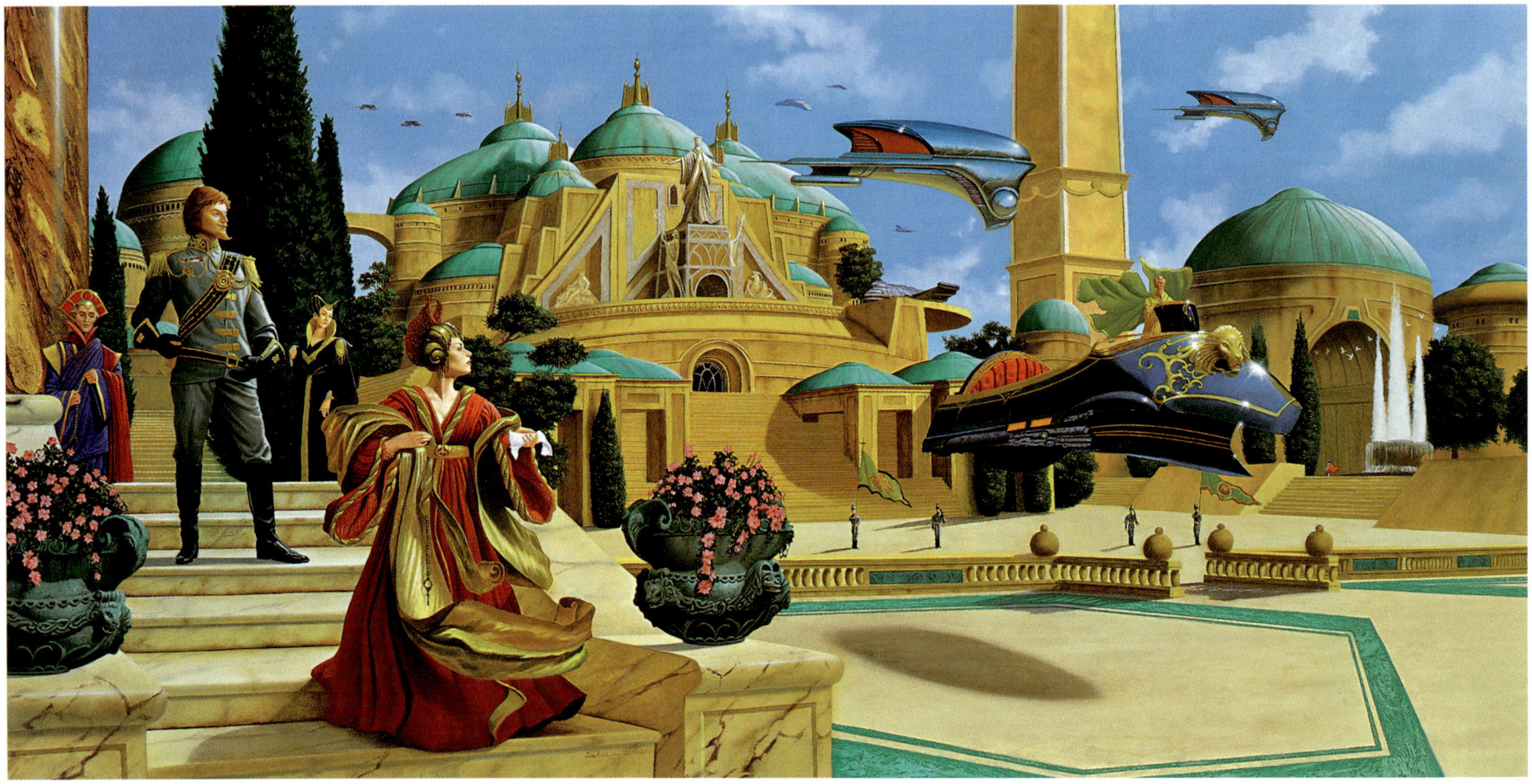

DUNE: HOUSE CORRINO
BRIAN HERBERT AND KEVIN J. ANDERSON, BANTAM, 2001
OIL ON MASONITE, 20¼ x 36in (51 x 91cm)

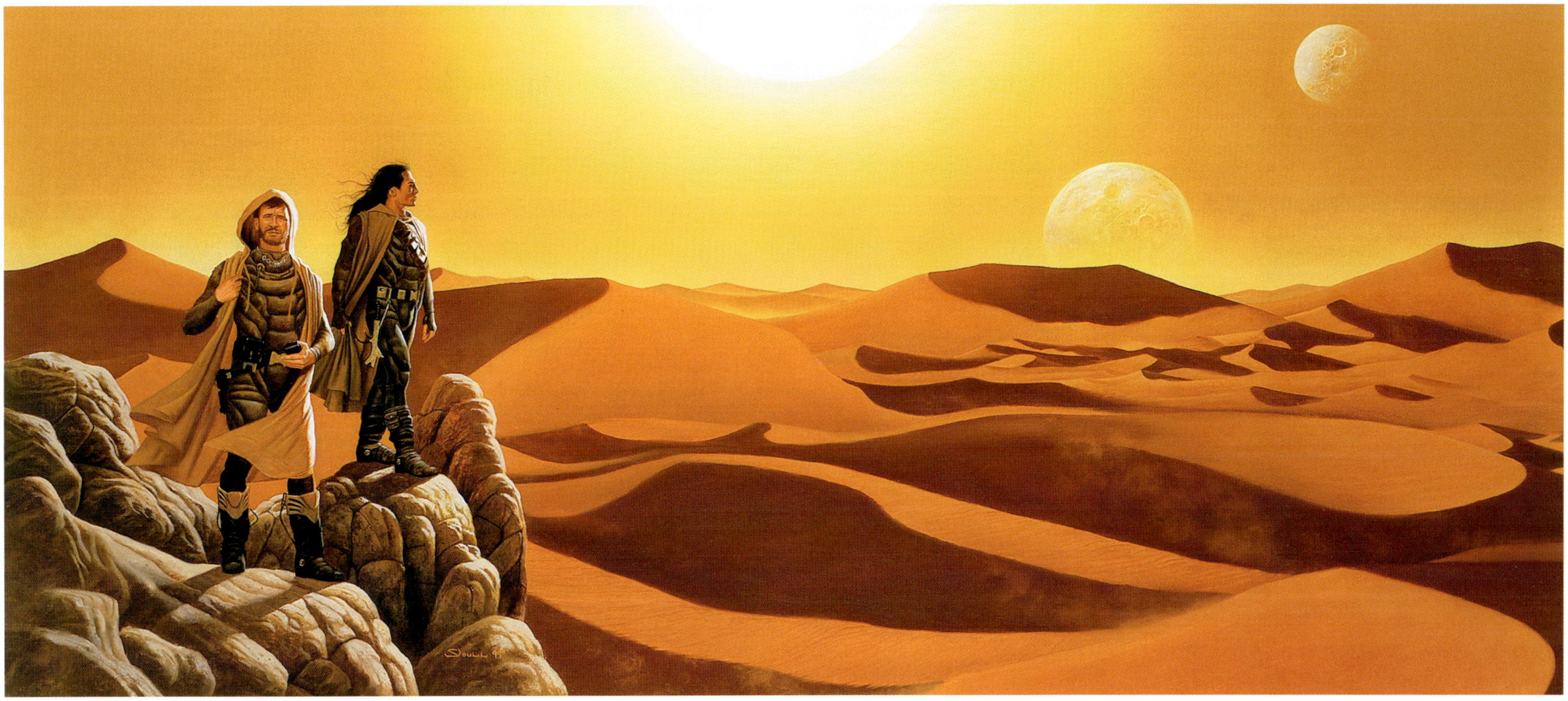

DUNE: HOUSE ATREIDES
BRIAN HERBERT AND KEVIN J. ANDERSON, BANTAM, 1999
OIL ON ILLUSTRATION BOARD, 16½ x 33½in (42 x 85cm)

THERE ARE NO BOUNDARIES

Science-fiction movies have always been a main driving force in my outlook as a person and in my growth as an artist. These movies not only inspire us to look beyond our petty differences but offer new horizons for us to strive towards. My favourite movies – the ones that have given me the most inspiration as an artist – have been the first *Star Wars* trilogy, *Dune,* the *Star Trek* series and *Blade Runner*. With the exception of *Star Trek,* I have been privileged to illustrate books based in the varied and colourful universes of all these.

When George Lucas's *Star Wars* came out in 1977 it changed many people's lives. Not only did it make movie history, it created new cultural icons. In 1991, Bantam obtained the rights to publish a collection of original novels based in the *Star Wars* universe and using the characters from the first three movies. I eagerly waited to see who would be doing the cover art for these novels, and was disheartened when only Lucasfilm movie-poster artists were hired.

At the 1993 World Science Fiction Convention in San Francisco I exhibited a number of paintings including *Speaking in Tongues* (see page 48), which depicts a highly realistic alien facing a human male.The creative director in charge of the book division of Lucasfilm was attending the convention as well, and this painting caught her eye. She expressed interest in my art, and the publisher at Bantam offered me a commission to paint the covers for three *Star Wars* anthologies centring on the various aliens in the movies. These were *Tales from the Mos Eisley Cantina, Tales from Jabba's Palace* and *Tales of the Bounty Hunters* (pages 90, 88 and 89), all edited by Kevin J. Anderson.

While at the convention I was invited to Skywalker Ranch and Industrial Light and Magic. This visit still remains a key memory in my life – practically a dream come true. Energized by it, I set about producing the best covers I could paint. I wanted to make the aliens as realistic as they had appeared on the big screen. The paintings were rendered in oils – they are not photographs, as some fans have erroneously surmised. It was my intention to illustrate the characters with an absolutely photorealistic conviction.

Bantam and Lucasfilm loved the paintings. These books remain the best-selling anthologies of all time, and I would like to think I had something to do with that.

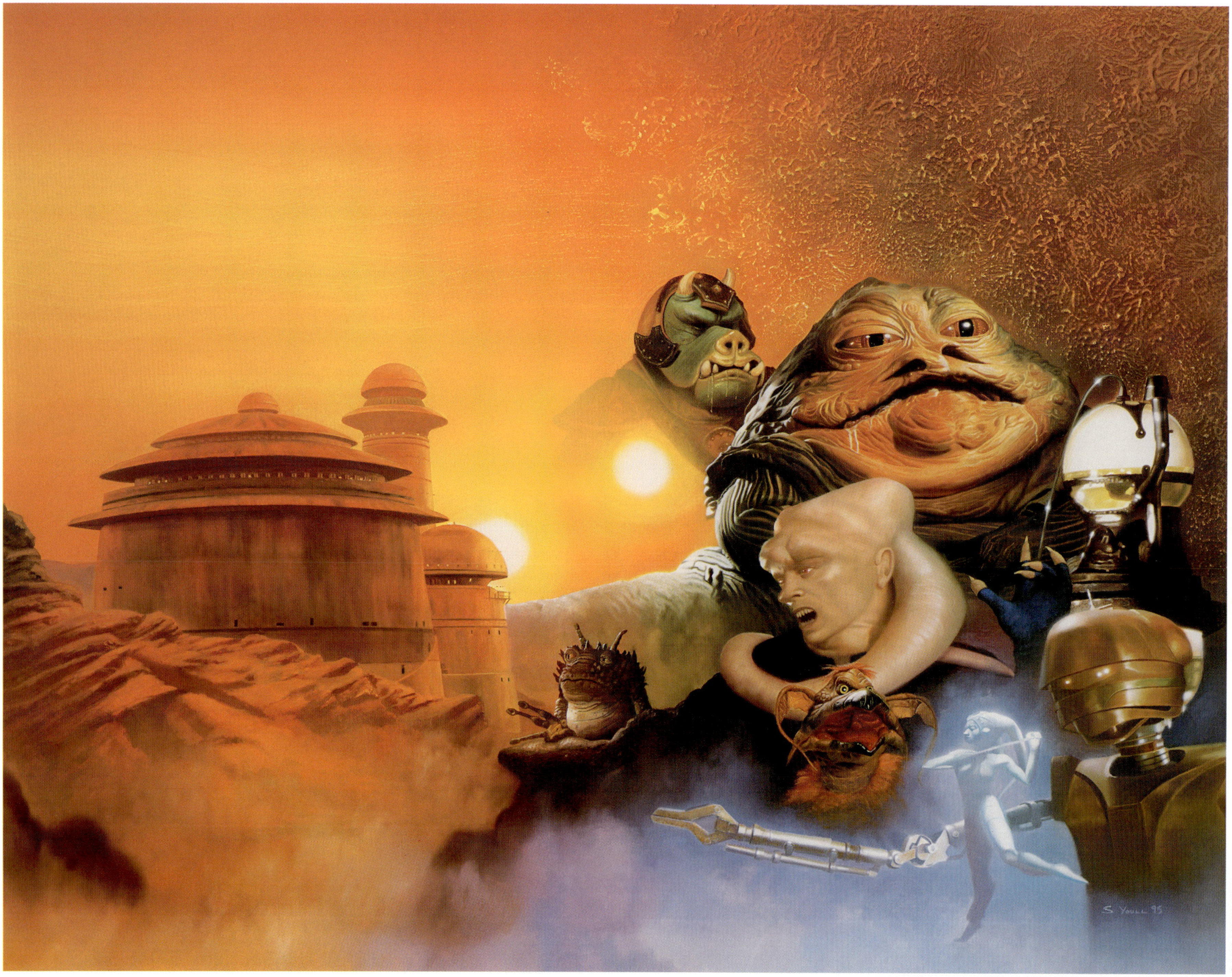

TALES FROM JABBA'S PALACE
EDITED BY KEVIN J. ANDERSON, BANTAM, 1995
OIL ON ILLUSTRATION BOARD, 16½ x 26½in (42 x 67cm)

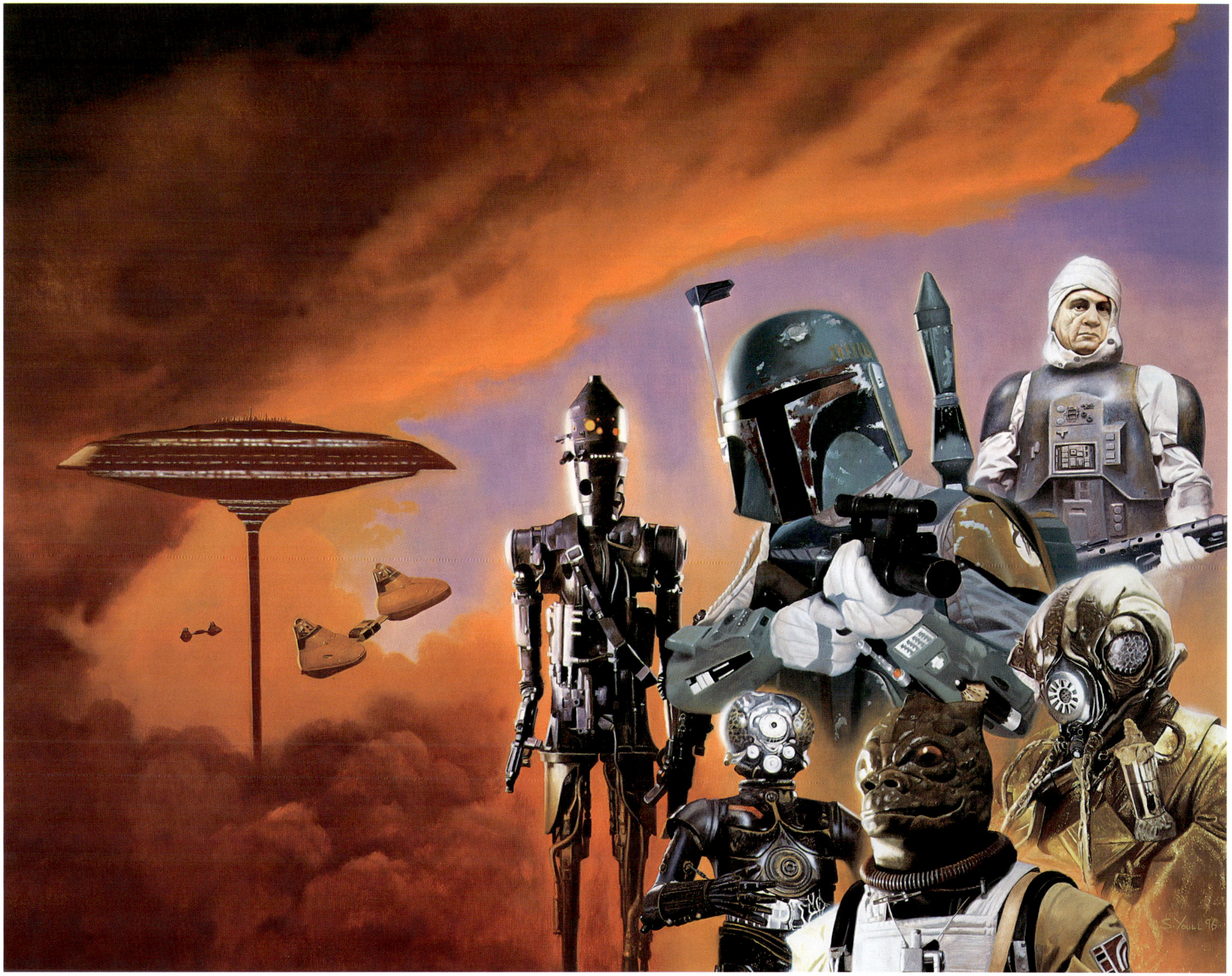

TALES OF THE BOUNTY HUNTERS

EDITED BY KEVIN J. ANDERSON, BANTAM, 1996

OIL ON ILLUSTRATION BOARD, 22 x 28in (56 x 71cm)

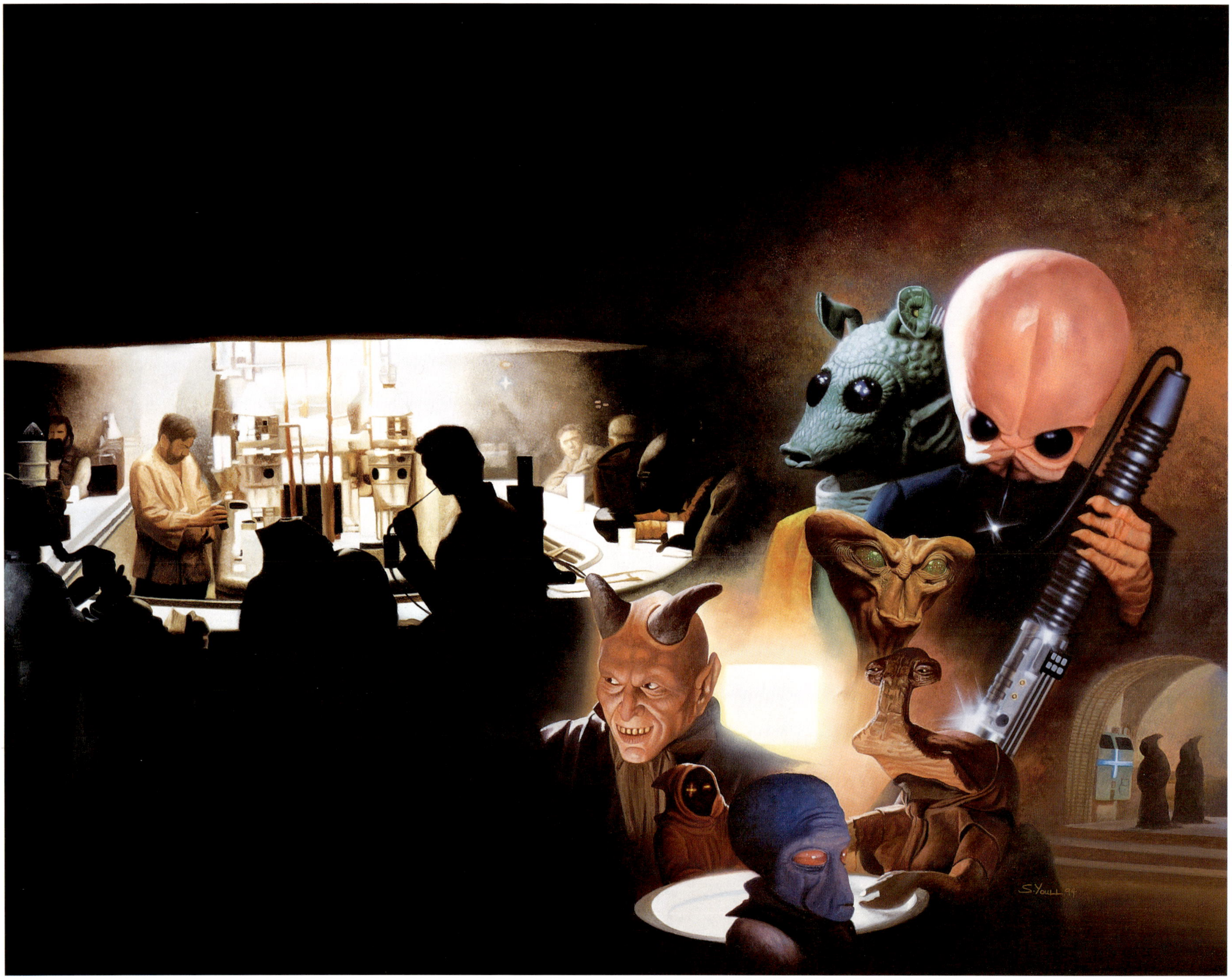

TALES FROM THE MOS EISLEY CANTINA

EDITED BY KEVIN J. ANDERSON, BANTAM, 1994

ACRYLIC ON ILLUSTRATION BOARD, 22 x 28in (56 x 71cm)

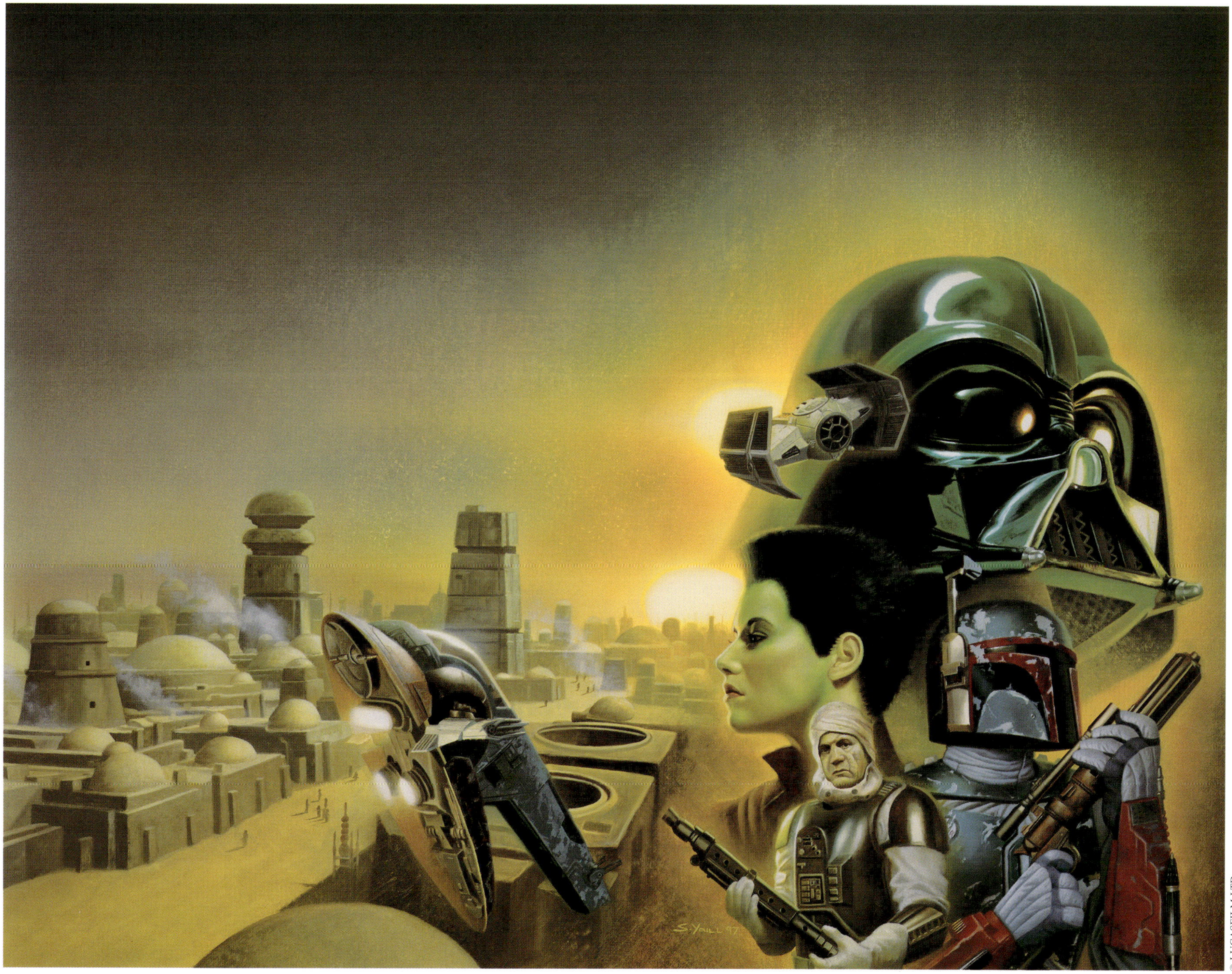

THE MANDALORIAN ARMOR

K.W. JETER, BANTAM, 1997

OIL ON ILLUSTRATION BOARD, 18½ x 24½in (47 x 62cm)

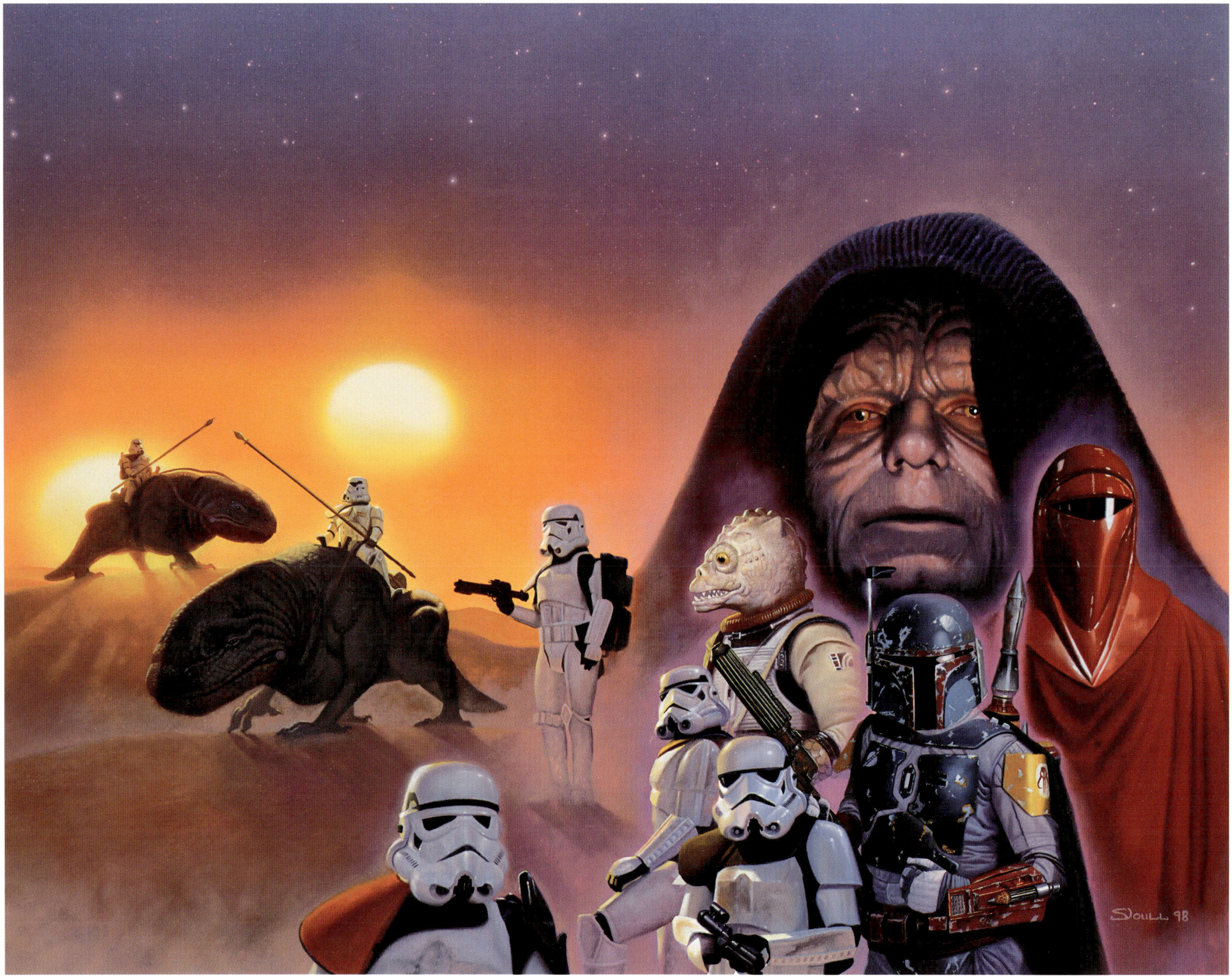

HARD MERCHANDISE

K.W. JETER, BANTAM, 1998

OIL ON MASONITE, 16 x 24in (41 x 61cm)

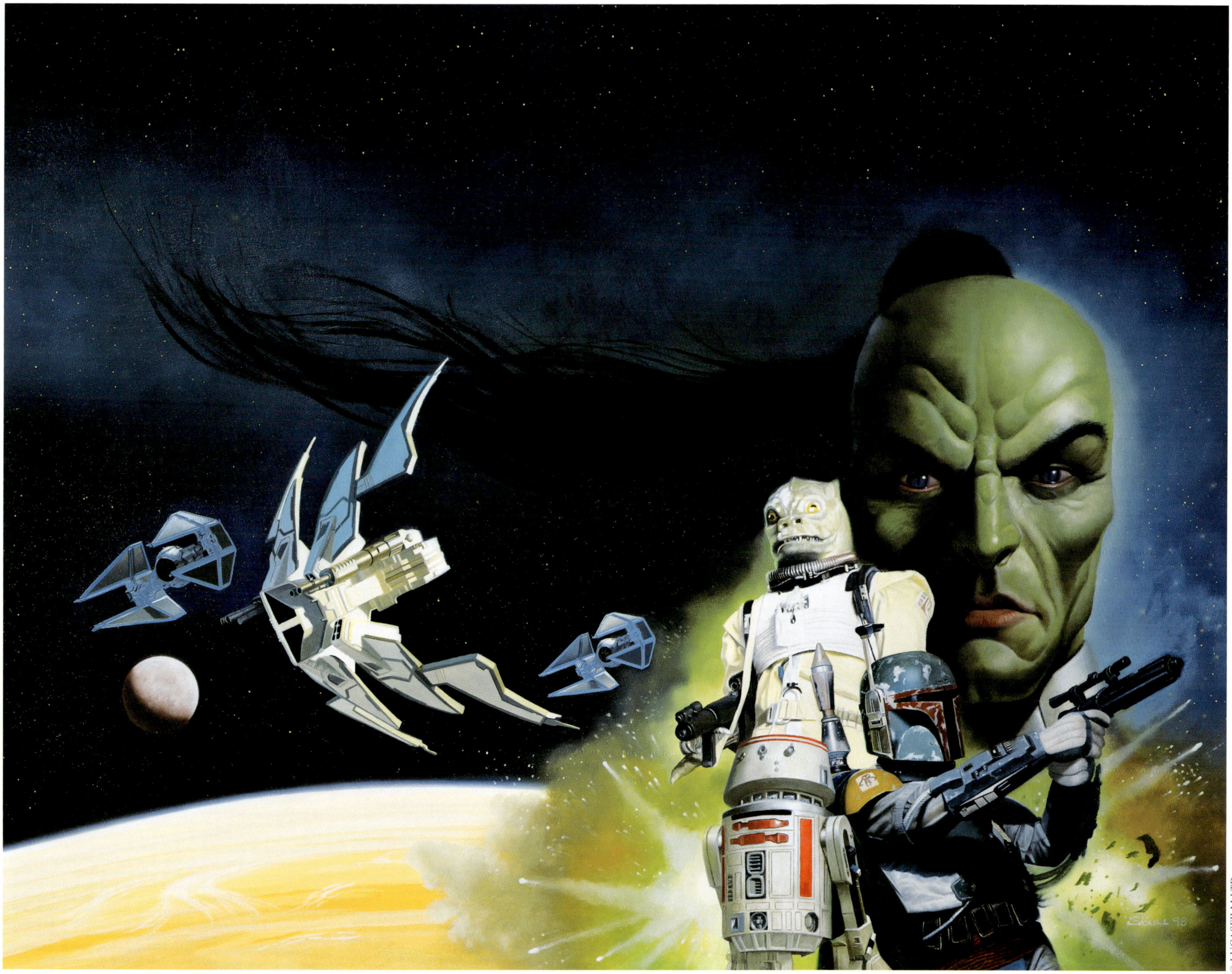

SLAVE SHIP

K.W. JETER, BANTAM, 1998

OIL ON ILLUSTRATION BOARD, 21 x 27in (53 x 69cm)

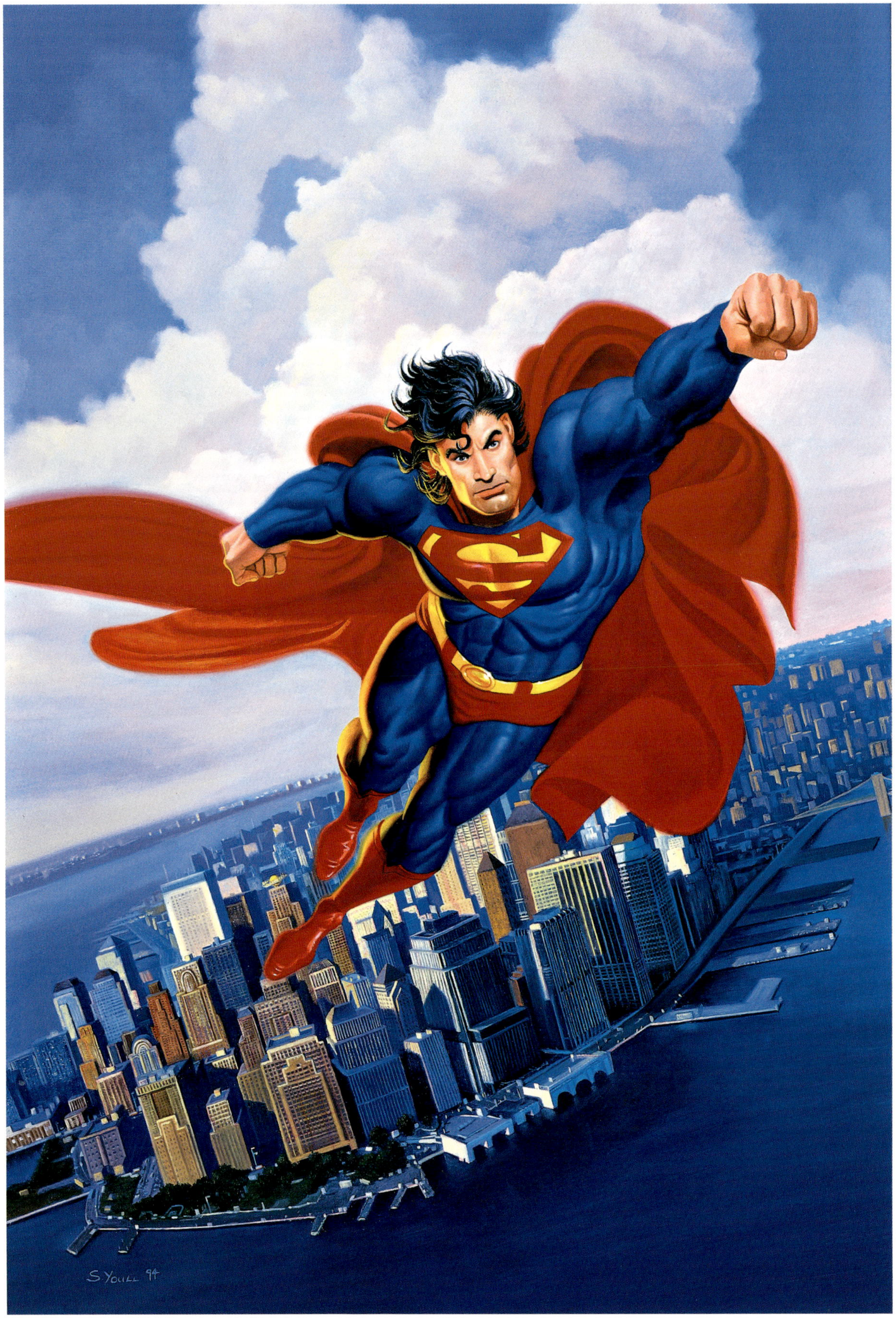

THE DEATH AND LIFE OF SUPERMAN
ROGER STERN, BANTAM, 1994
OIL ON MASONITE, 26½ x 16½in (67 x 42cm)

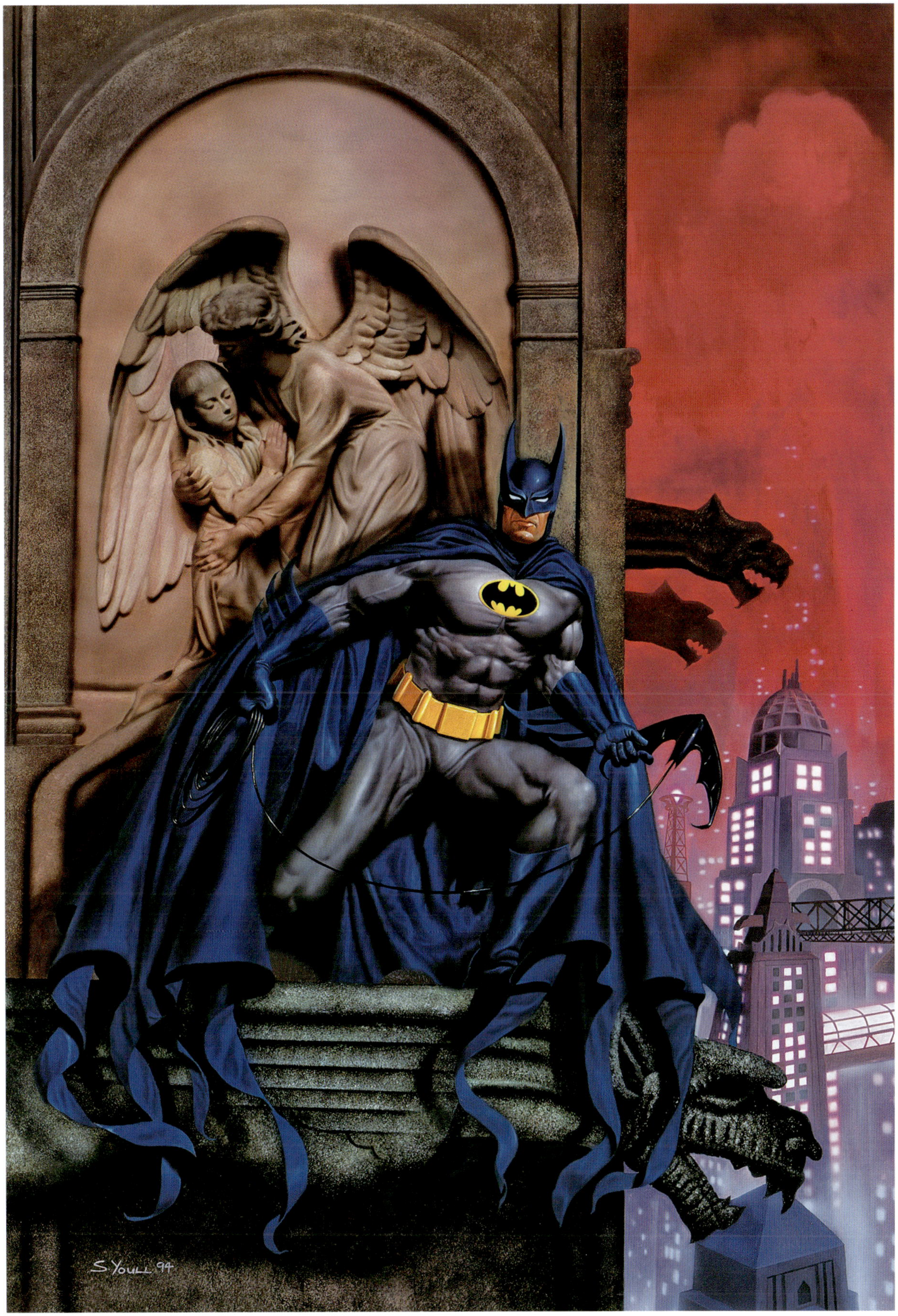

BATMAN: KNIGHTFALL

DENNIS O'NEIL, BANTAM, 1994

OIL ON MASONITE, 32 x 20in (81 x 51cm)

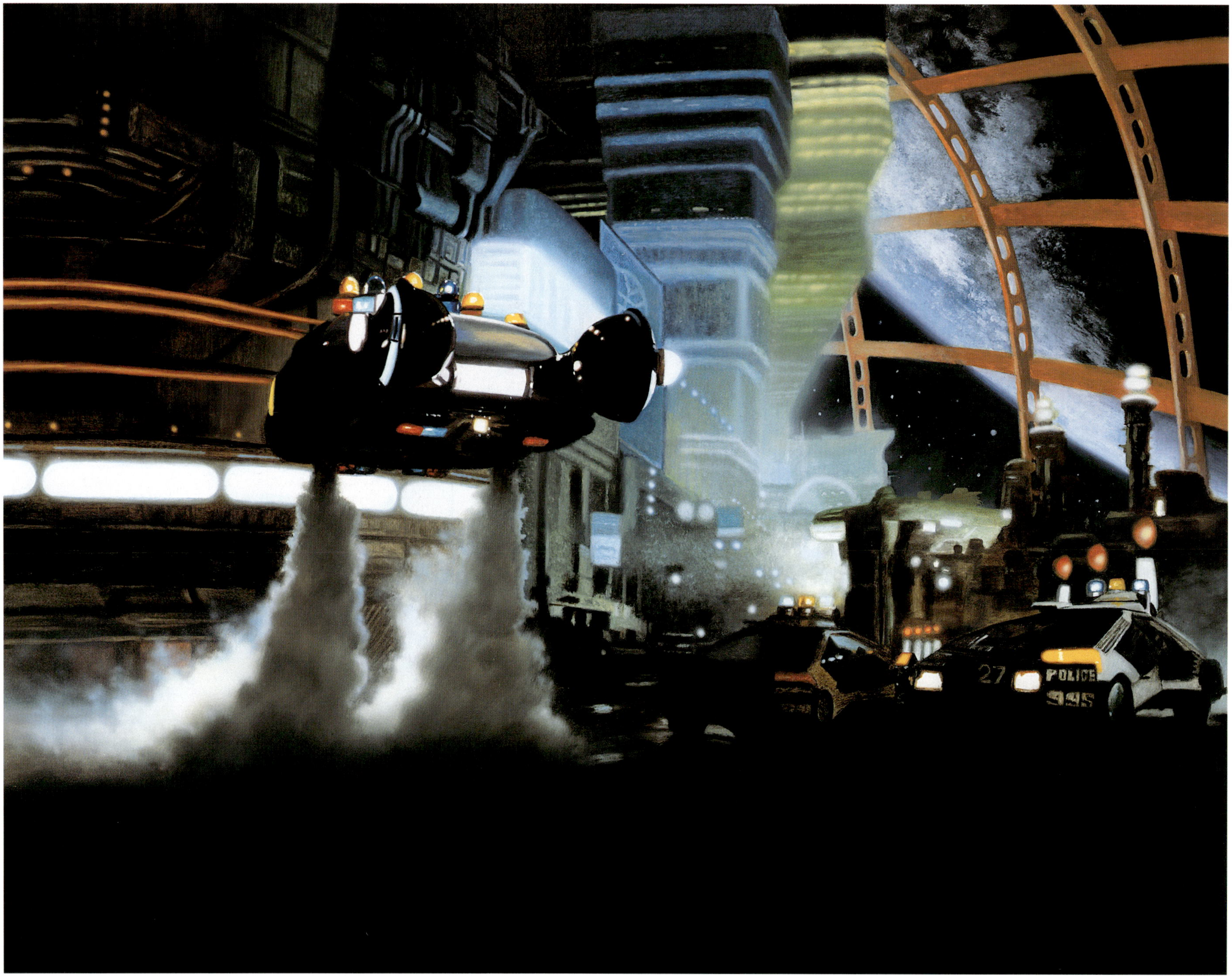

BLADE RUNNER: REPLICANT NIGHT

K.W. JETER, BANTAM, 1996

OIL ON MASONITE, 10¾ x 13½in (27 x 34cm)

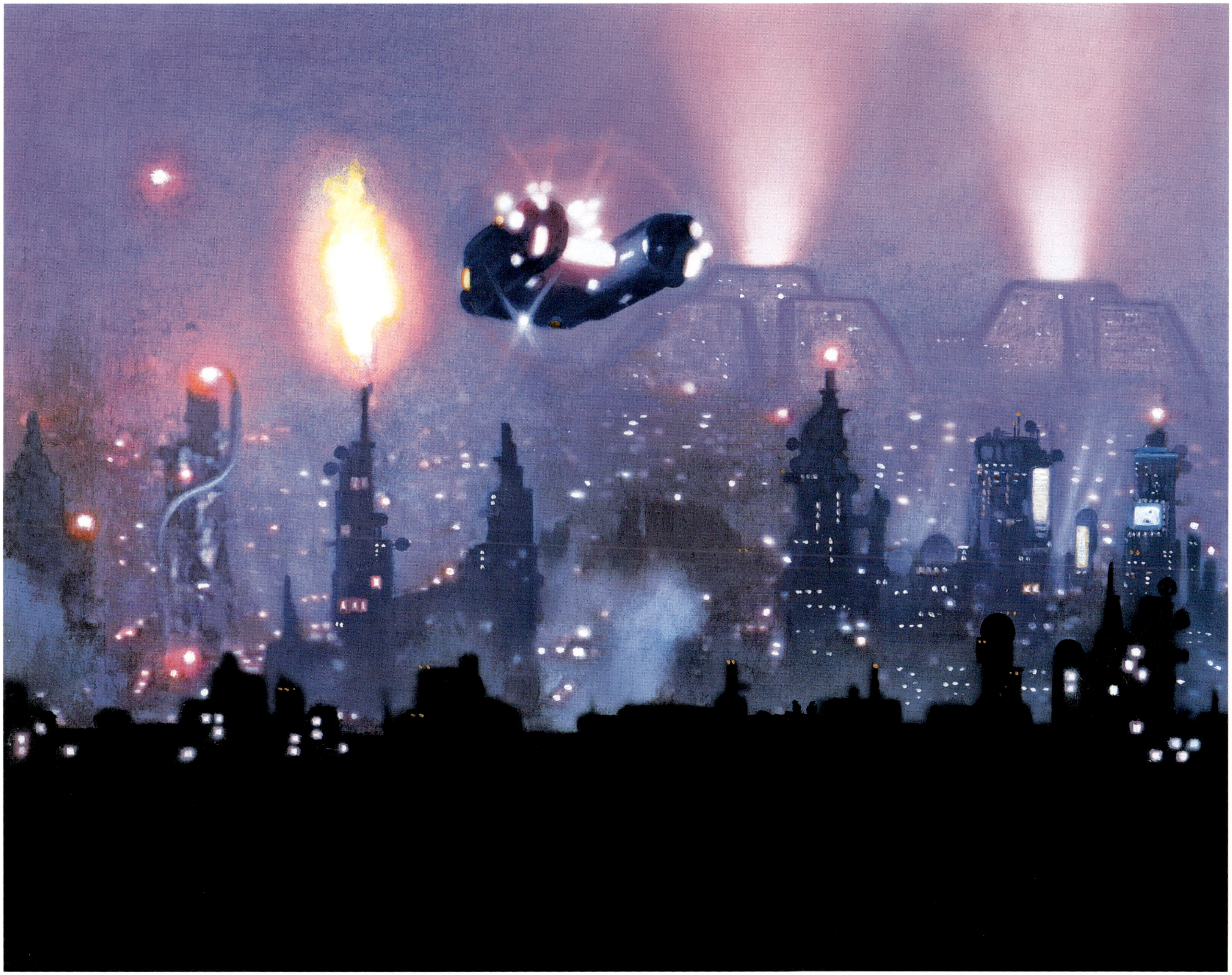

BLADE RUNNER 2: THE EDGE OF HUMAN

K.W. JETER, BANTAM, 1995

OIL ON ILLUSTRATION BOARD, 10 x 16in (25 x 41cm)

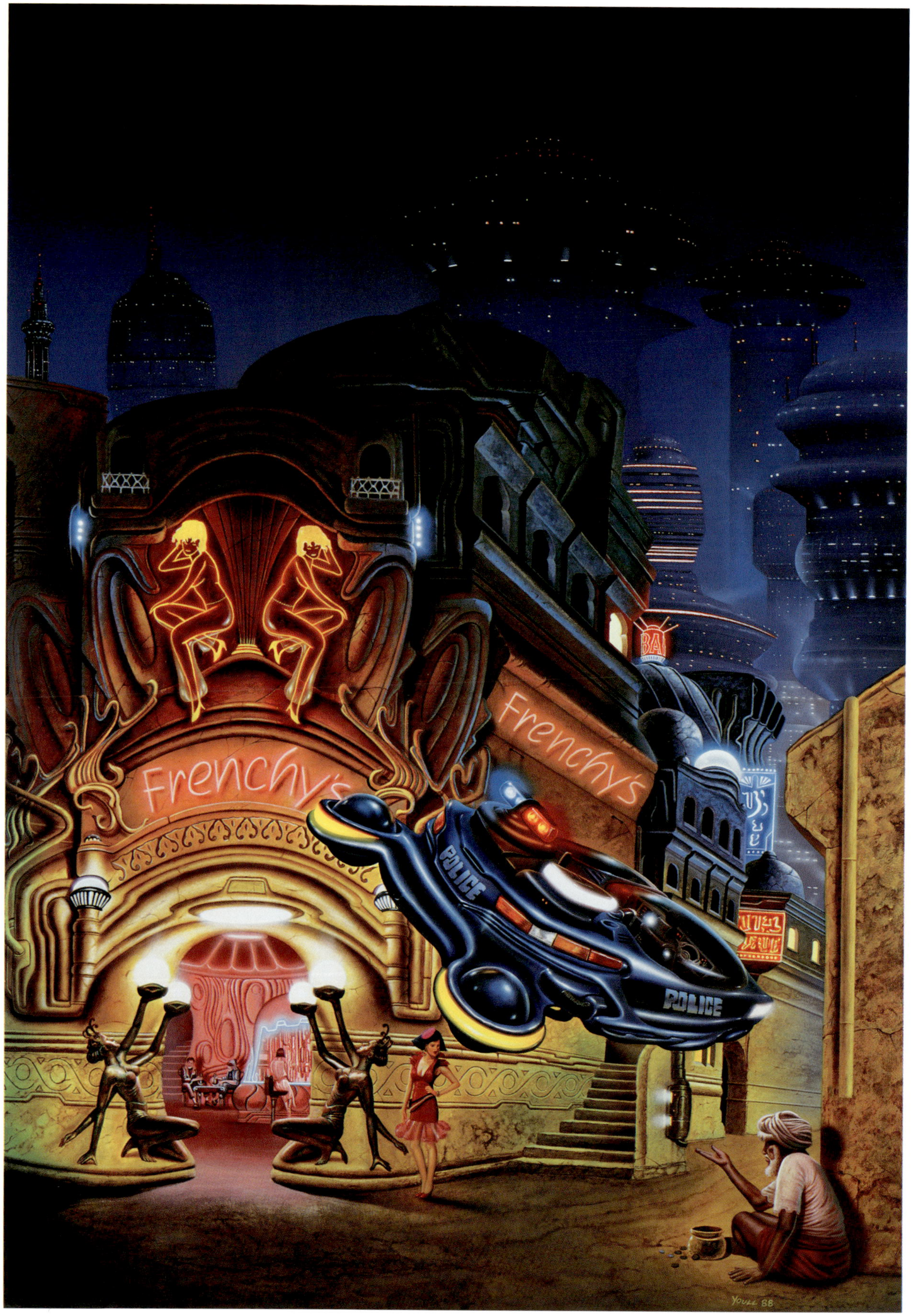

A FIRE IN THE SUN

GEORGE ALEC EFFINGER, BANTAM, 1988

ACRYLIC ON ILLUSTRATION BOARD, 32½ x 22in (83 x 56cm)

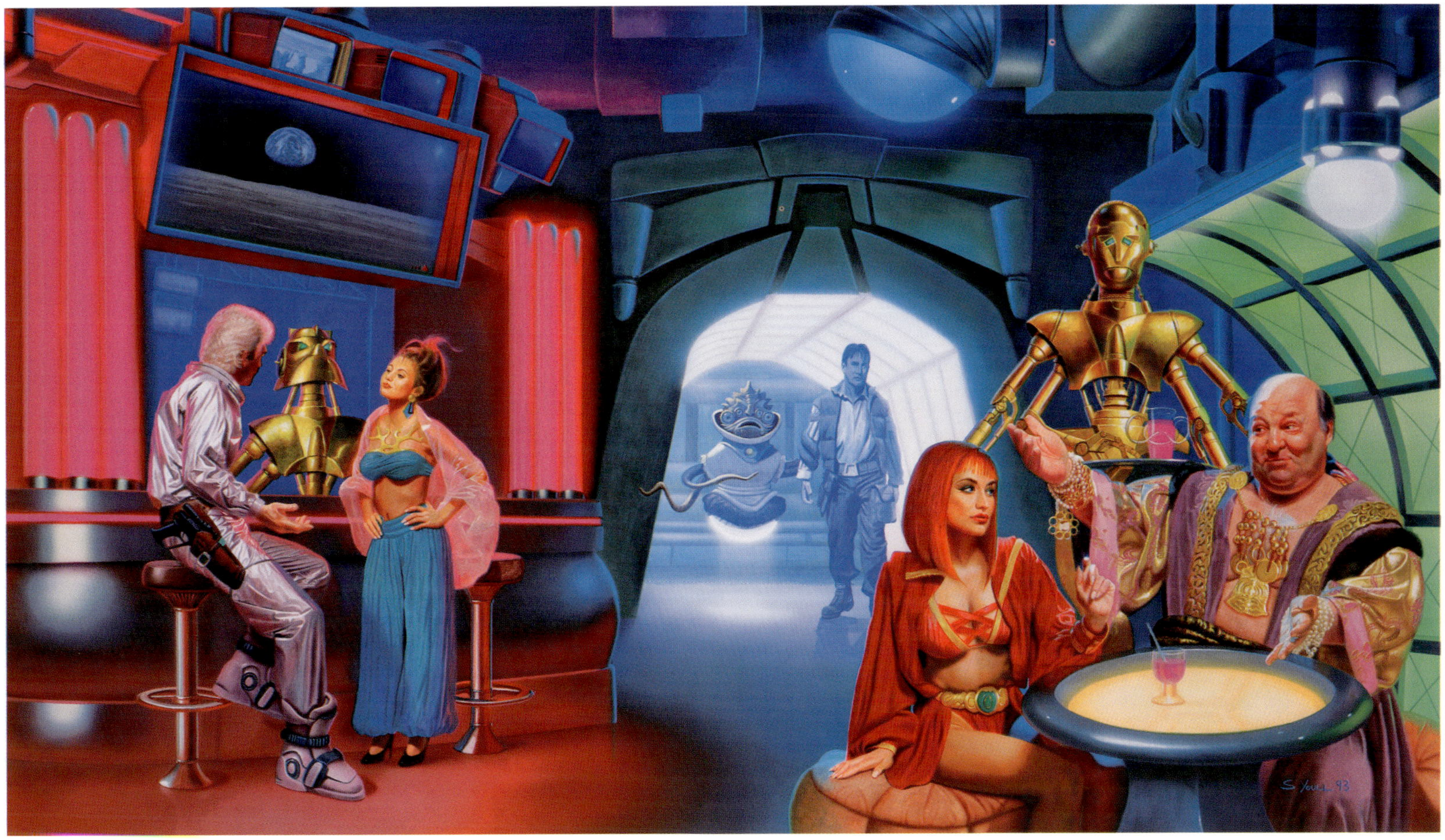

SAM GUNN UNLIMITED
BEN BOVA, BANTAM, 1993
ACRYLIC AND OIL ON MASONITE, 22 x 32in (56 x 81cm)

FUTURESCOPIC

One of the most challenging – though fun – aspects of science-fiction art is the creation of believable and credible worlds. It's my responsibility as cover artist to capture the universe in which the story takes place while at the same time enhancing and elevating the narrative, to bring that universe to life. Ideally the end result is a cover that not only compels the reader to pick up the book but also conveys an interesting visual story in its own right.

The one philosophy I've always believed in, as a cover artist working in a speculative medium, is that each work should be given careful consideration on its own terms. It is very easy to get comfortably stuck into a repetitive approach to cover art, using the same colours, similar compositions or whatever, but I have always striven to hear each author's individual voice, and thereby allow the cover art to reflect that particular story.

I read everything I illustrate, making careful notes regarding character descriptions, plot, mood and texture. If there is no copy of the manuscript available, or only a partial one, I discuss the book with the art director and sometimes the editor or the author until I get enough information for me to have a feeling for the book.

Even the symbolism or metaphor of the writing can greatly affect the images I propose for the cover. Before I even start any preliminary sketches I ask myself a number of questions about the novel: Is it moody? Or fast-paced? Or surreal? And so on. The overall feeling of the book will influence the composition and even the use of colour.

However, the most important thing that gives rise to the art is the story. In all of the alternative futures I've visited through the many wonderful stories I've read, the cover just waits to be discovered.

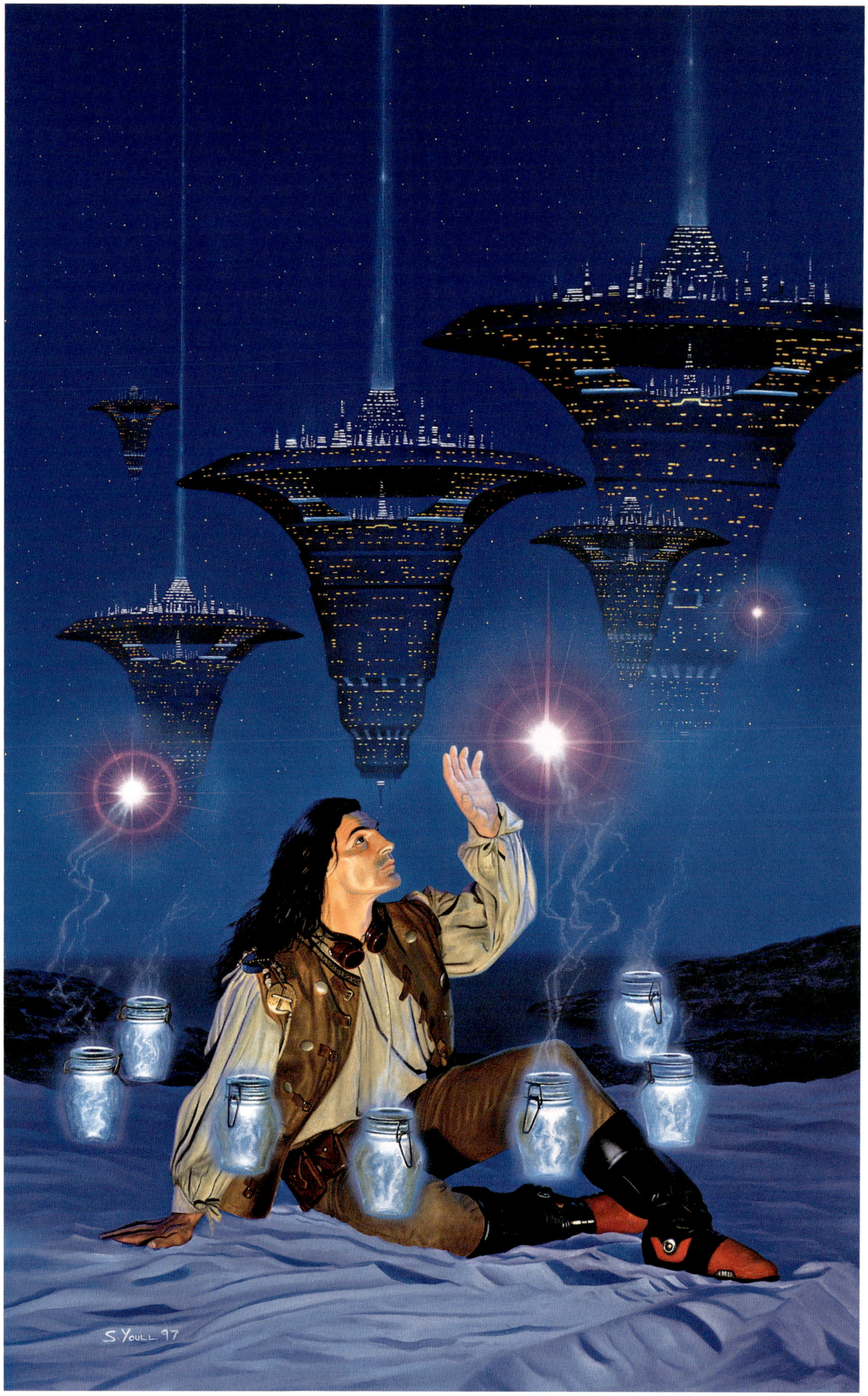

ALIEN INFLUENCES

KRISTINE KATHRYN RUSCH, BANTAM, 1997

OIL ON ILLUSTRATION BOARD, 24 x 14in (61 x 36cm)

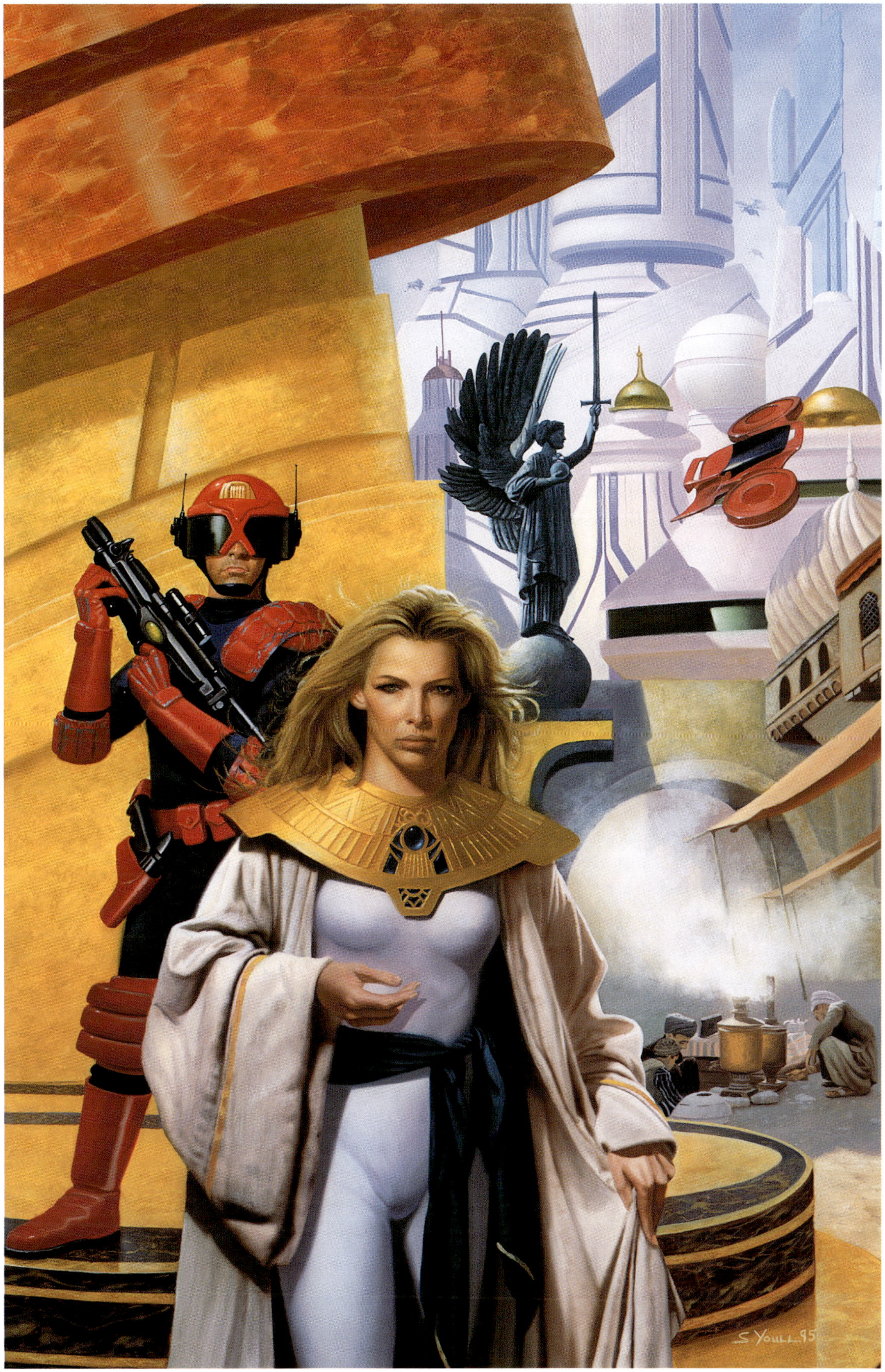

BLINDFOLD

KEVIN J. ANDERSON, WARNER, 1995

OIL ON ILLUSTRATION BOARD, 24 x 15in (61 x 38cm)

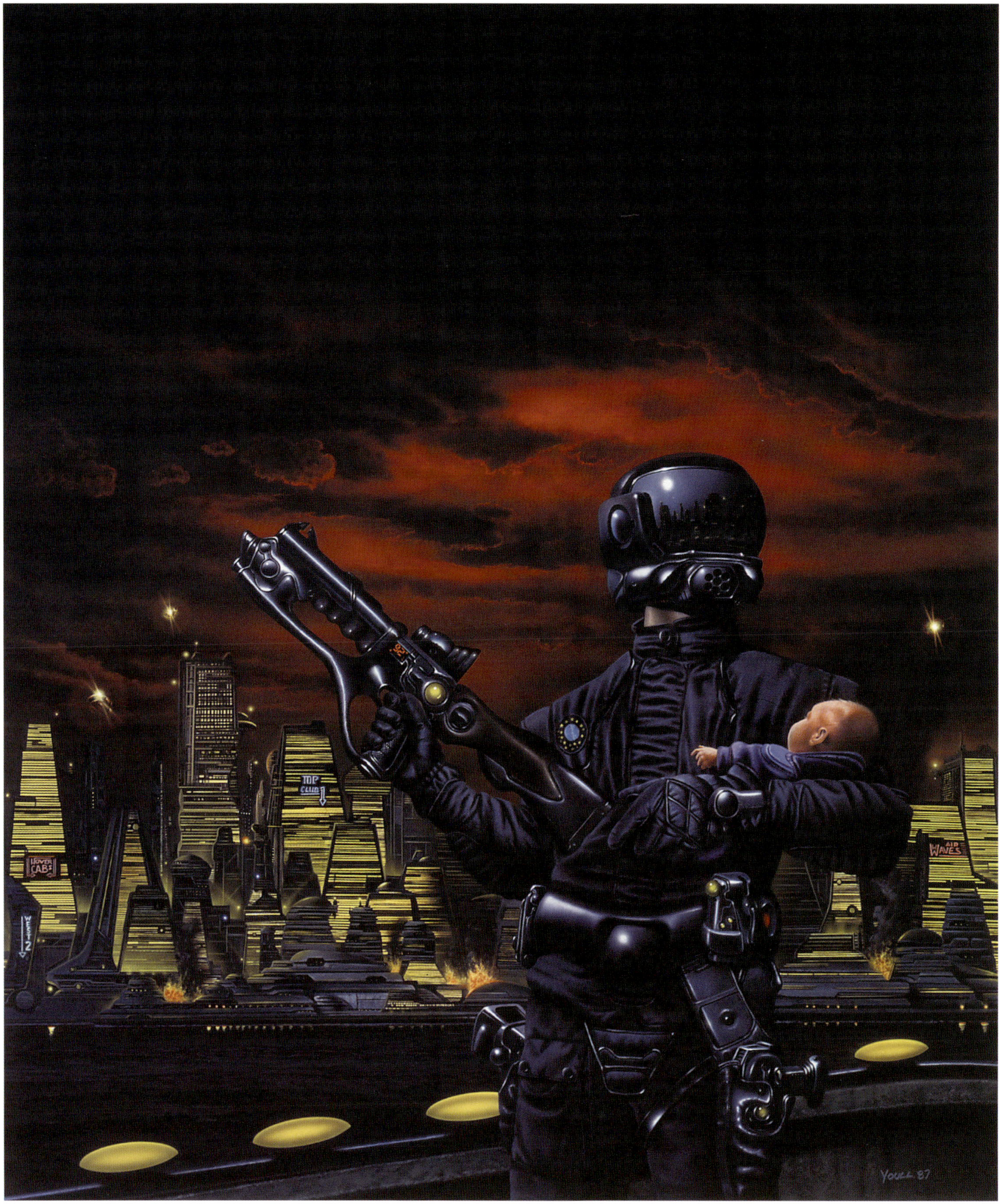

EMERALD EYES

DANIEL KEYS MORAN, BANTAM, 1987

ACRYLIC ON ILLUSTRATION BOARD, 38 x 28in (97 x 71cm)

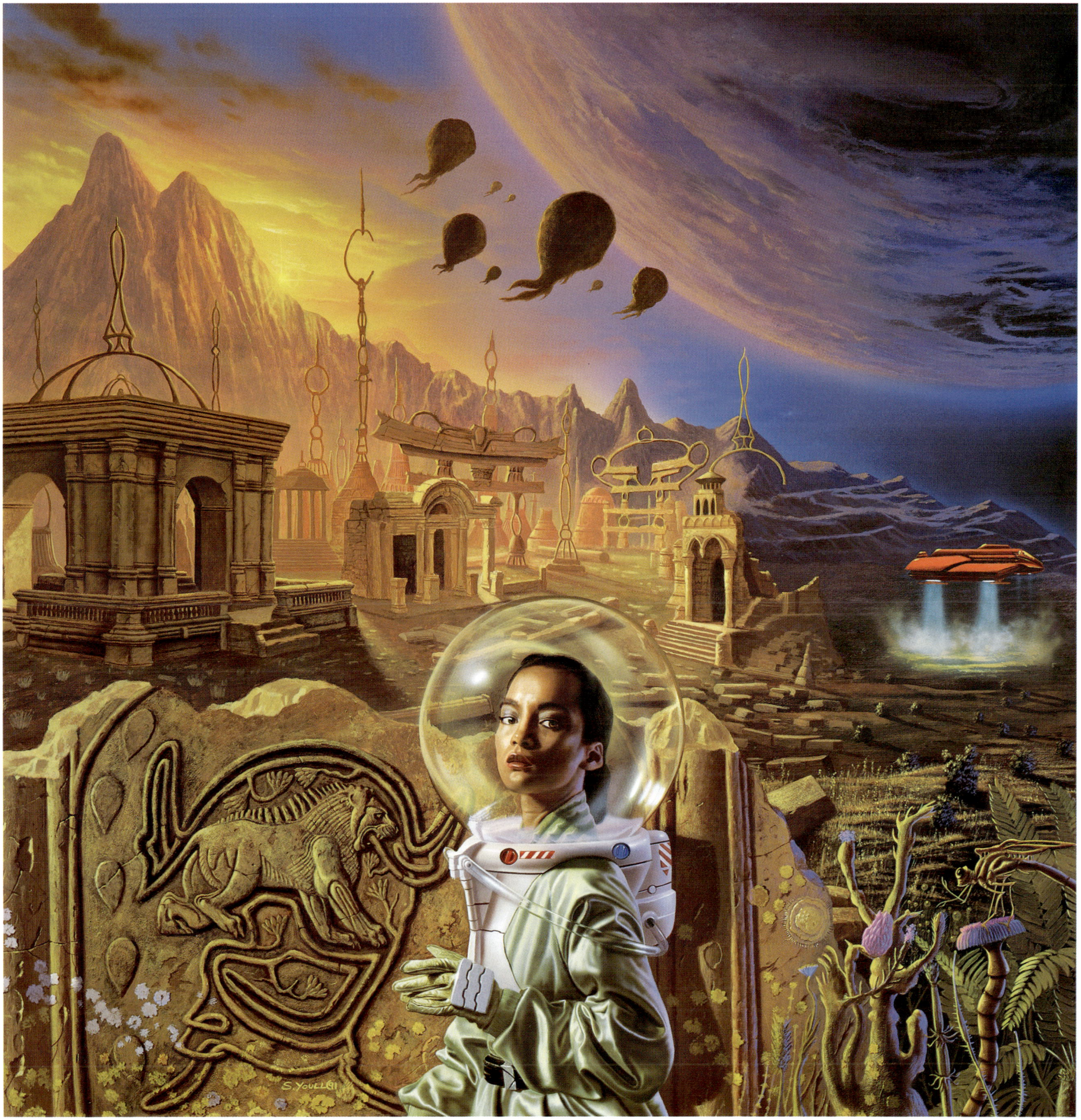

MURASAKI

EDITED BY ROBERT SILVERBERG, BANTAM, 1991
ACRYLIC ON ILLUSTRATION BOARD, 18 x 28in (46 x 71cm)

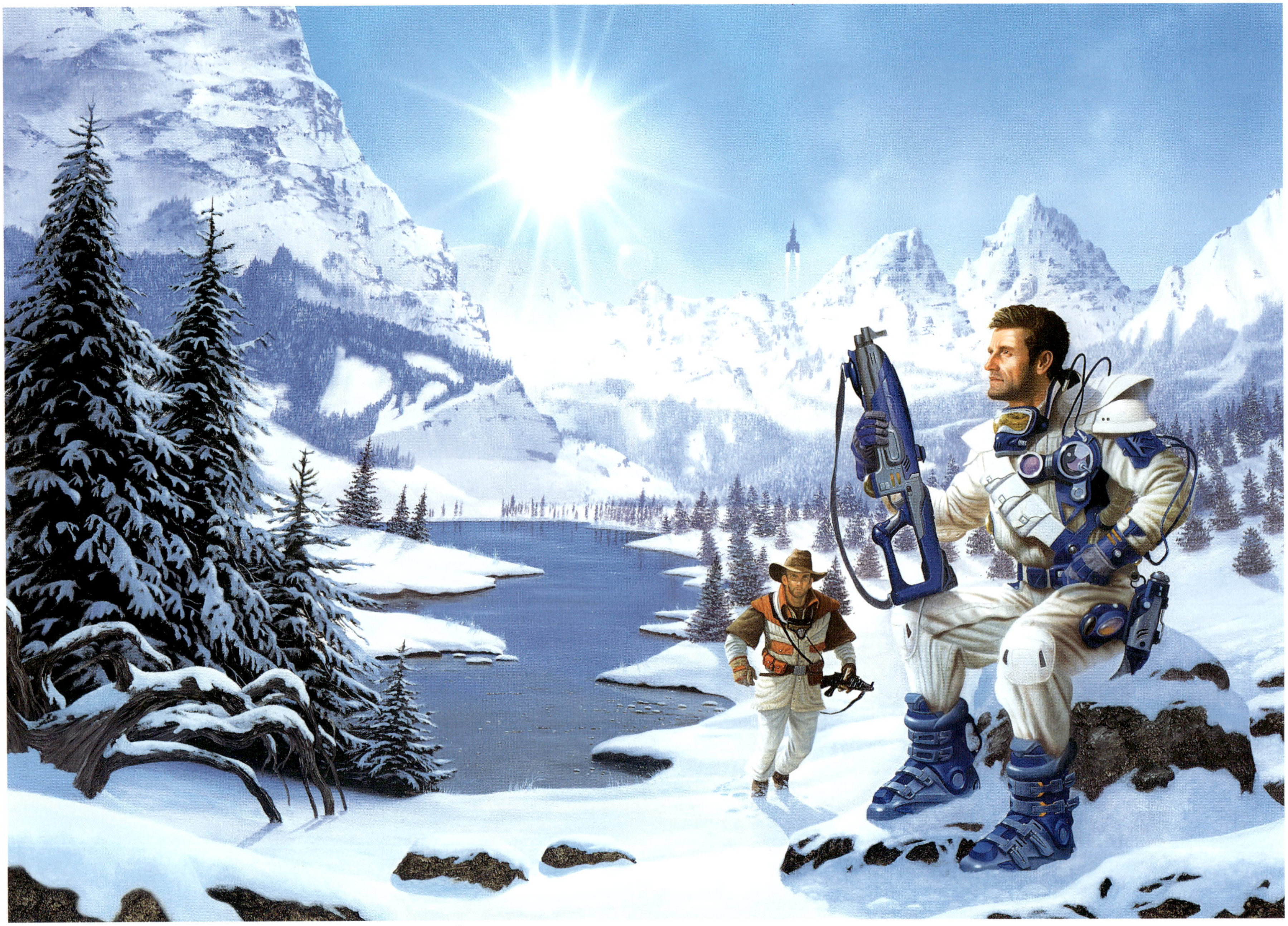

CANDLE

JOHN BARNES, TOR, 1999

OIL ON ILLUSTRATION BOARD, 22 x 32in (56 x 81cm)

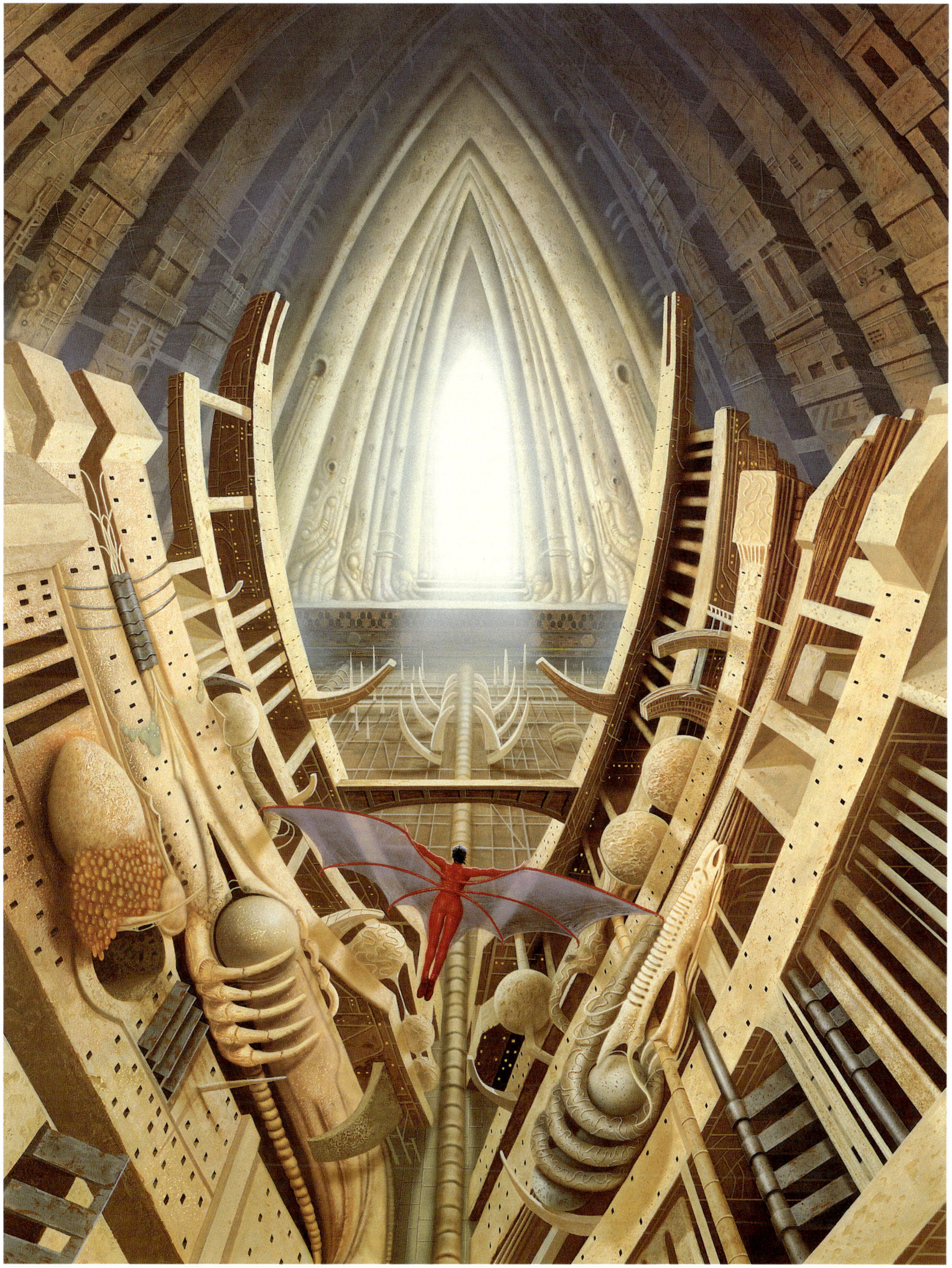

TERMINAL CAFÉ

IAN McDONALD, BANTAM, 1994

ACRYLIC ON CANVAS, 40 x 30in (102 x 76cm)

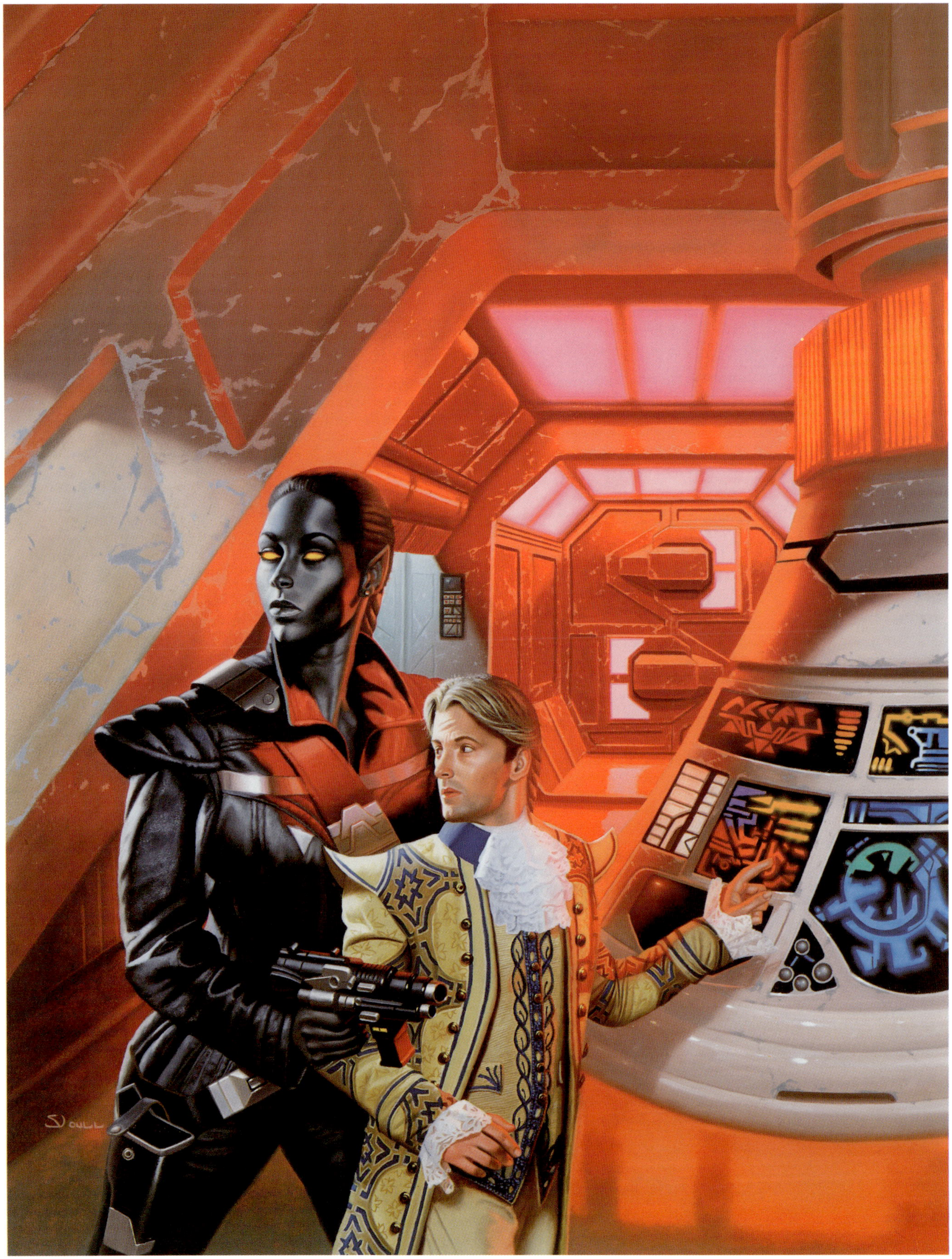

DEFENDER

C.J. CHERRYH, DAW, 2000

OIL ON MASONITE, 25 x 15in (64 x 38cm)

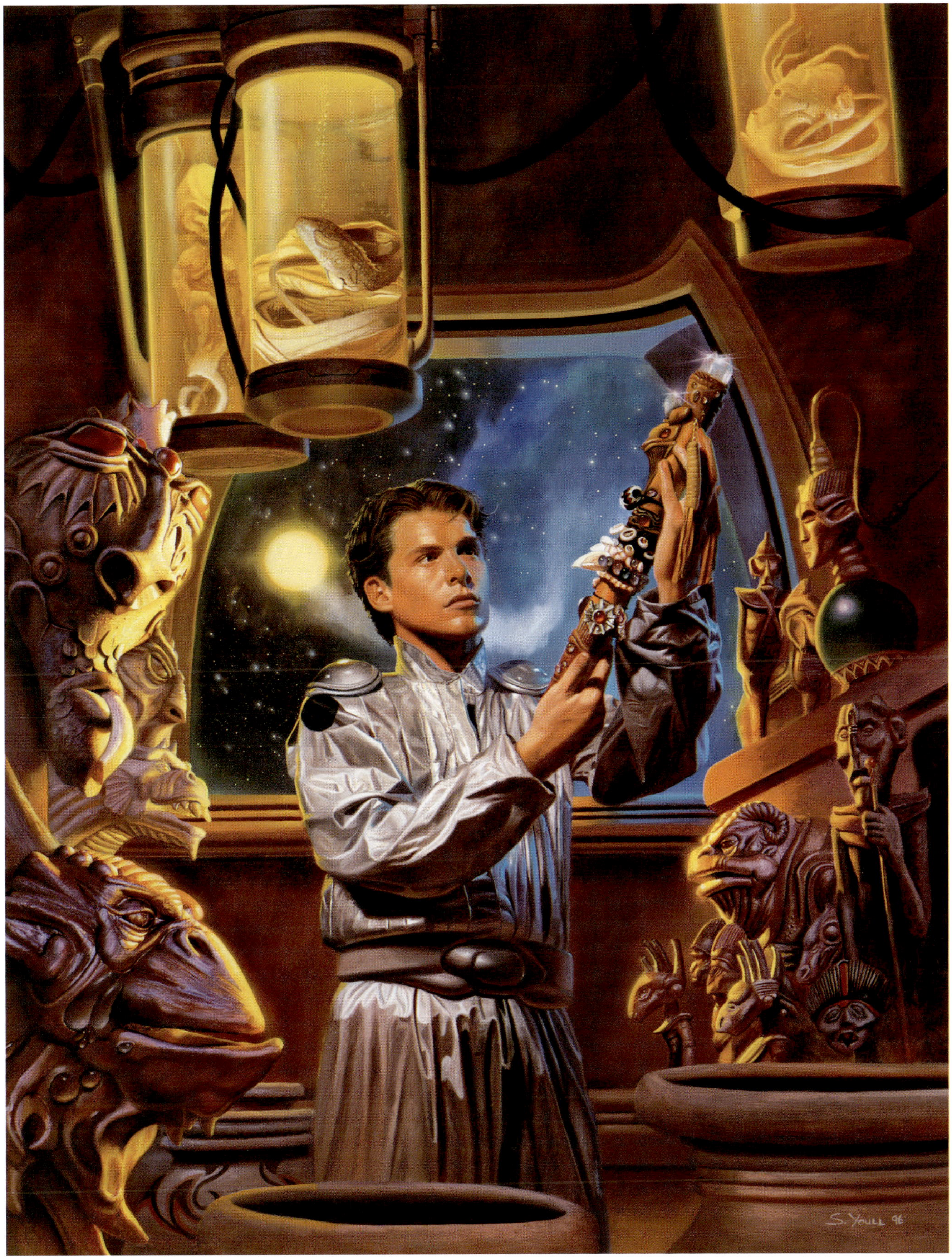

FINITY'S END

C.J. CHERRYH, WARNER, 1996

OIL ON ILLUSTRATION BOARD, 21 x 15½in (53 x 39cm)

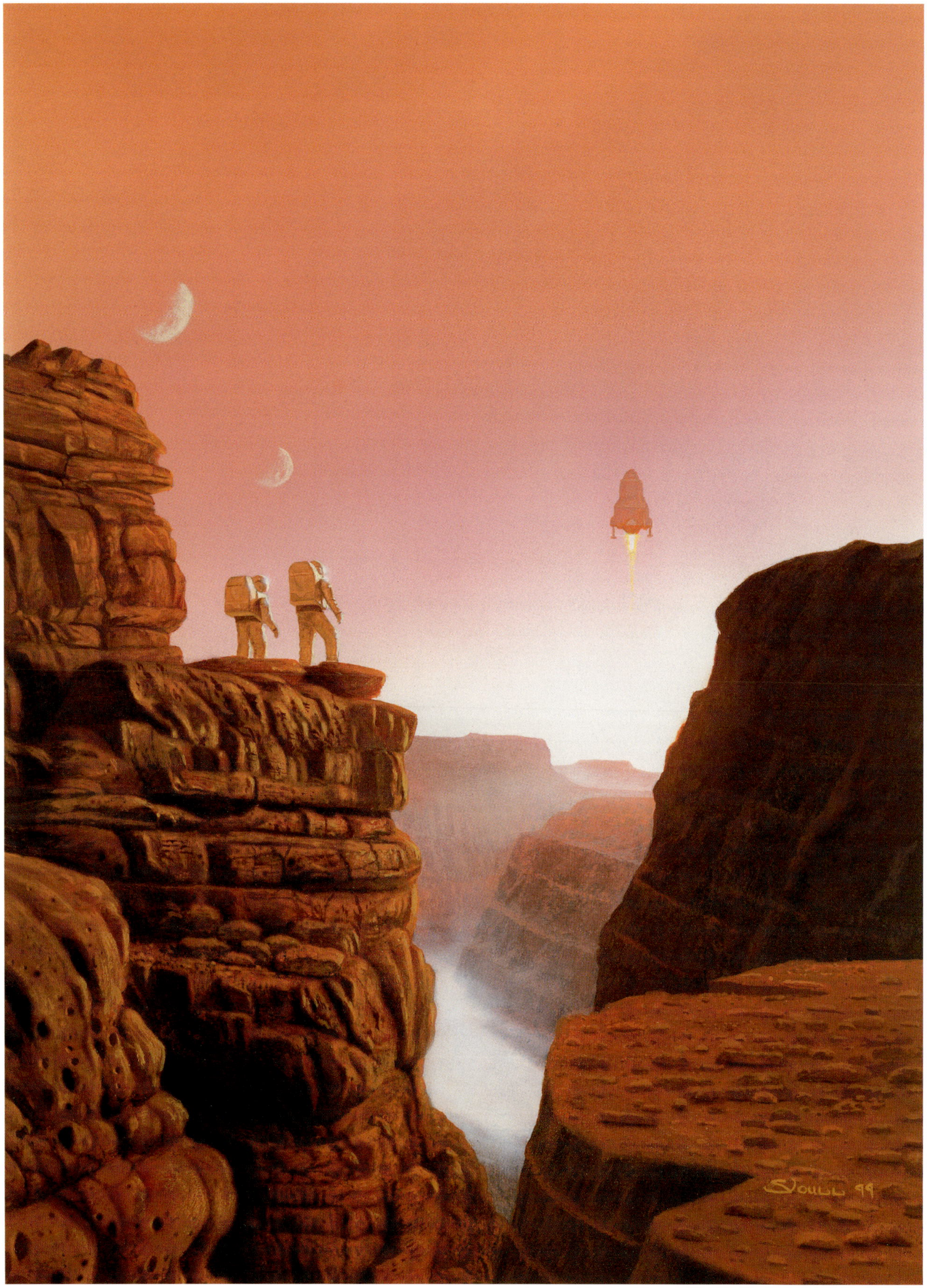

THE MARTIAN RACE

GREGORY BENFORD, WARNER, 1999

ACRYLIC AND OIL ON ILLUSTRATION BOARD, 17 x 10in (43 x 25cm)

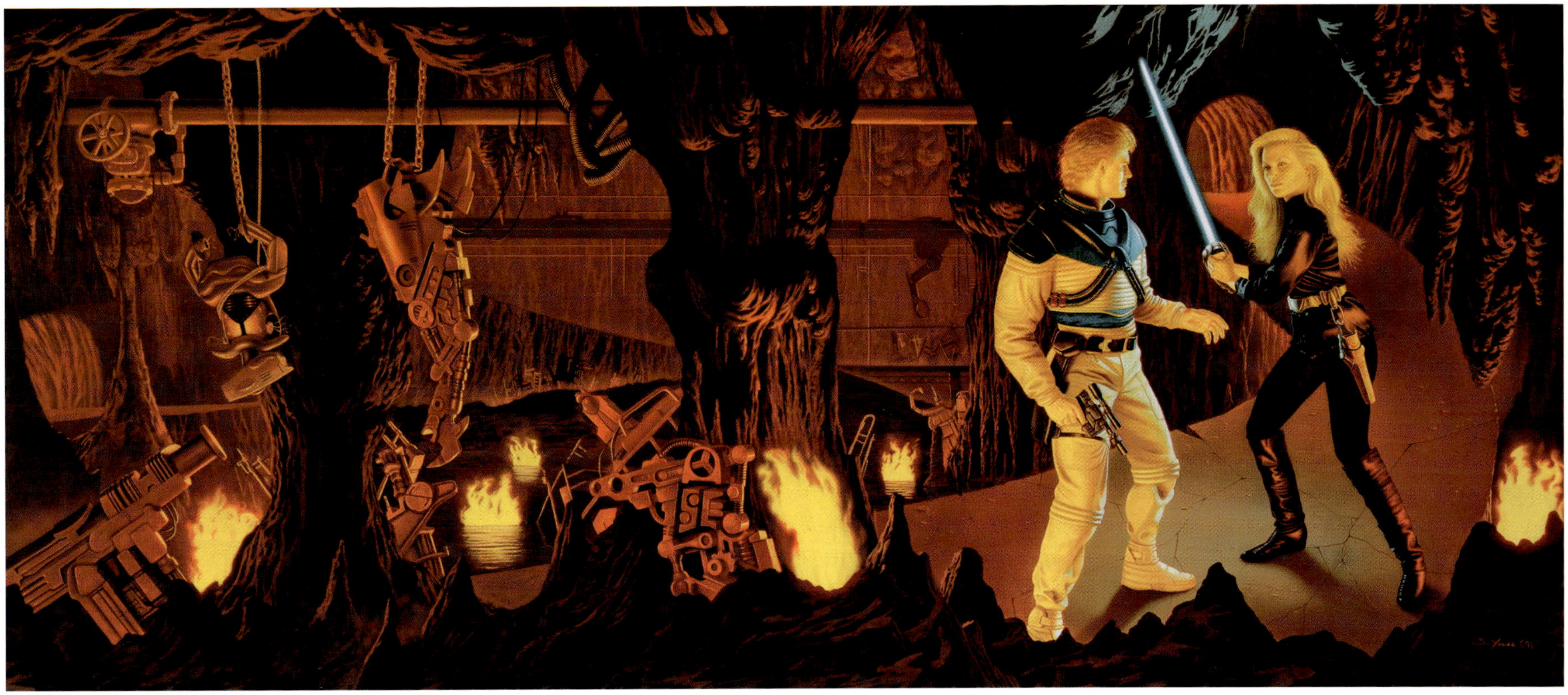

KING'S SACRIFICE
MARGARET WEIS, BANTAM, 1991
ACRYLIC ON MASONITE, 18 x 40½in (46 x 103cm)

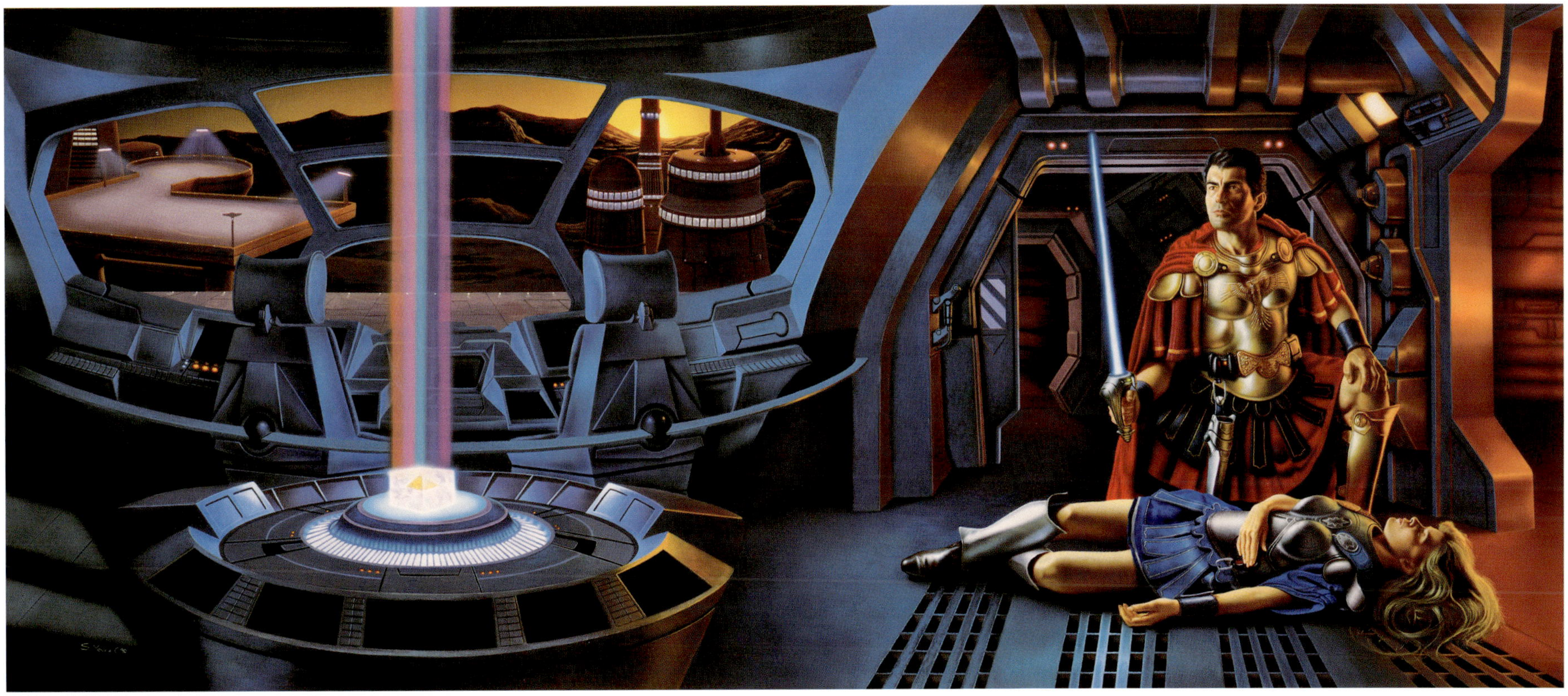

KING'S TEST
MARGARET WEIS, BANTAM, 1990
ACRYLIC ON MASONITE, 18 x 40½in (46 x 103cm)

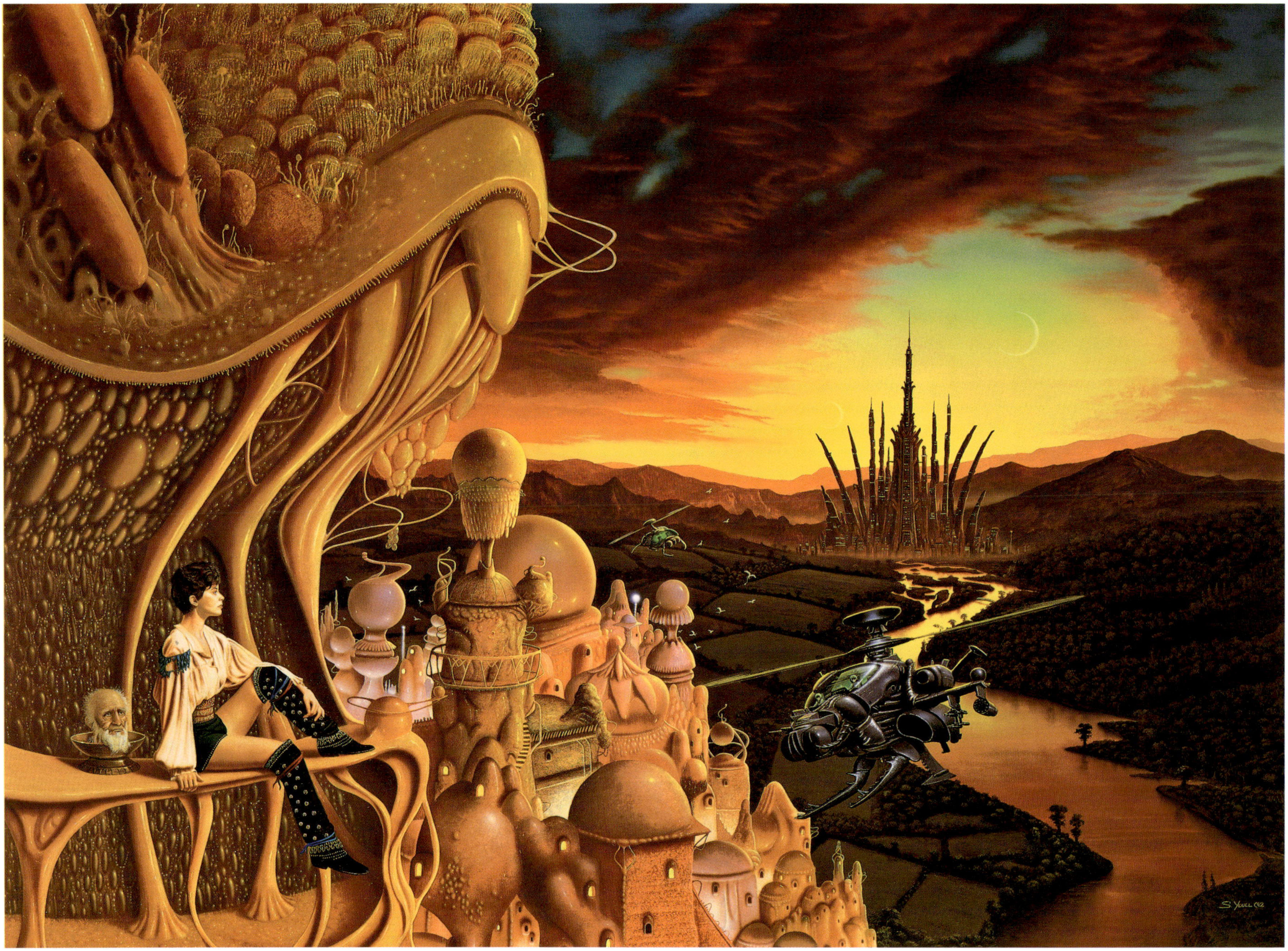

THE BROKEN LAND

IAN McDONALD, BANTAM, 1992
ACRYLIC AND OIL ON ILLUSTRATION BOARD, 27½ x 33in (70 x 84cm)

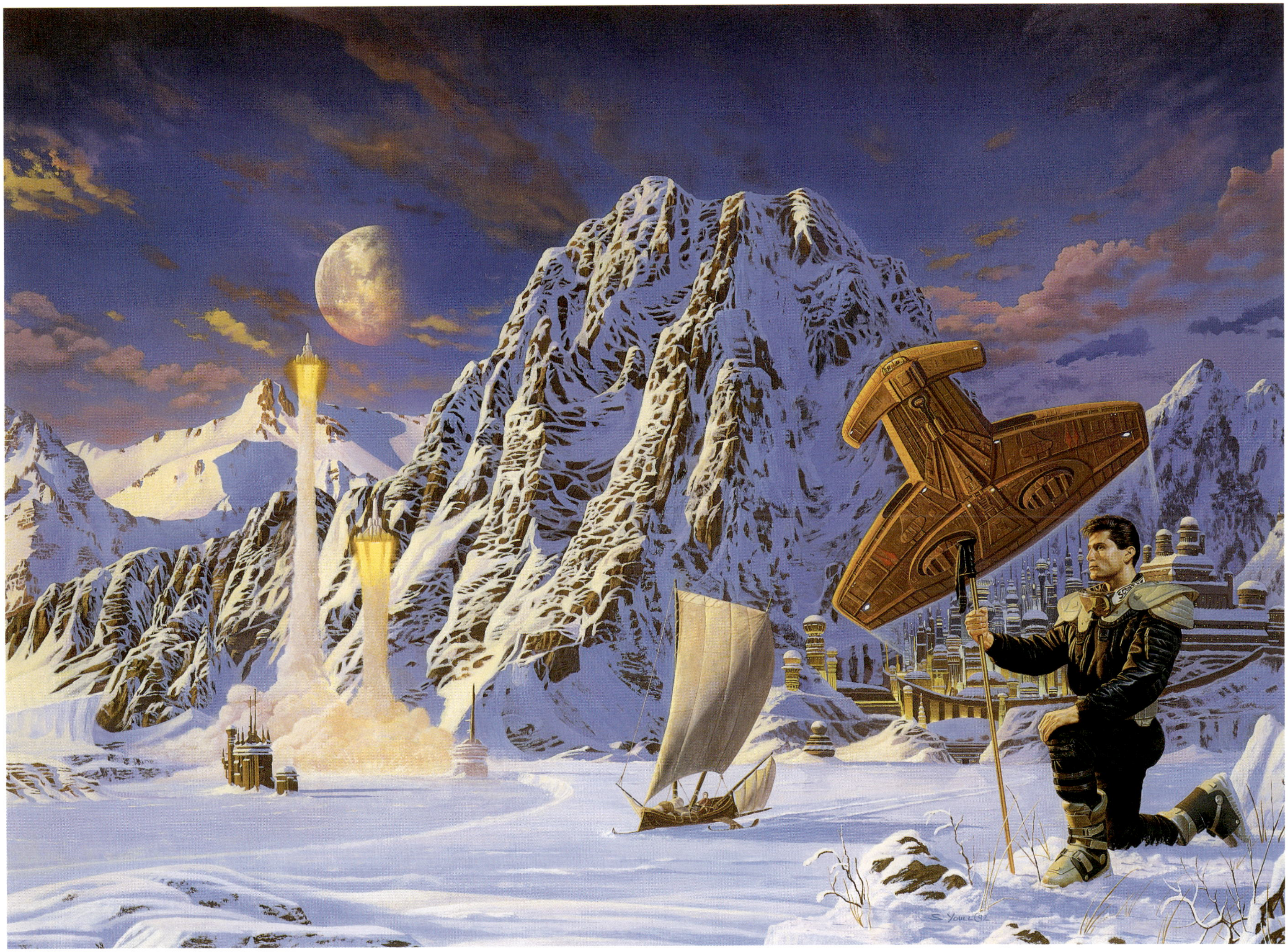

THE BROKEN GOD

DAVID ZINDEL, BANTAM, 1992

ACRYLIC AND OIL ON ILLUSTRATION BOARD, 30 x 40in (76 x 102cm)

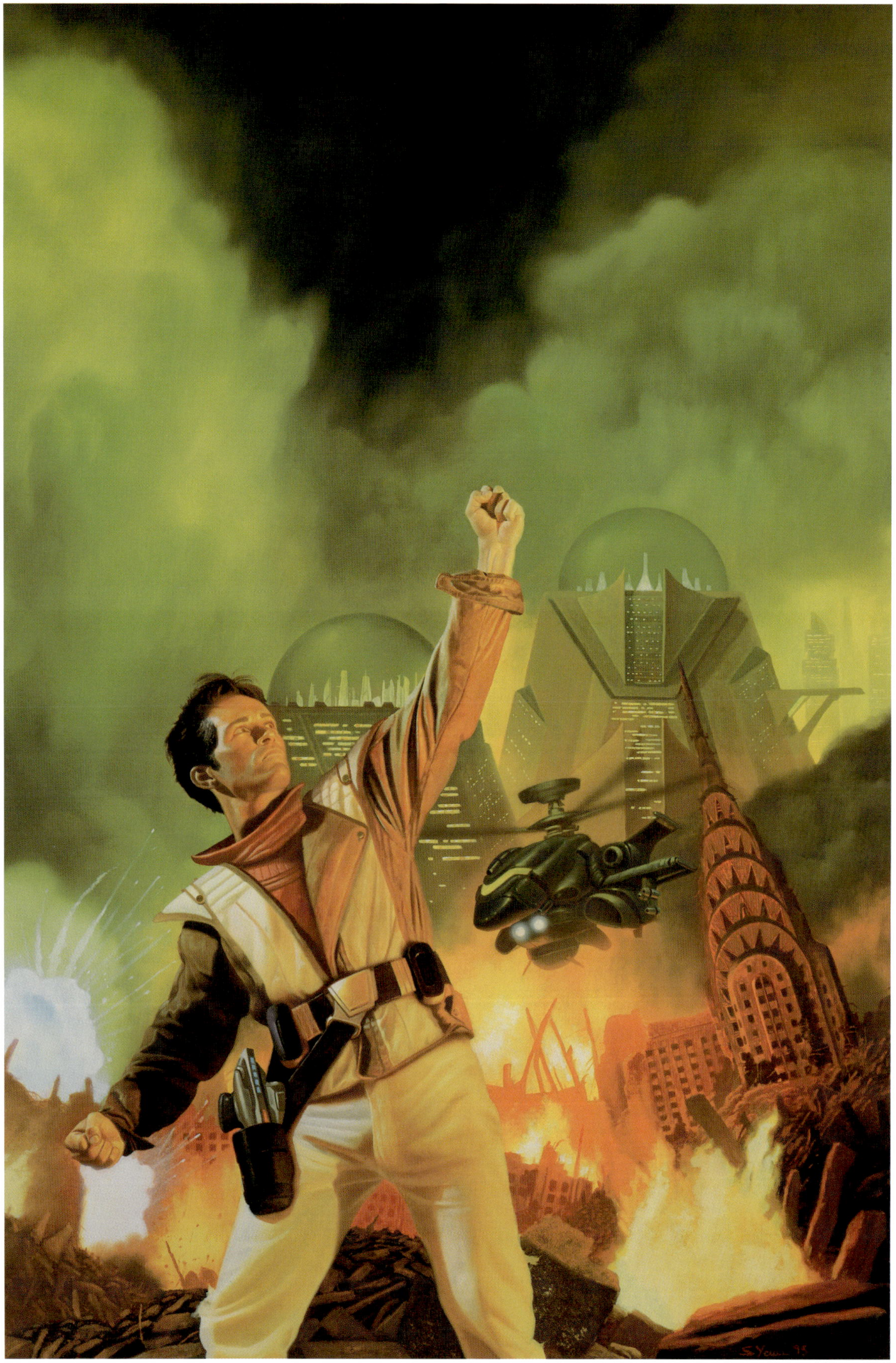

VOICES OF HOPE

DAVID FEINTUCH, WARNER, 1995

OIL ON MASONITE, 27½ x 17¼in (70 x 44cm)

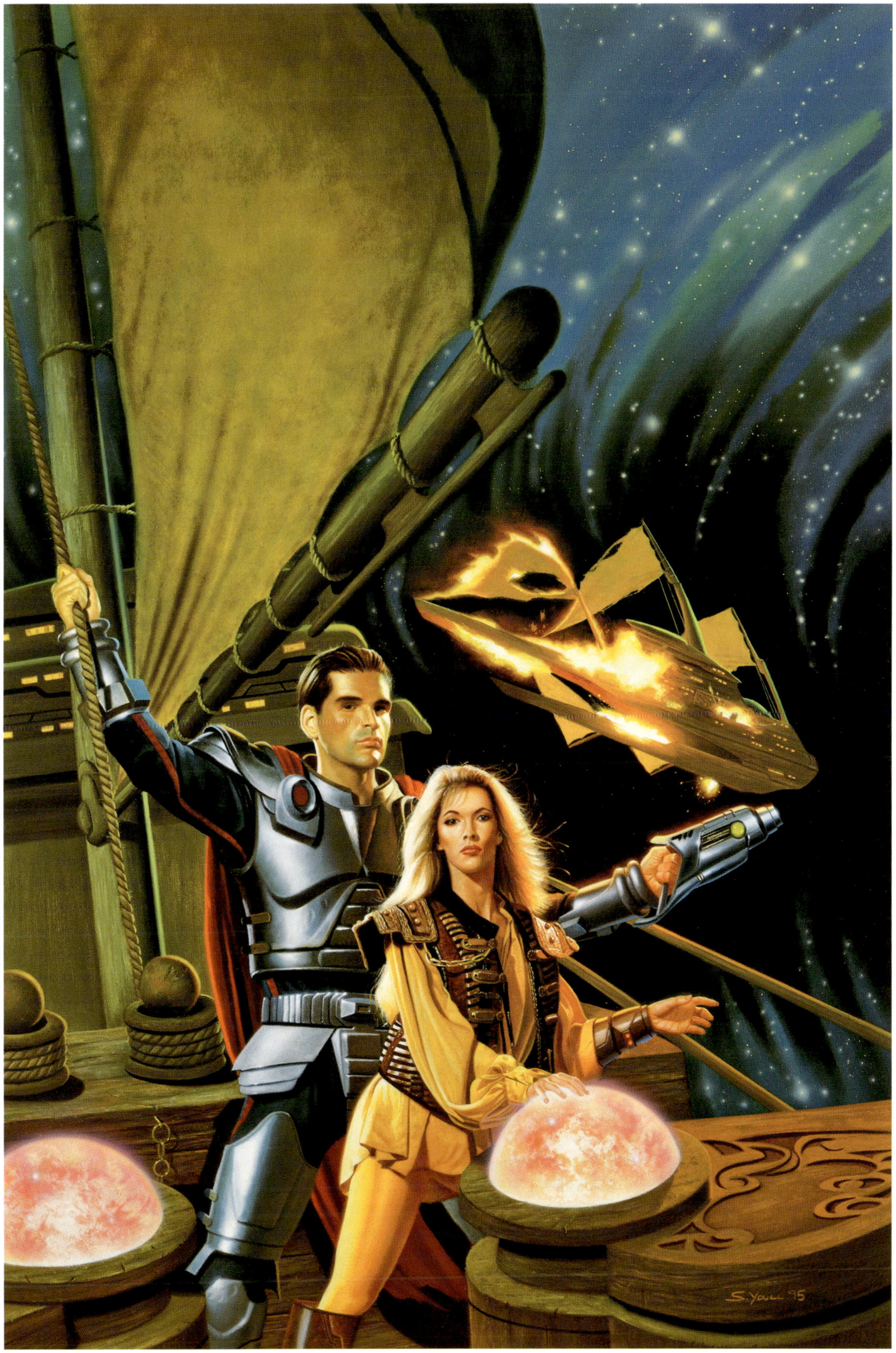

REQUIEM OF STARS

TRACY HICKMAN, BANTAM, 1995

OIL ON ILLUSTRATION BOARD, 29½ x 18½in (75 x 48cm)

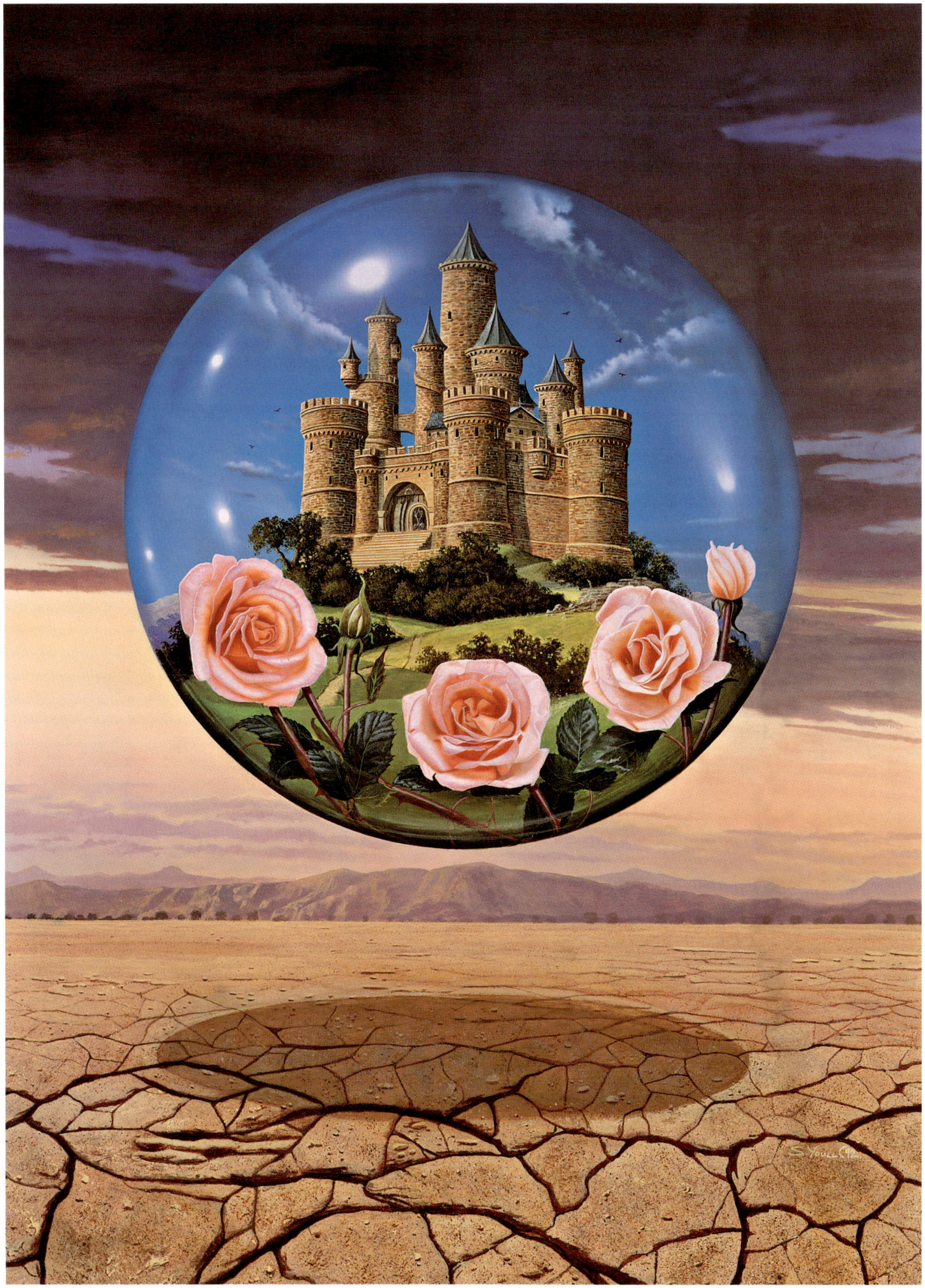

BEAUTY

SHERI S. TEPPER, BANTAM, 1992

ACRYLIC ON MASONITE, 26 x 19in (66 x 48cm)

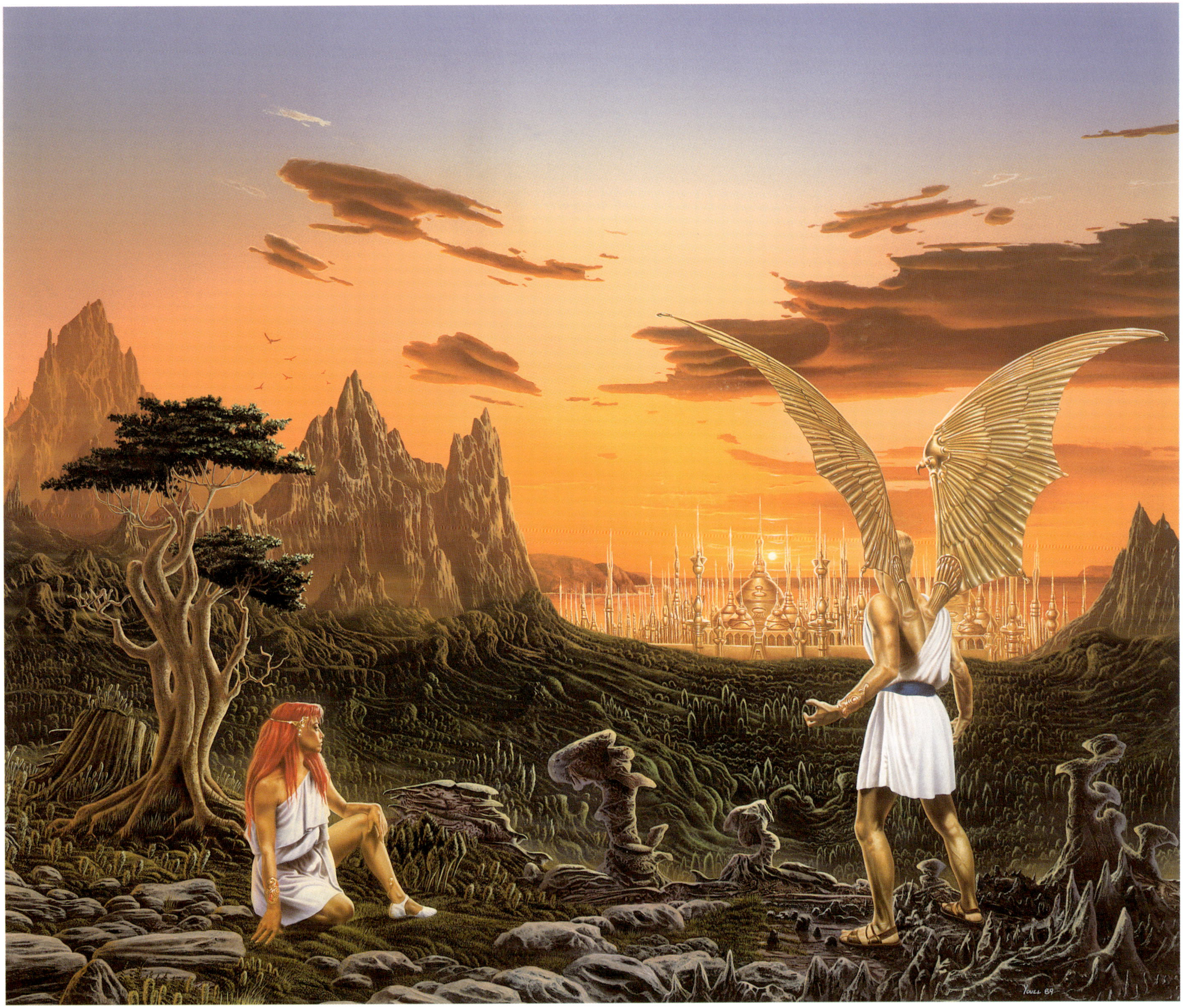

GARDEN OF THE SHAPED

SHEILA FINCH, BANTAM, 1989

ACRYLIC ON ILLUSTRATION BOARD, 27½ x 33in (70 x 84cm)

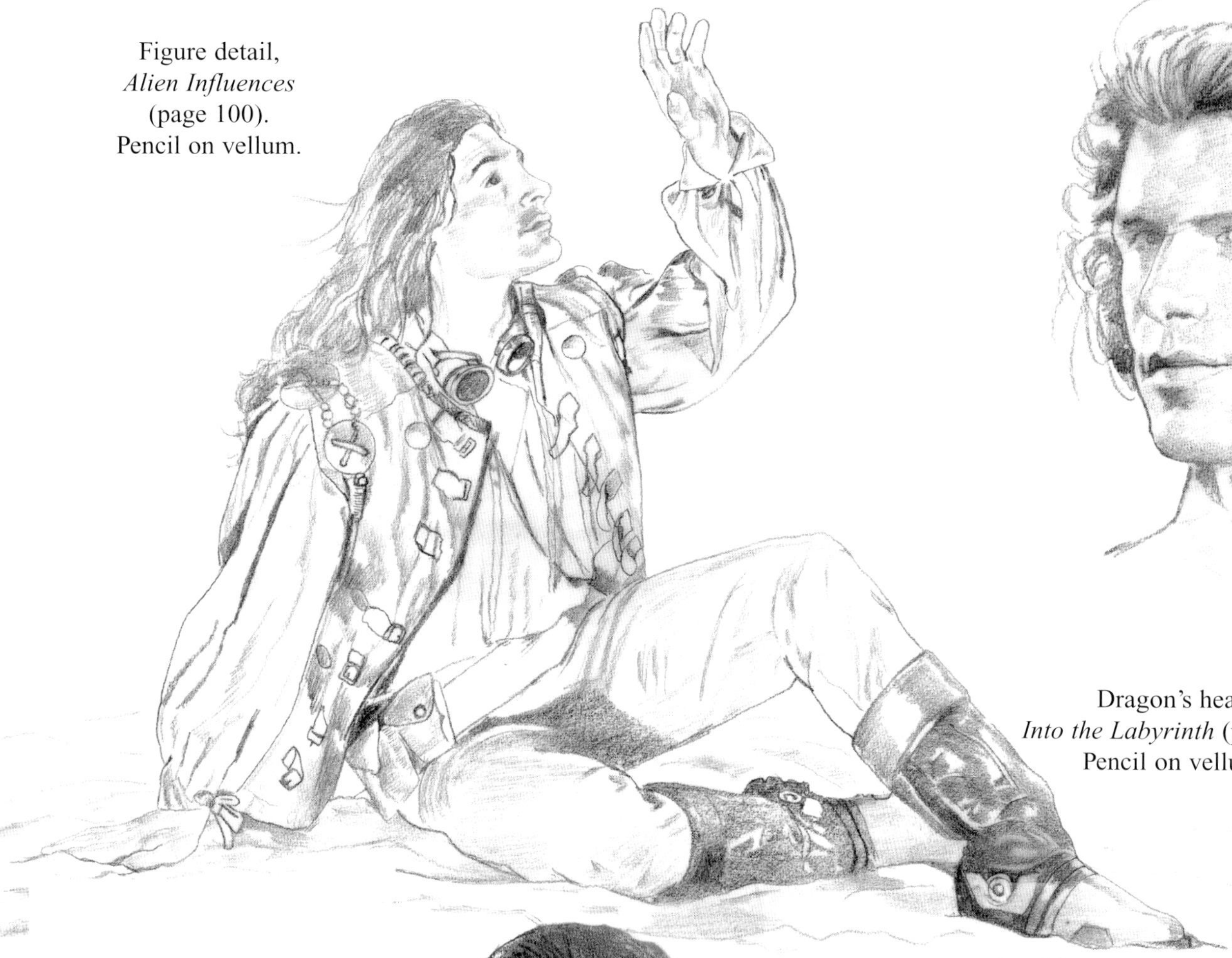

Figure detail,
Alien Influences
(page 100).
Pencil on vellum.

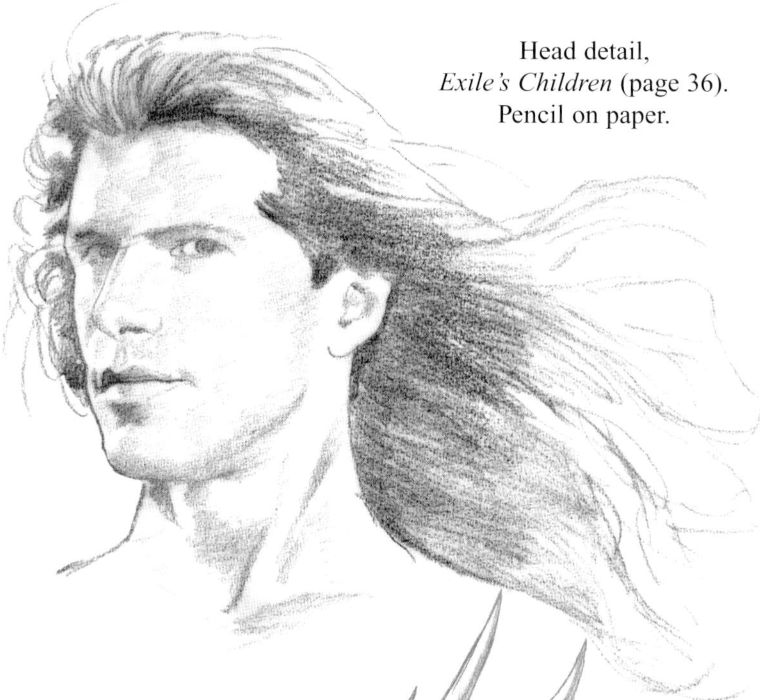

Head detail,
Exile's Children (page 36).
Pencil on paper.

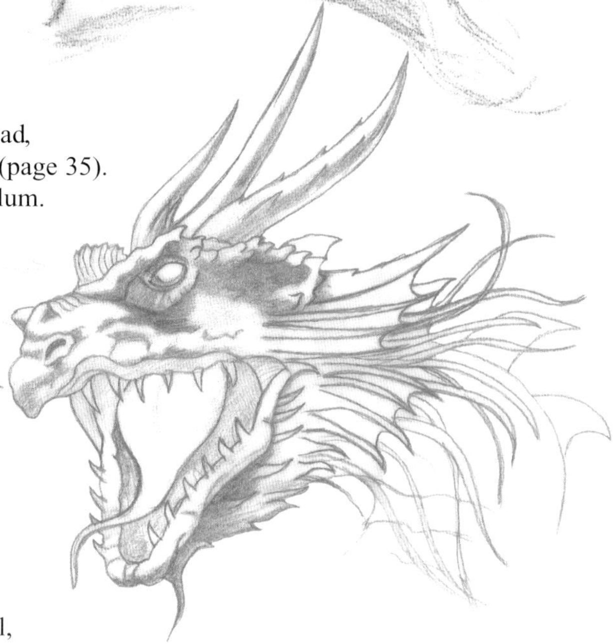

Dragon's head,
Into the Labyrinth (page 35).
Pencil on vellum.

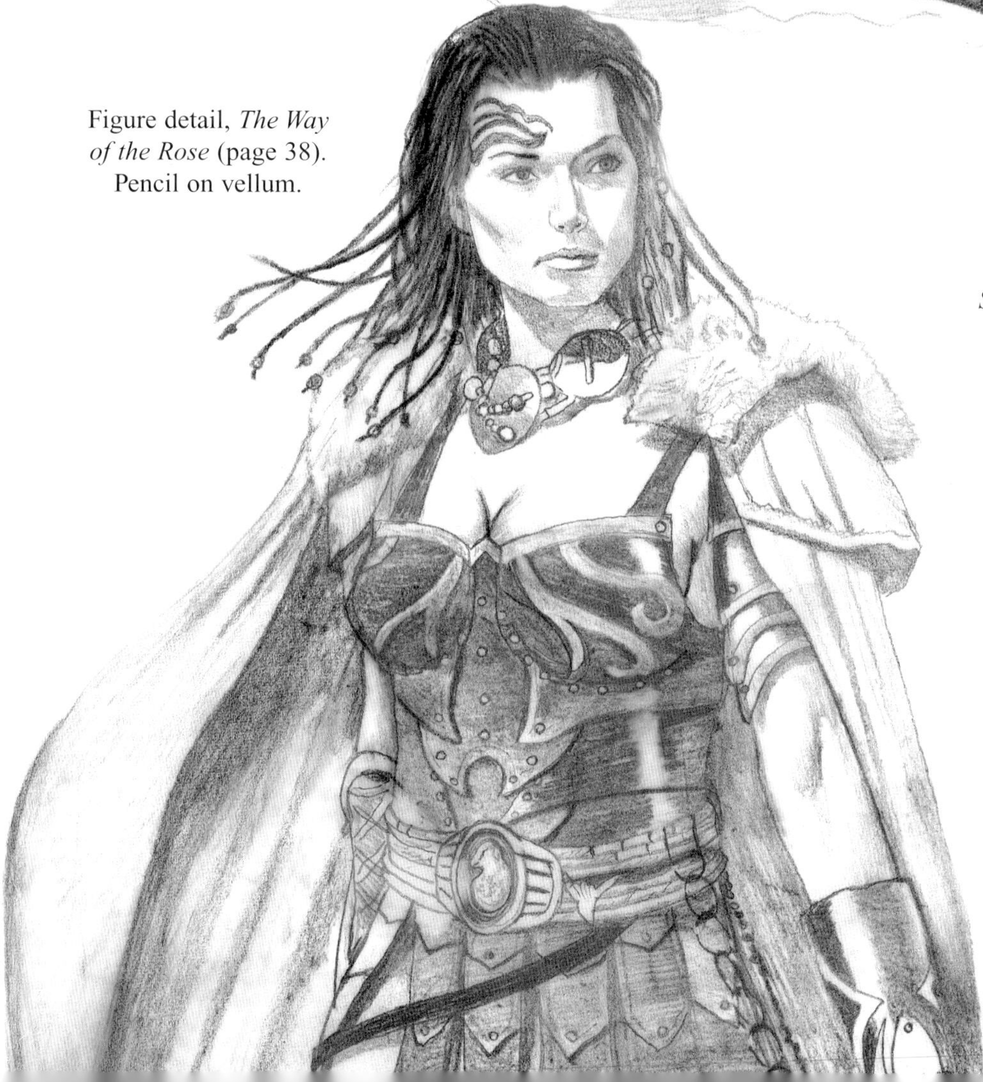

Figure detail, *The Way of the Rose* (page 38).
Pencil on vellum.

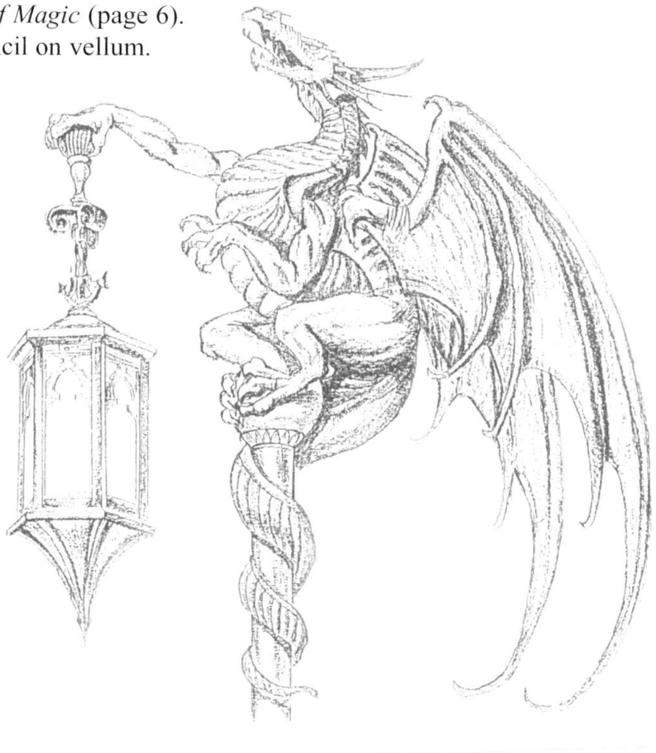

Background detail,
Ship of Magic (page 6).
Pencil on vellum.

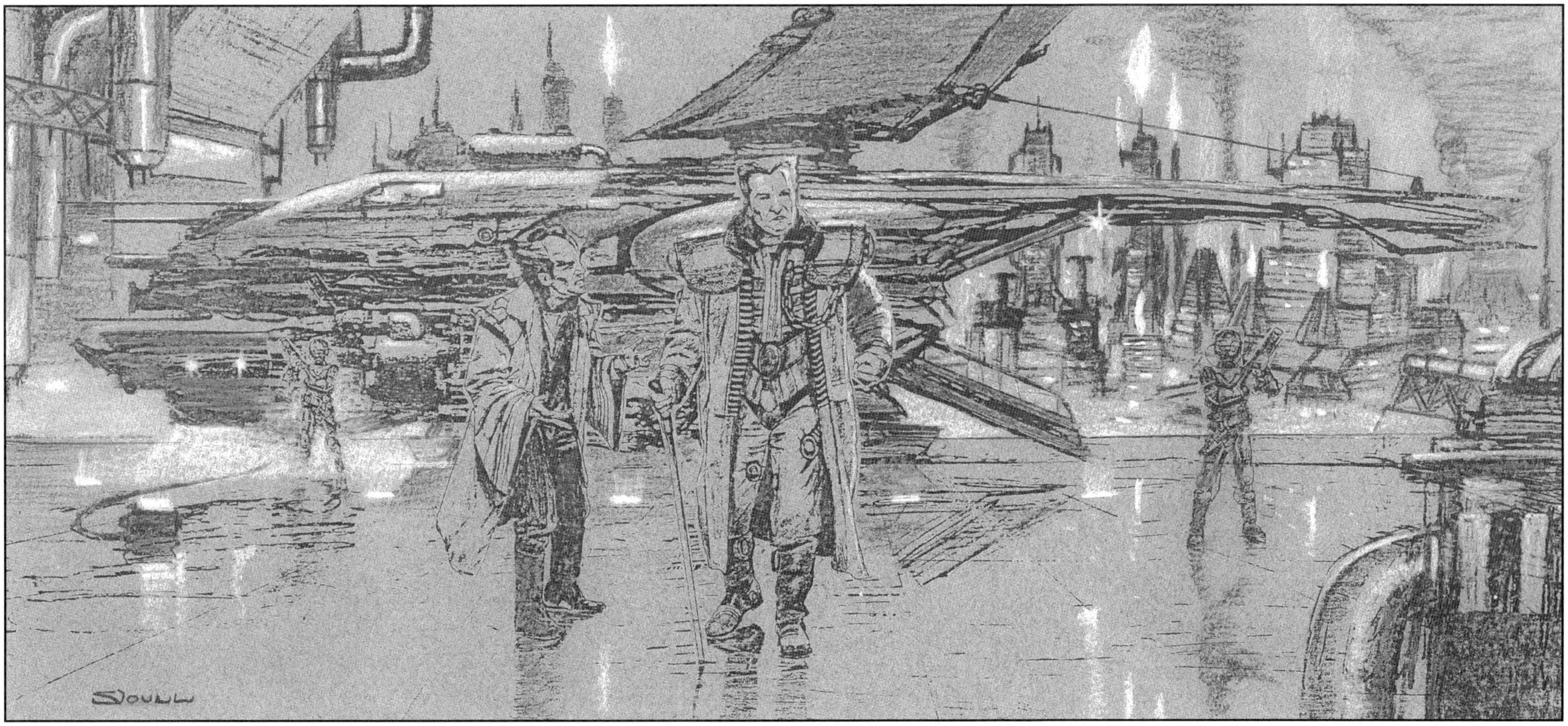

Alternative sketch idea, *Dune: House Harkonnen* (page 86).
Ink and charcoal on charcoal paper.

METAMORPHOSIS

The constant struggle to improve my art has been a personal journey of evolution. As part of that journey I have changed my choice of medium a number of times. In my early days I used pastels before switching to gouache, then acrylics and finally oil paints, moving from one medium to another because each time I felt I must or I could no longer improve as an artist.

During the years 1985 through 1992 most of my paintings were done in acrylics. At this time I was obsessed with the finished surface of my art. I found that painting and airbrushing onto an extremely smooth surface (frequently I would wet-sandpaper a gessoed board) made the blending of the acrylics appear flawless and gave the painting a glass-like finish. It was fun to watch people go right up to the painting, scrutinize it for any signs of brushwork and decide it probably was really a print! The whole process was rewarding, but very time-consuming.

After six or seven years, however, the limits of my patience were being rather stretched. I was also becoming increasingly aware of the limitations of acrylics with regard to the way I wanted my figurative work to look. In 1992 I moved over to oils and discovered an extremely rewarding new medium. Not only did I find I could achieve the same level of finish I was used to, but I could complete a painting in half the time. I also found a multitude of techniques that add texture and unusual effects to my work and take very little time to render. Oils are the medium in which I still work.

Though I have always loved to paint, my favourite part of the creative process is the sketch and design stage. I feel more comfortable sketching on a train or in a park than in my studio, consciously trying to create. While I'm designing something I like to be distracted in some way, so that my subconscious thoughts can take over. I find I rarely need to do colour sketches unless I'm working on a particularly complicated image.

Most of the time I work from background to foreground, but on occasion I've painted a major figure in the middle of an unfinished background. I also like to finish one area at a time rather than work into the entire painting at once.

The next few pages contain various sketches, from rough concepts to finished drawings, plus a step-by-step example to show the way I work.

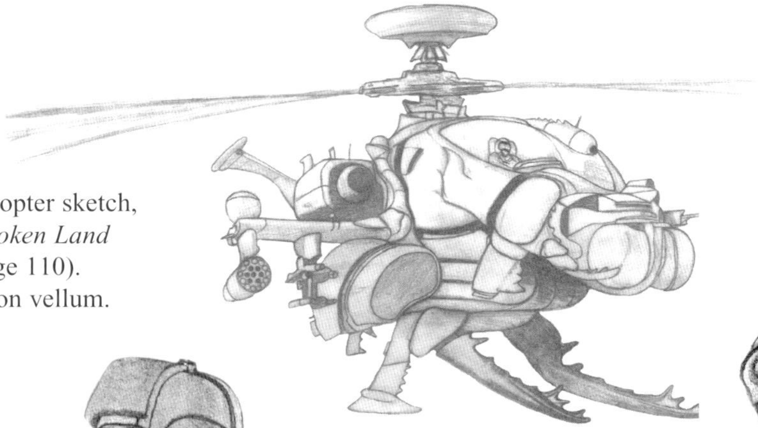

Bug helicopter sketch,
The Broken Land
(page 110).
Pencil on vellum.

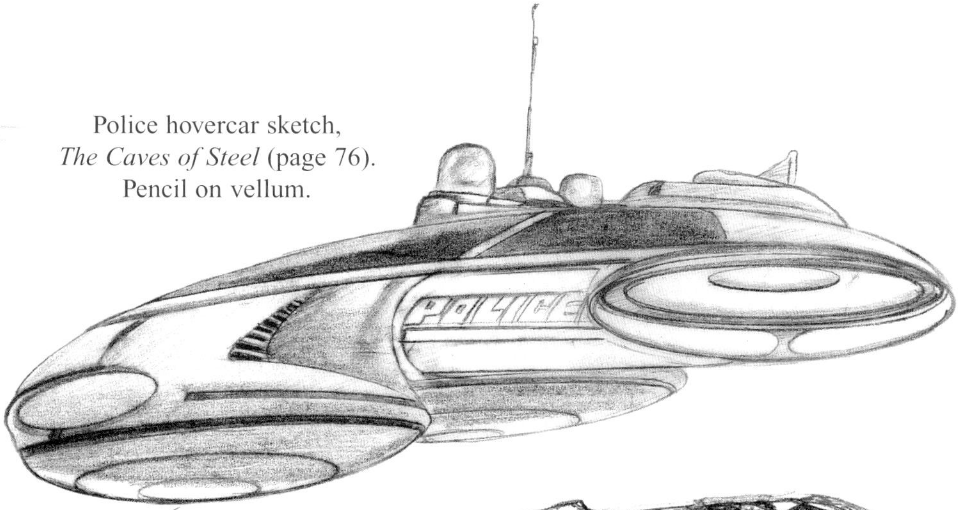

Police hovercar sketch,
The Caves of Steel (page 76).
Pencil on vellum.

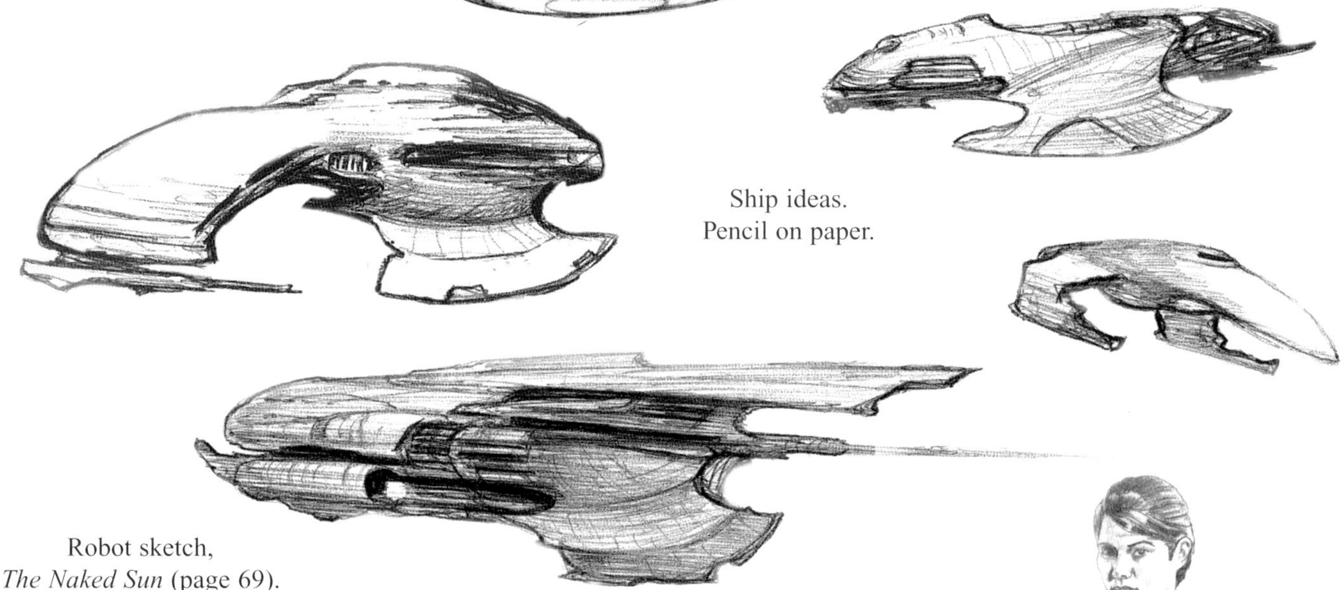

Ship ideas.
Pencil on paper.

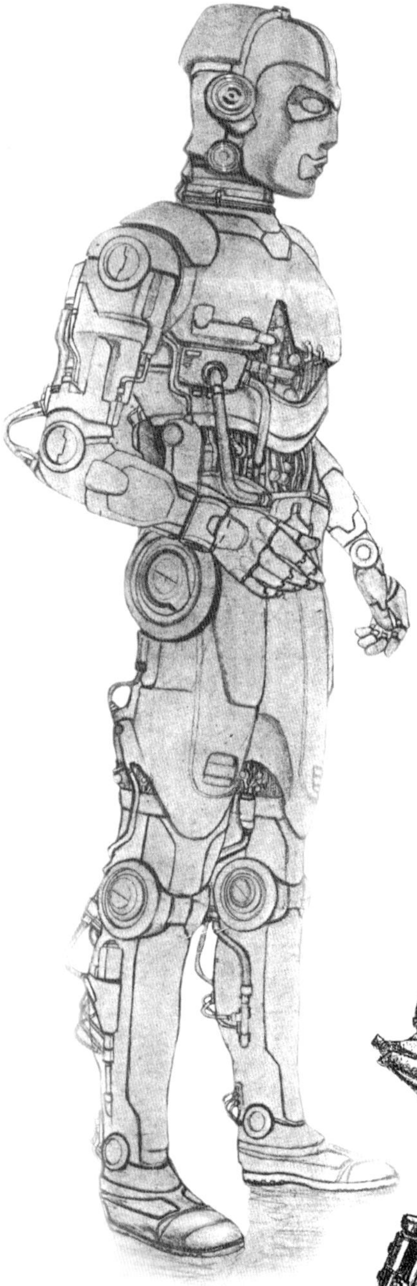

Robot sketch,
The Naked Sun (page 69).
Pencil on vellum.

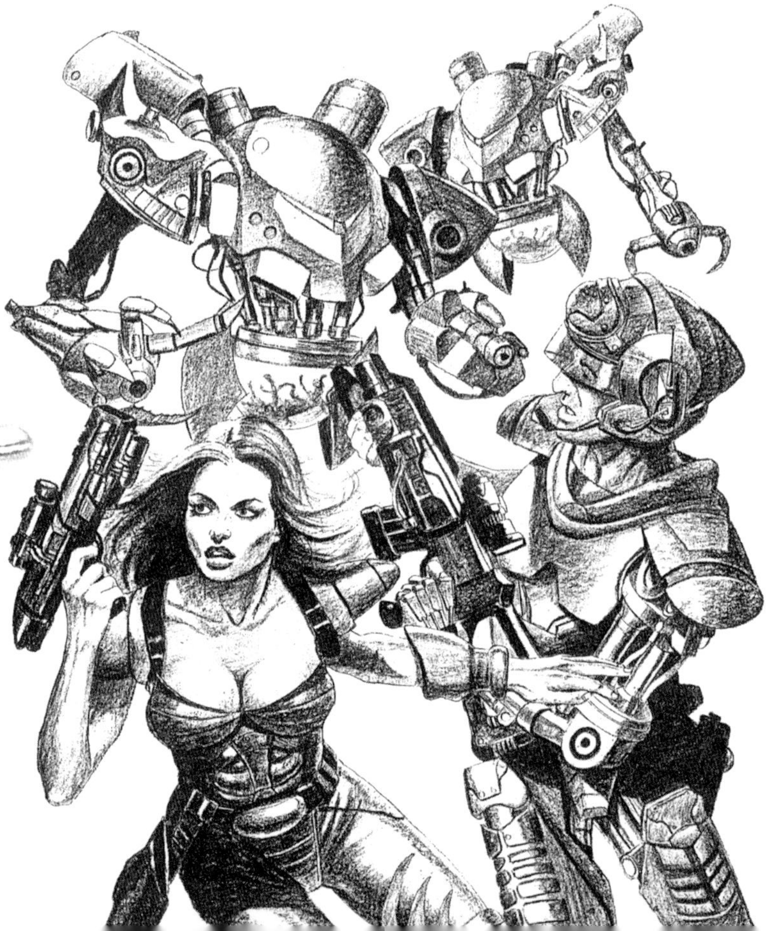

Figures and robot sketch,
Robot Blues (page 64).
Ink and charcoal on
charcoal paper.

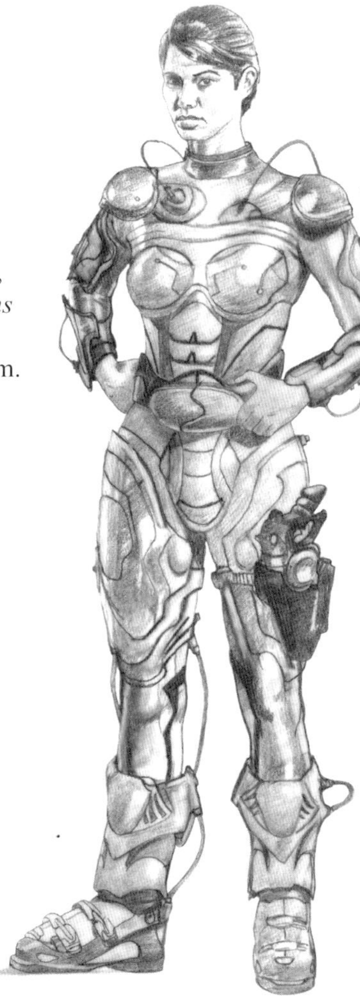

Figure sketch,
Gravity Dreams
(page 52).
Pencil on vellum.

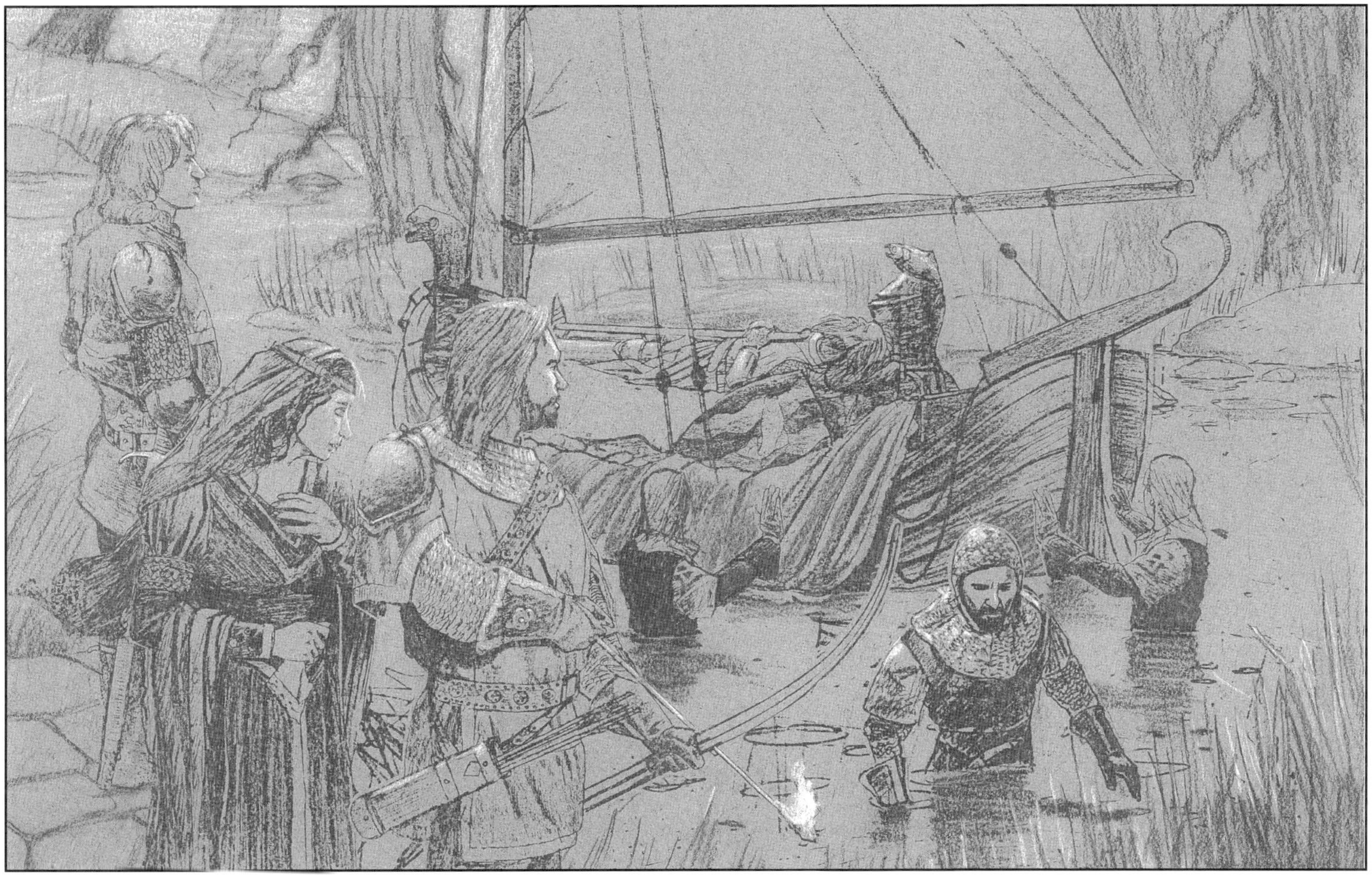

Sketch, *A Storm of Swords* (page 26). Ink and charcoal on charcoal paper.

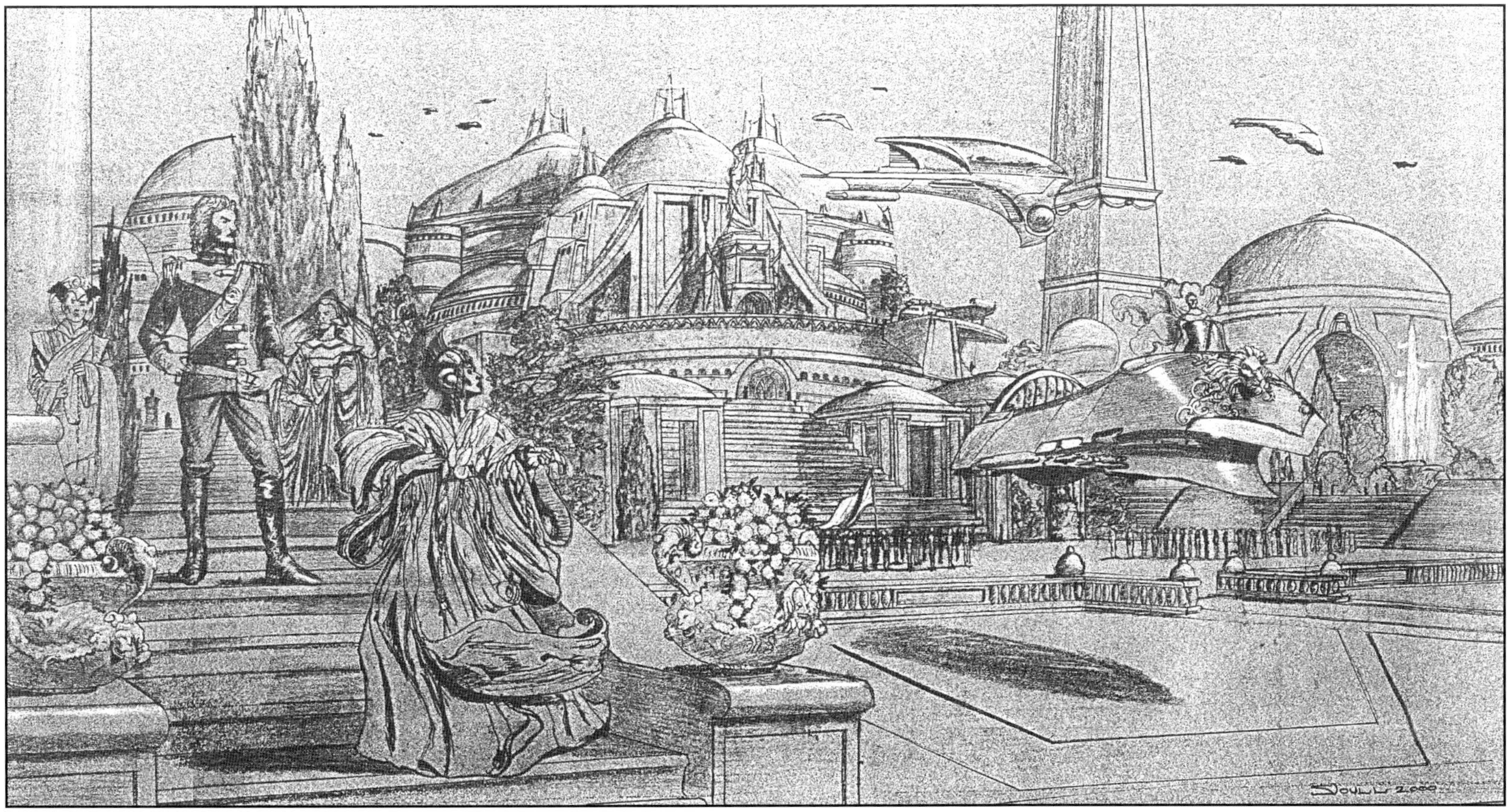

Sketch, *Dune: House Corrino* (page 86). Ink and charcoal on charcoal paper.

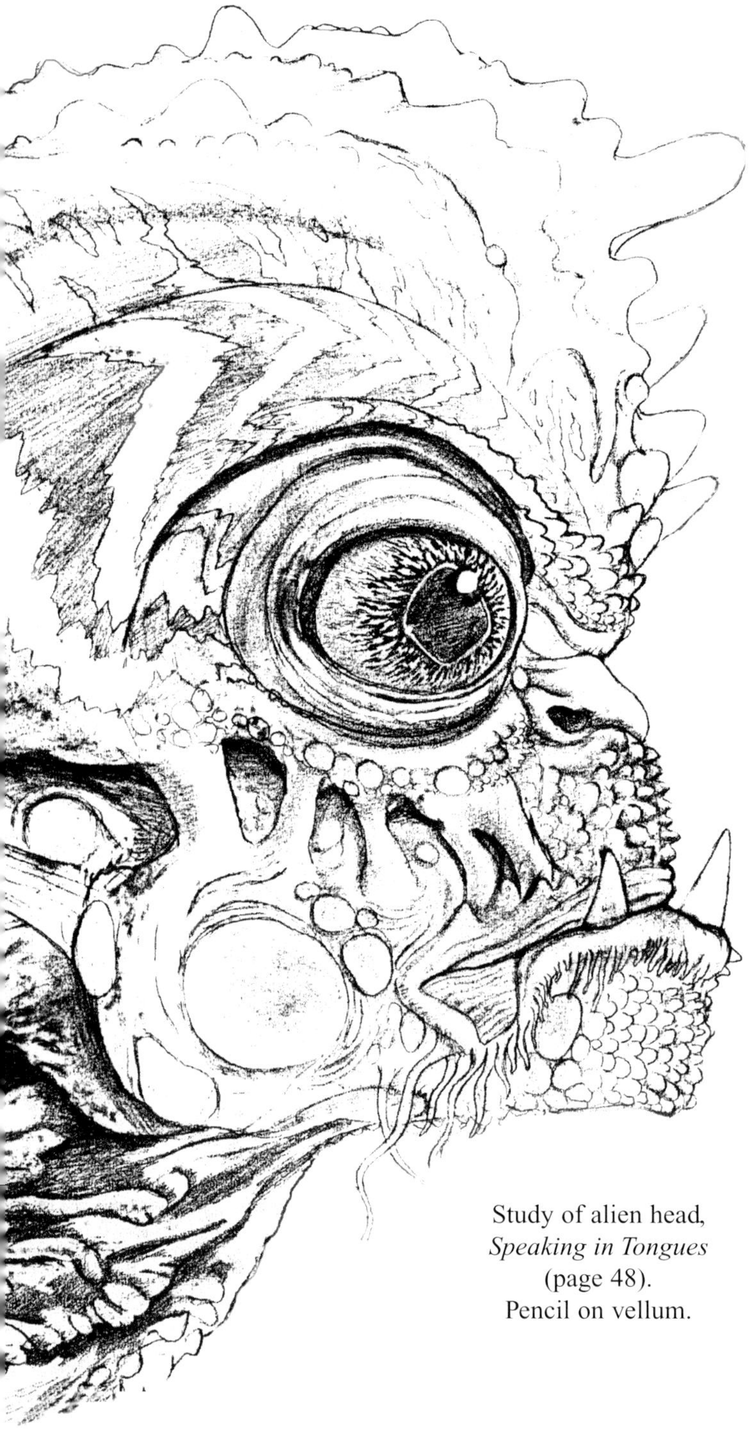

Study of alien head,
Speaking in Tongues
(page 48).
Pencil on vellum.

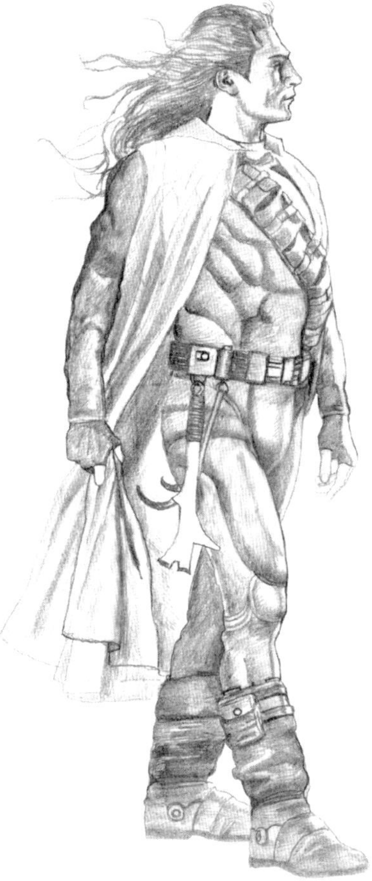

Fremen sketch,
Dune: House Atreides (page 87).
Pencil on vellum.

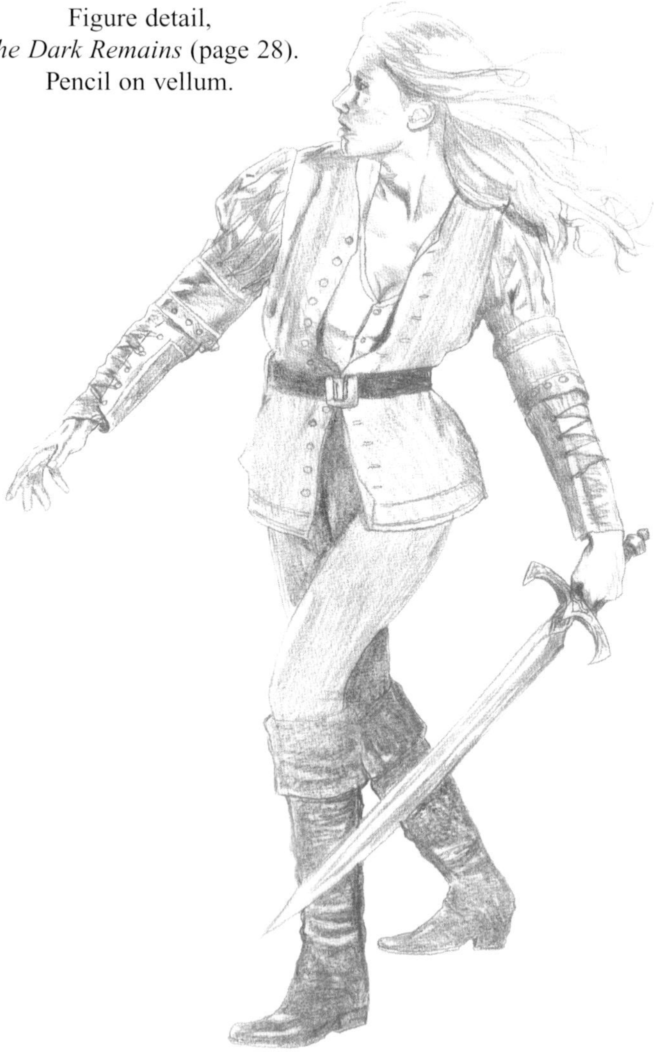

Figure detail,
The Dark Remains (page 28).
Pencil on vellum.

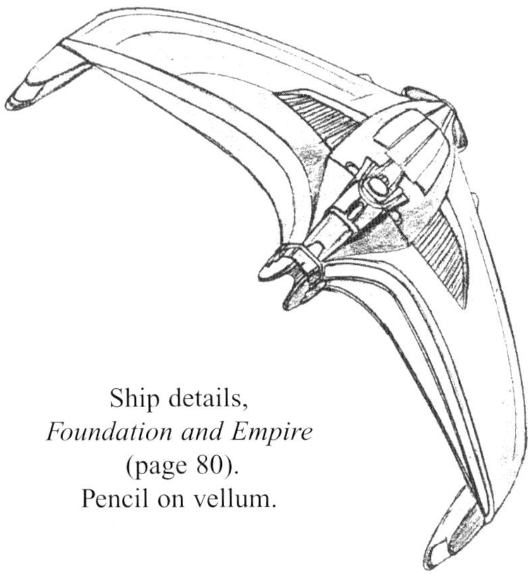

Ship details,
Foundation and Empire
(page 80).
Pencil on vellum.

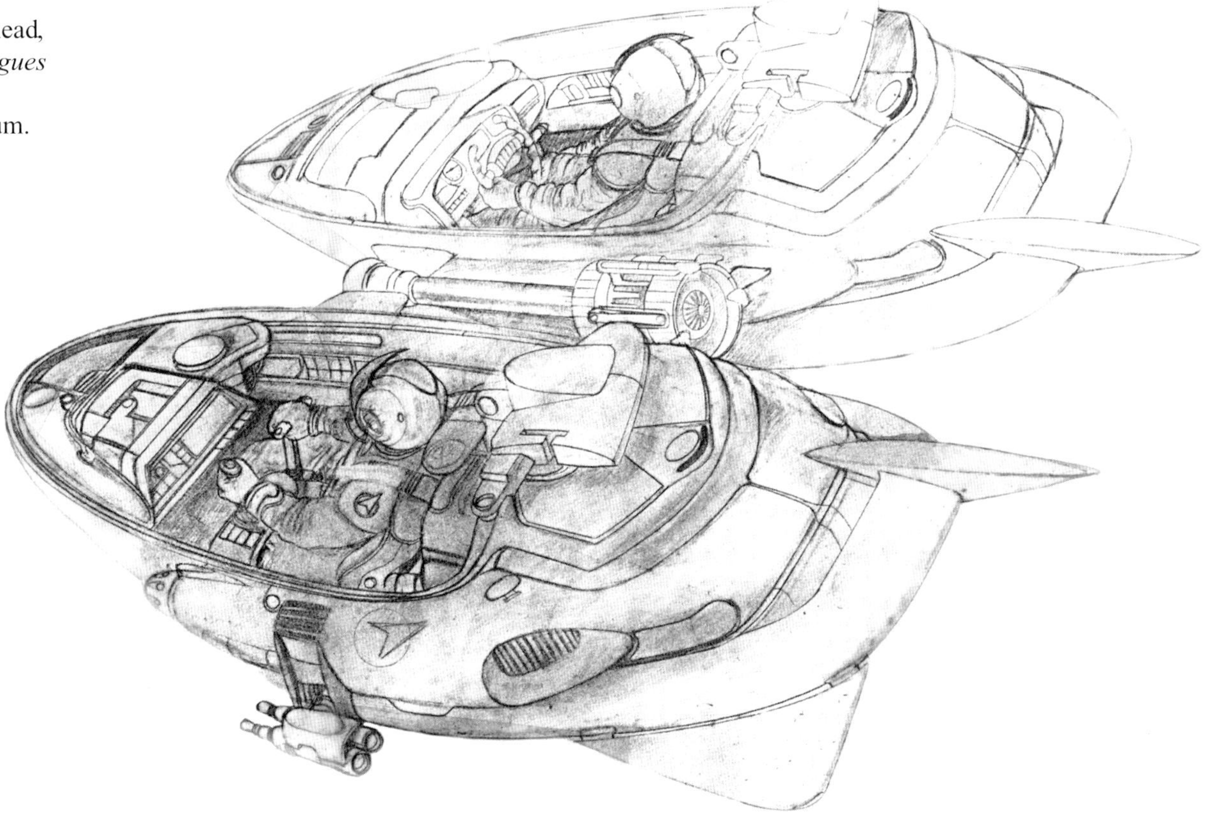

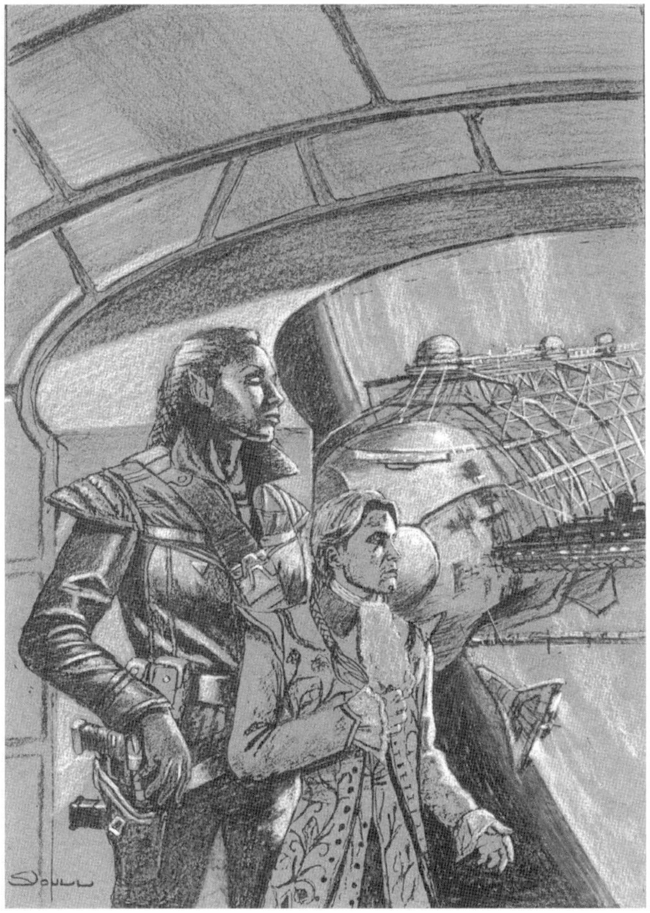

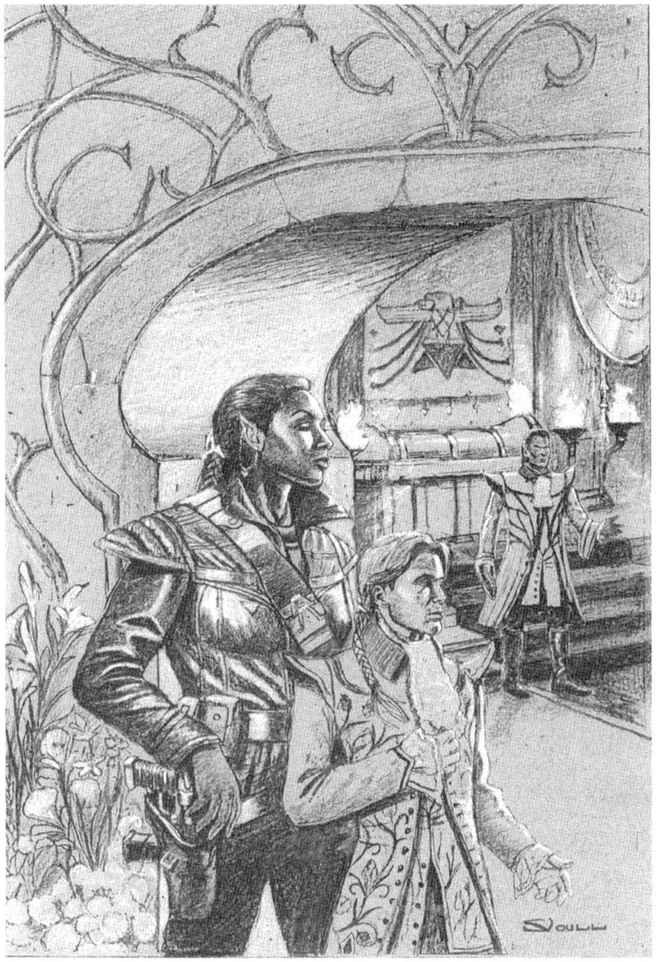

Two alternative sketch ideas, *Defender* (page 106). Ink and charcoal on charcoal paper.

Robot study, *The Positronic Man* (page 72). Pencil on vellum.

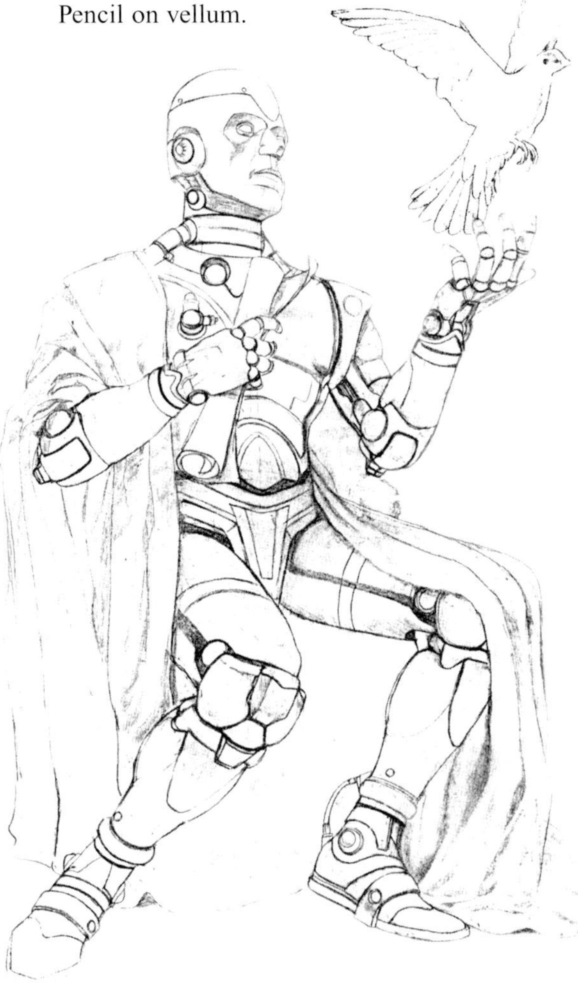

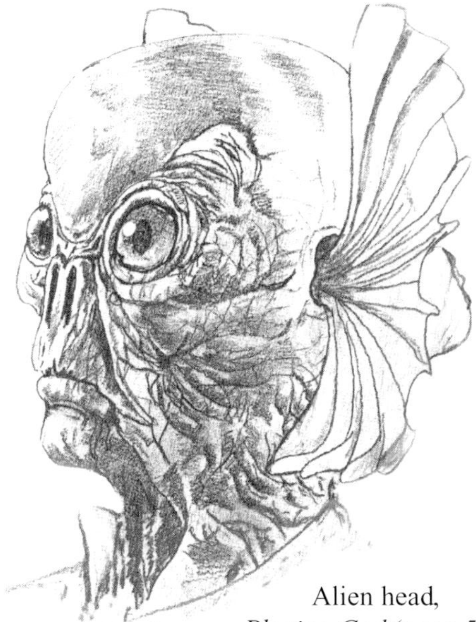

Alien head, *Playing God* (page 51). Pencil on vellum.

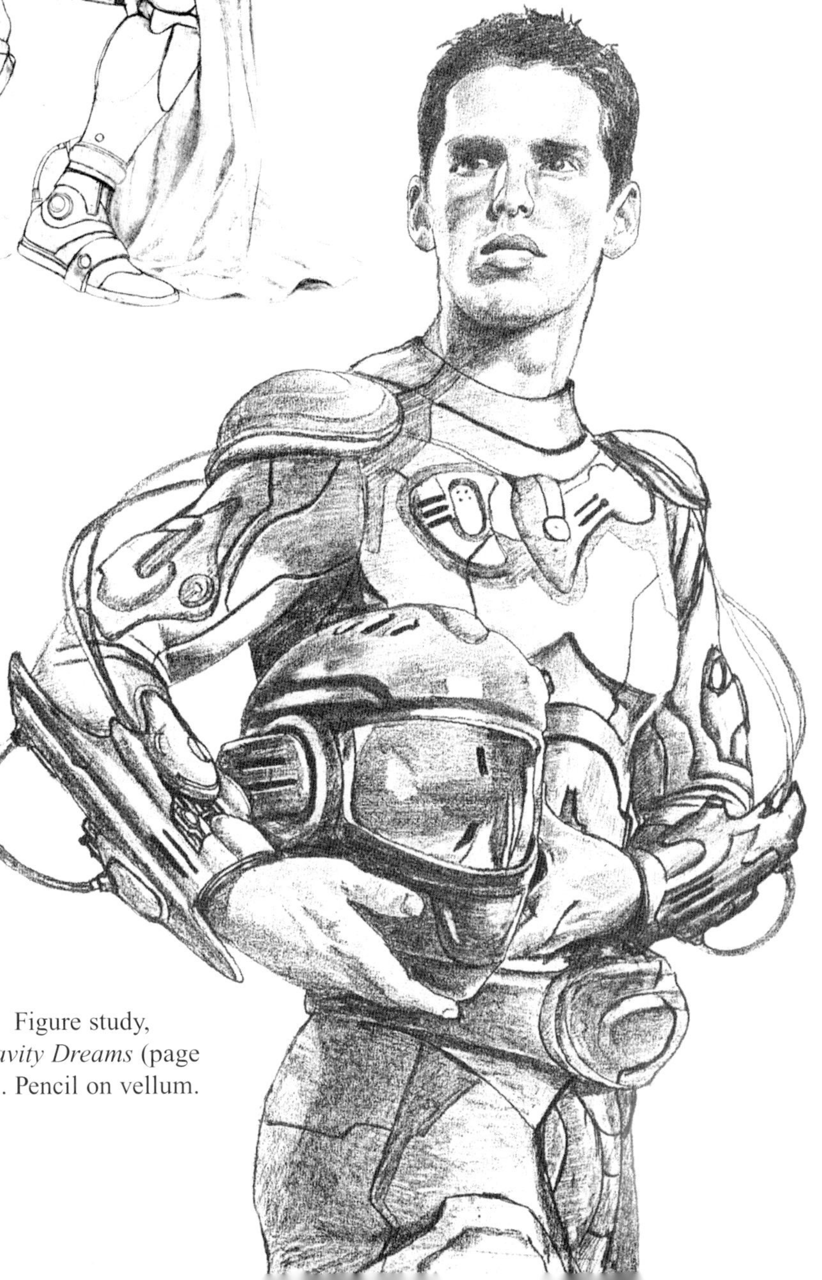

Figure study, *Gravity Dreams* (page 52). Pencil on vellum.

Data monitor concept sketch.
Pencil on paper.

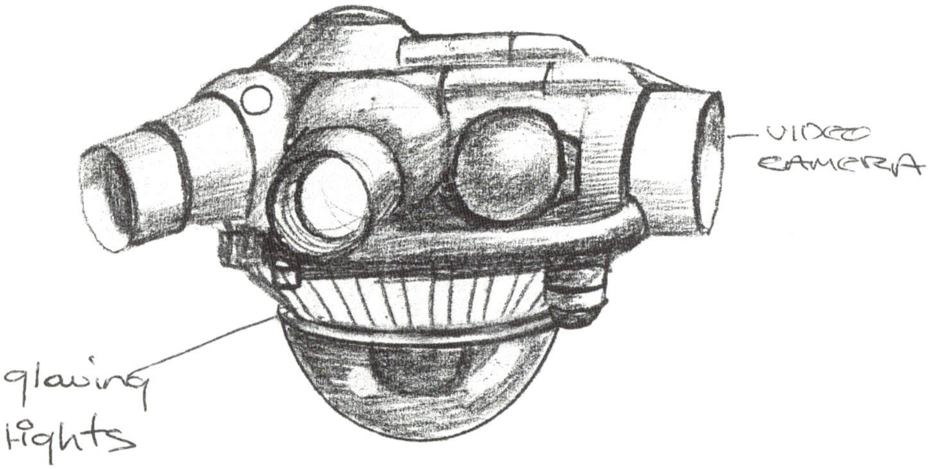

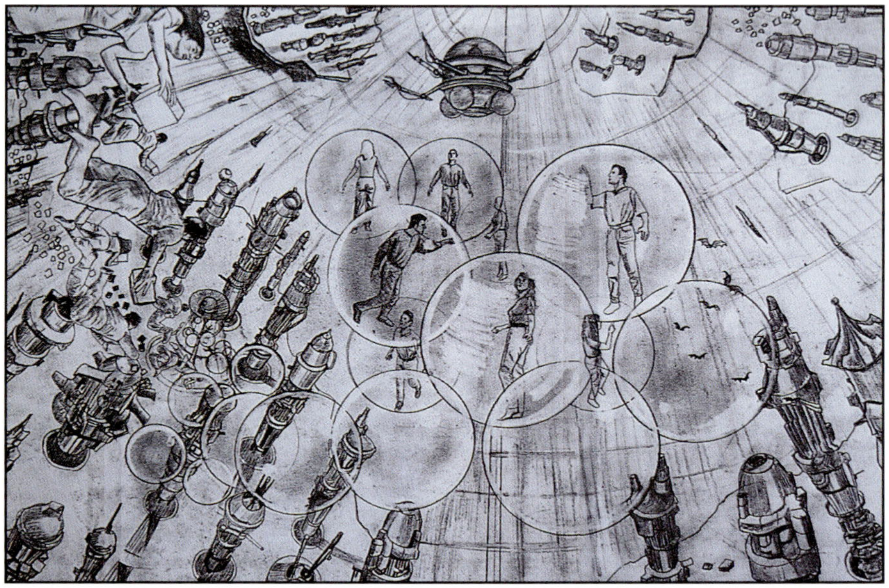

One of the beginning sketch ideas for *WOM Planet.*

Details from conceptual stage.
Pencil on paper.

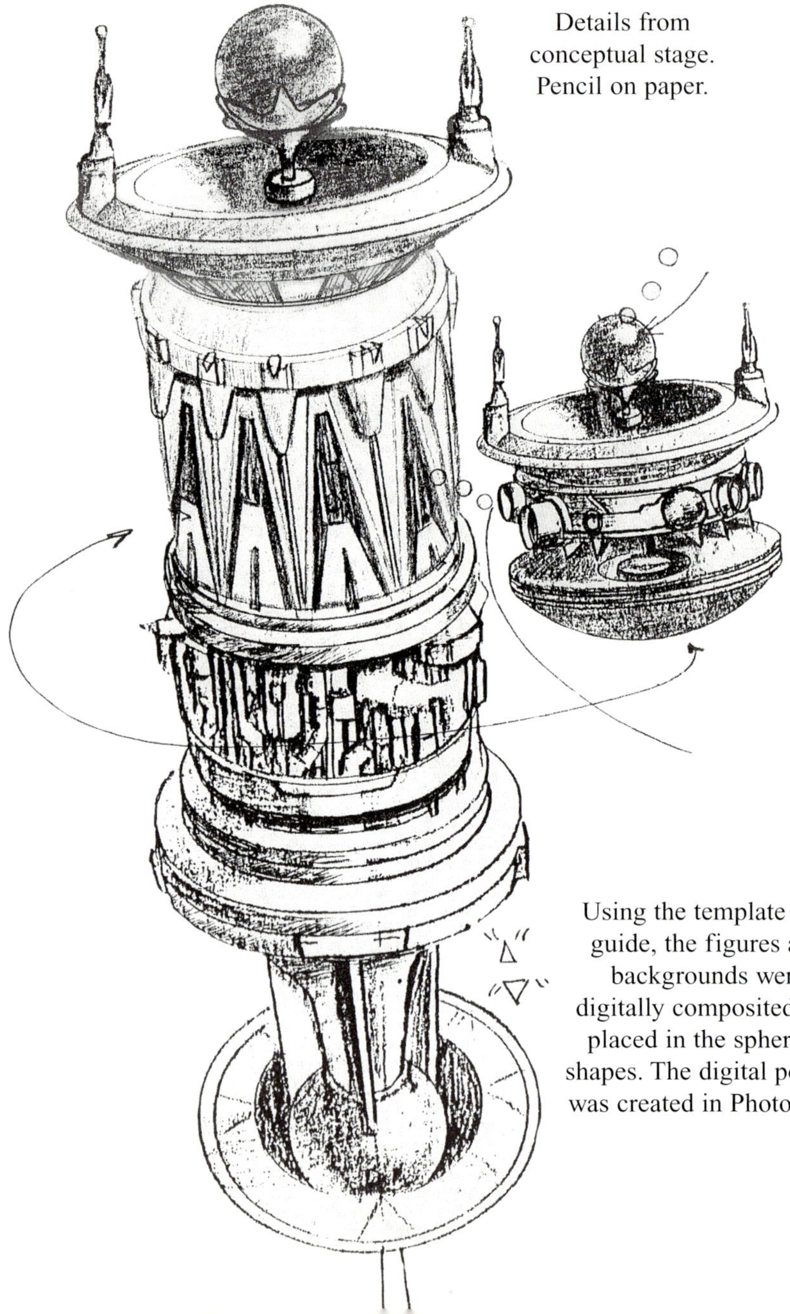

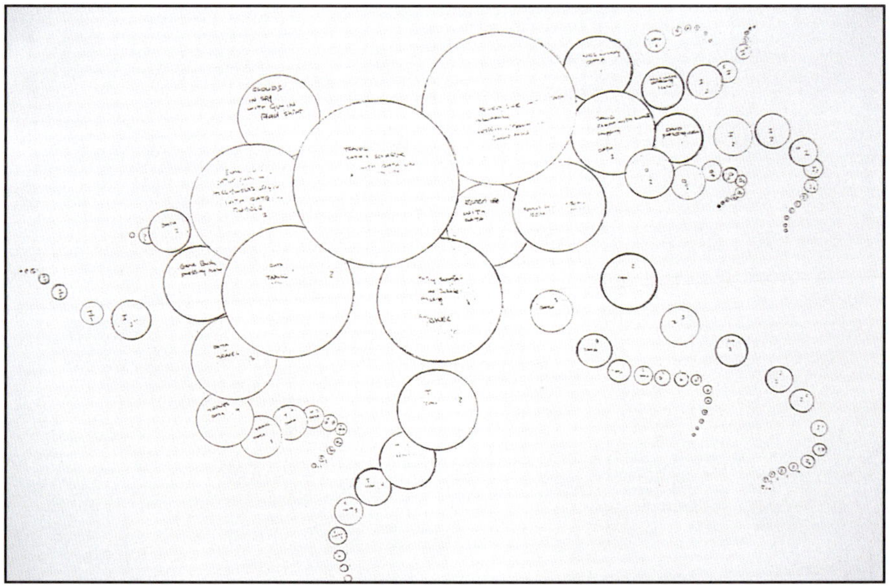

Plotting the bubble path; this acted as a visual template for the digital positioning.

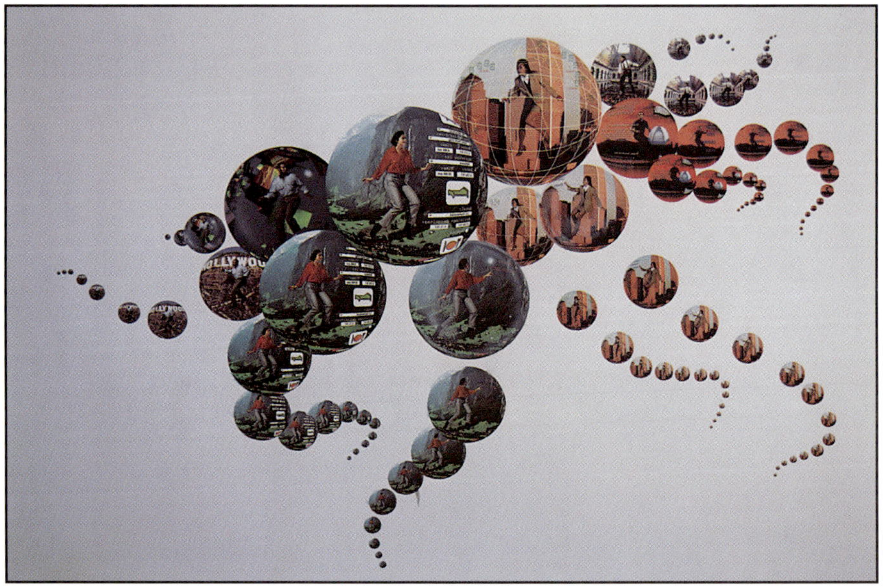

Using the template as a guide, the figures and backgrounds were digitally composited and placed in the spherical shapes. The digital portion was created in Photoshop.

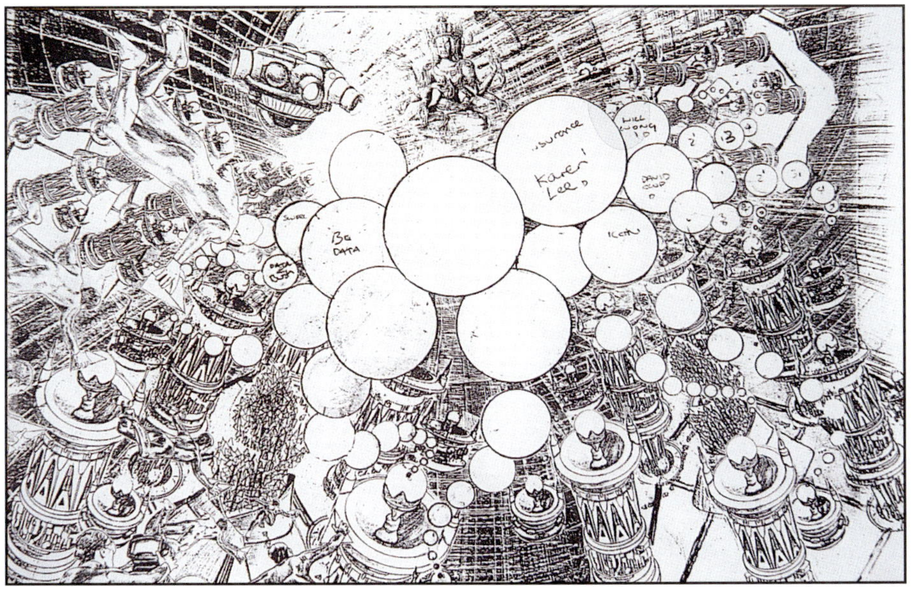

Close-up of finished sketch. Pencil on paper.

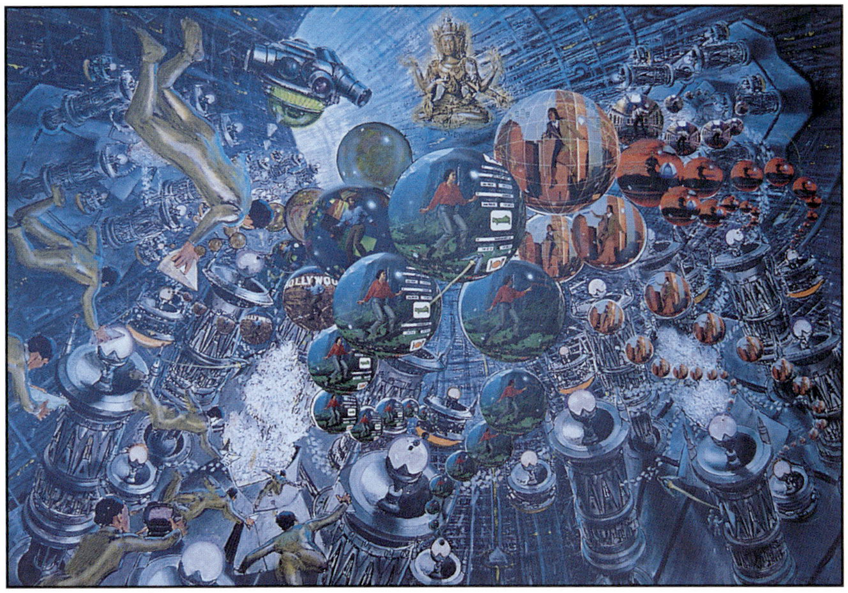

Rough oil colour sketch for finished painting.

WOM PLANET

This is a multi-step concept to show visually how a new piece of software functioned. This is the only painting I've ever done this way. I scanned photographs into a computer and converted them into circular shapes, then printed them out on watercolour paper. I next redrew the rest of the art and painted over the whole illustration. The painting, from conceptual meetings to finished art, took almost a year, because the software was being developed at the time and thus was constantly changing. The finished painting is shown on pages 70–71.

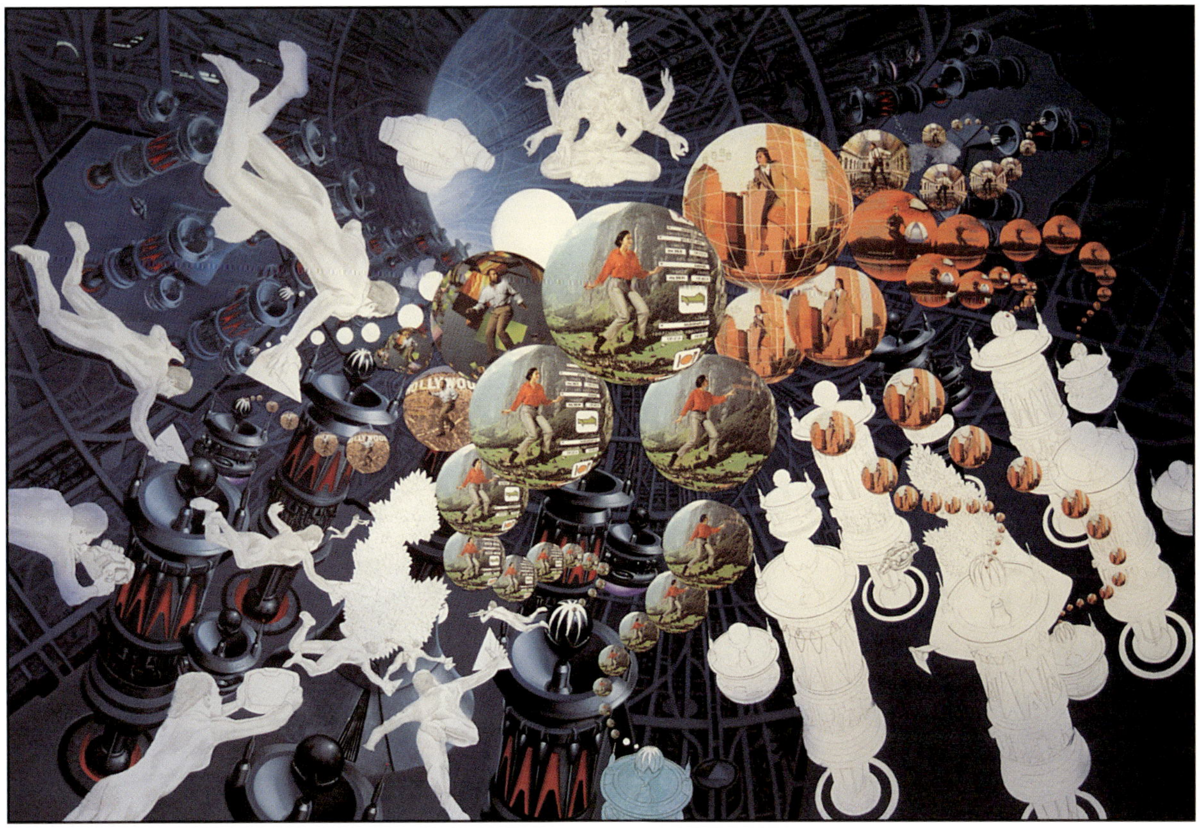

The painting in a partially finished state.

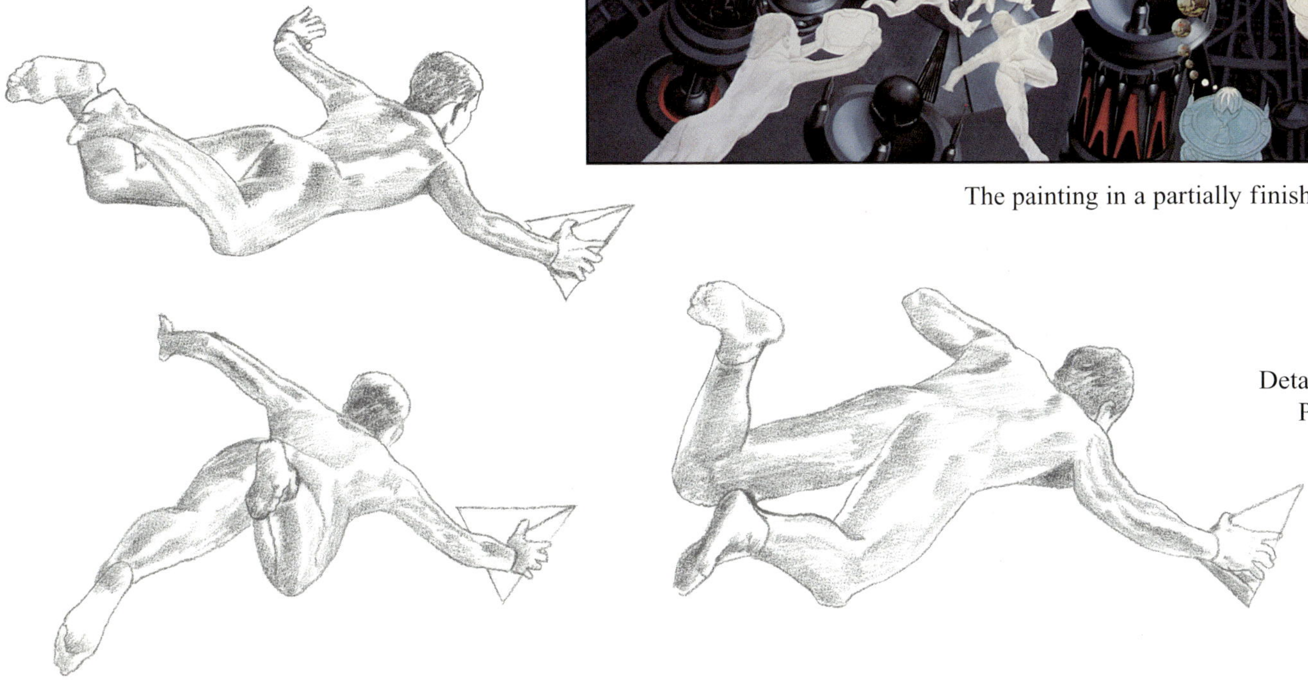

Details of flying figures.
Pencil on vellum.

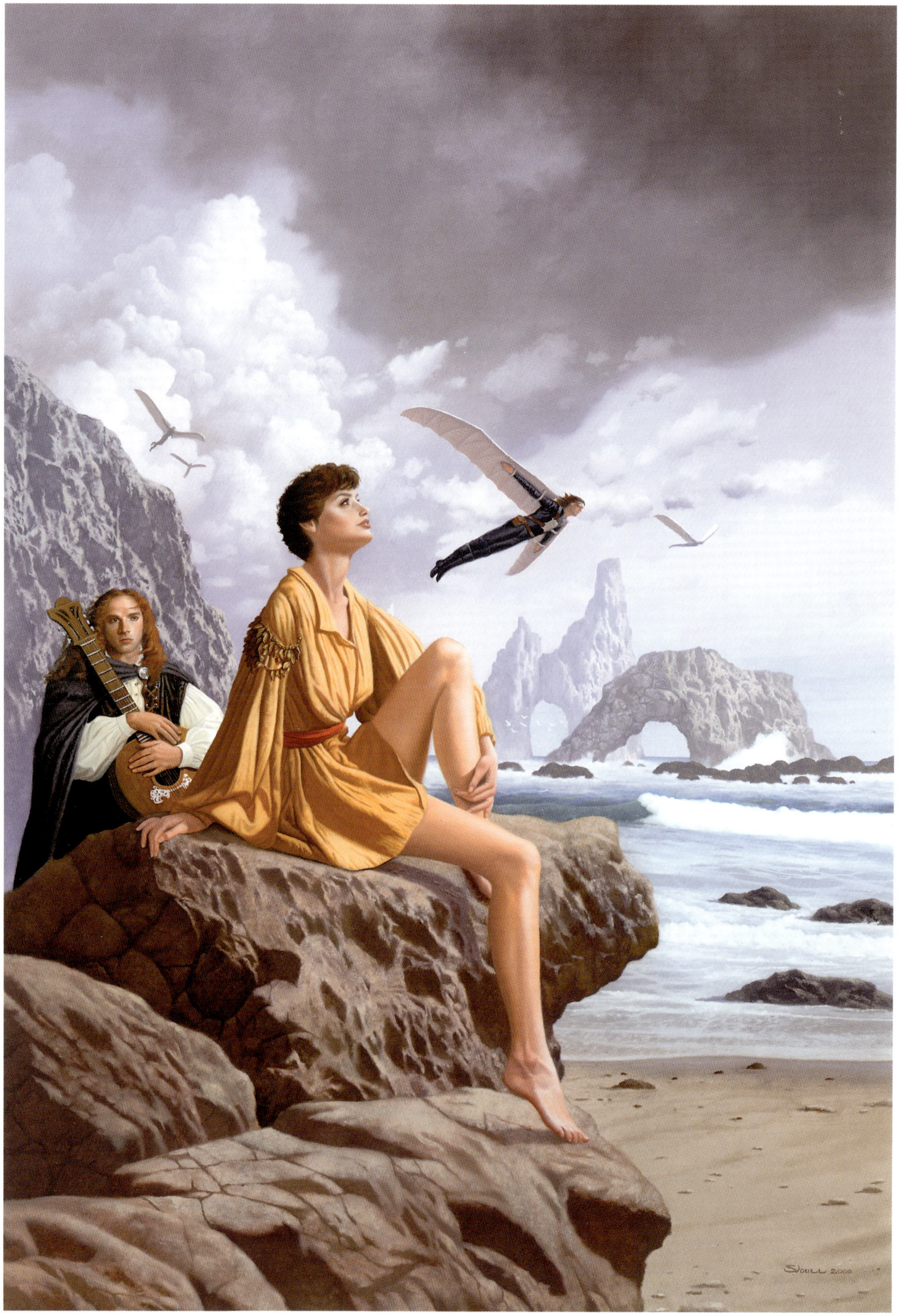

WINDHAVEN

GEORGE R. R. MARTIN AND LISA TUTTLE, BANTAM, 2001

OIL ON MASONITE, 28 x 19in (71 x 48cm)

INDEX OF WORKS

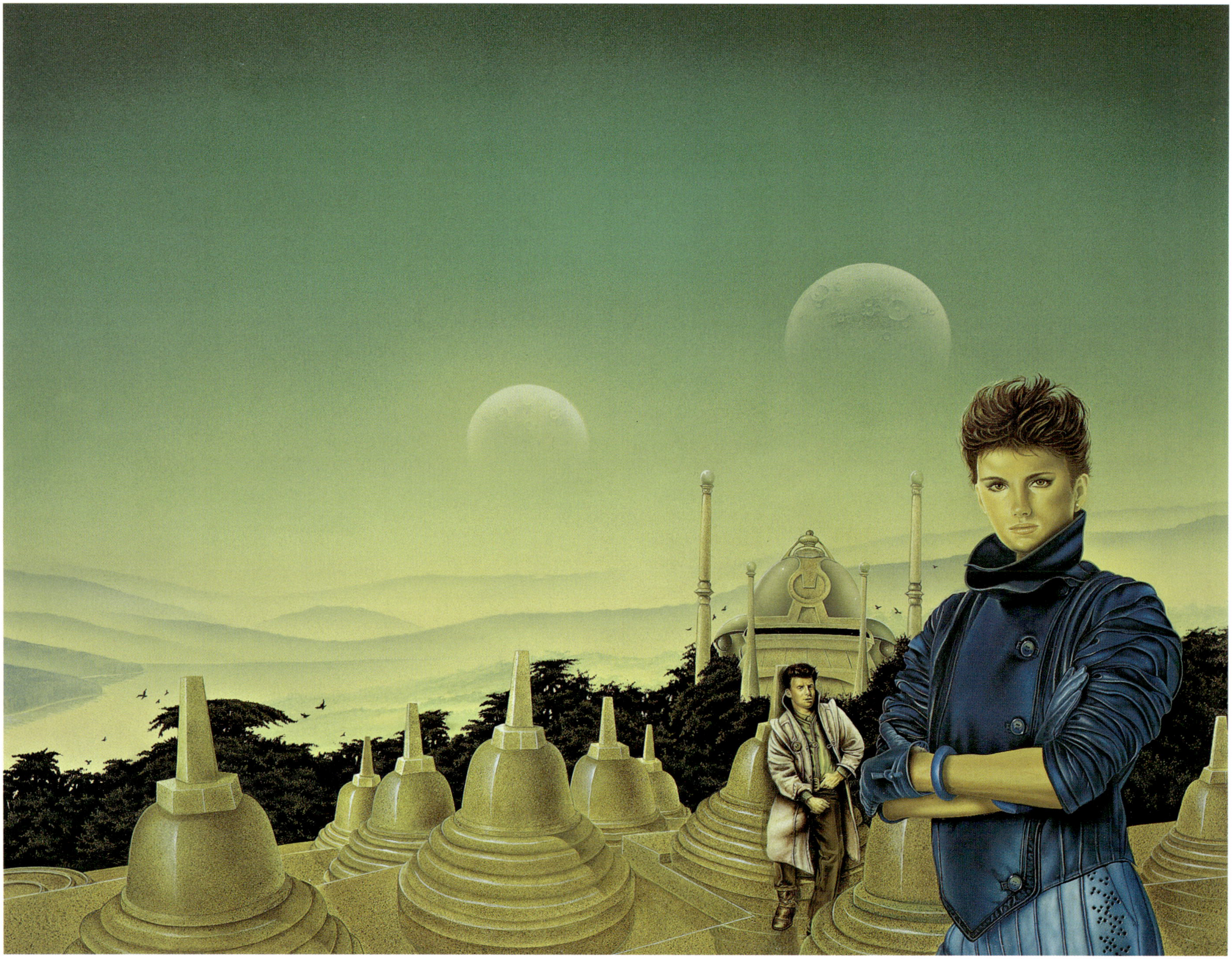

BLUE

SELF-PROMOTION, 1987

ACRYLIC ON ILLUSTRATION BOARD, 17 x 22in (43 x 56cm)

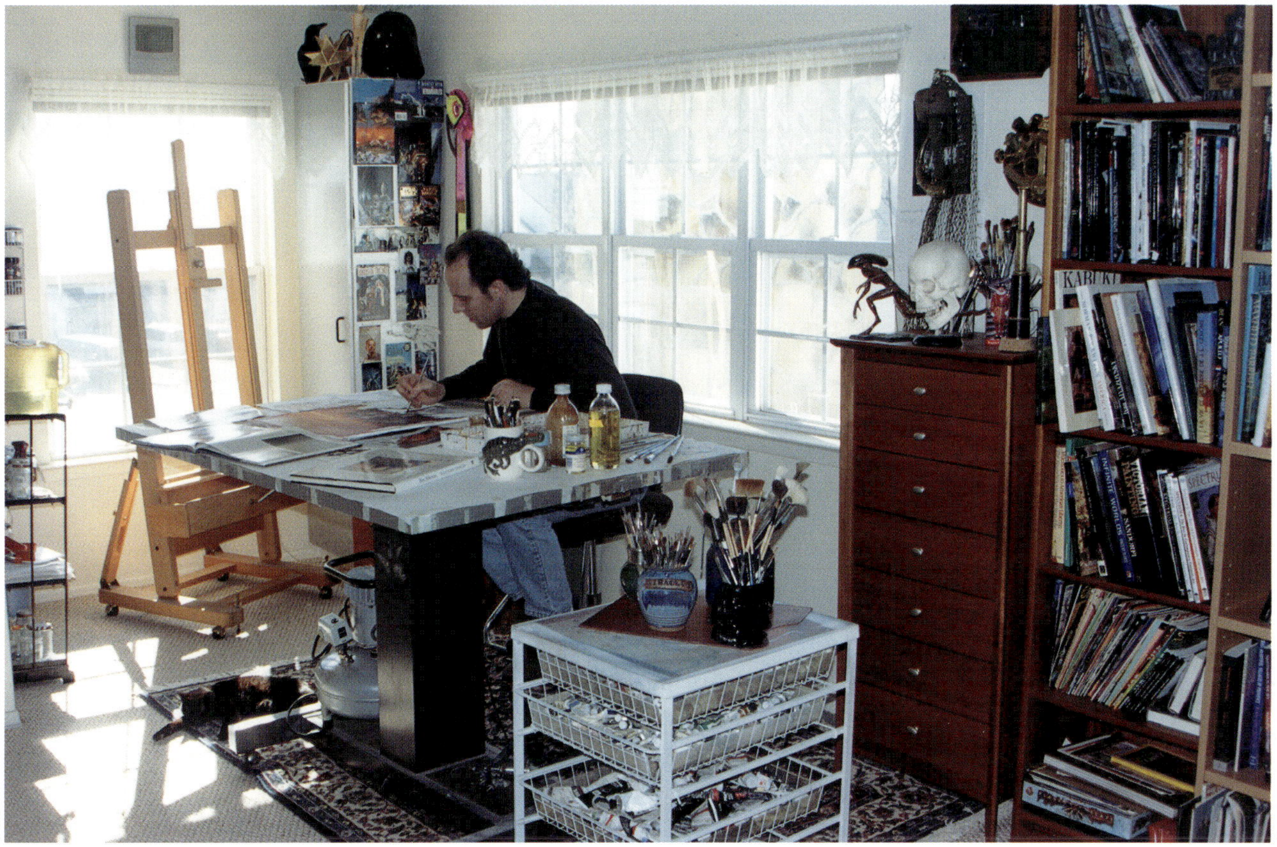

ACKNOWLEDGEMENTS

None of us are born with paintbrushes and pencils in our hands. Many things have to happen before an artist finds his true path. A college instructor once told me, ‘When you venture out into the world, you run the risk of being hired. After that it’s up to you.’ I’ve found that you also need people who have confidence in your work and encourage you along the way, so I would like to offer special thanks to the following:

To Dennis Fox, my first art-school teacher, who shared and recognized my love for science fiction and art.

To my parents, Maurice and Dorothy Youll, and my family, a constant source of support and love.

To my twin brother, Paul, an incredible artist and my better half. Without his inspiration and tireless enthusiasm I could not have come this far.

To my wife and soulmate, Jamie, without question the hardest-working and most talented art director I have ever known. Thanks for designing and putting together this book, and for enriching my life beyond words.

To the artists, teachers and friends who have influenced and encouraged me throughout my life.

To Emma Baxter and Katie Hardwicke at Paper Tiger, for their patience and for wanting to publish my art book.

And to all the clients and art directors I’ve worked for. Without them this book would not have been possible.

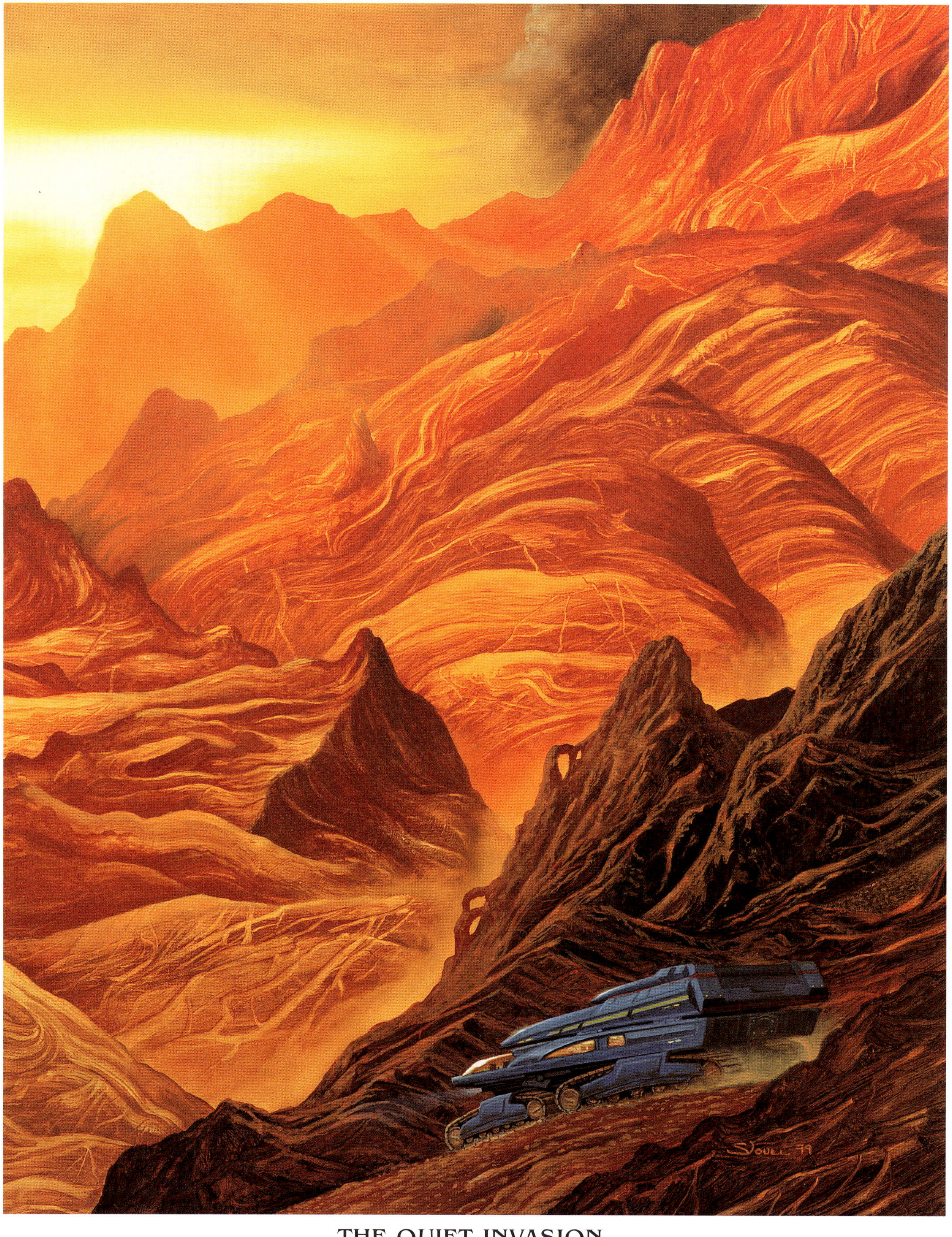

THE QUIET INVASION

SARAH ZETTEL, WARNER, 1999

OIL ON MASONITE, 15 X 21in (38 X 53cm)